William Henry Johnson

Summer excursion routes and rates

Delaware, Lackawanna and western railroad company

William Henry Johnson

Summer excursion routes and rates
Delaware, Lackawanna and western railroad company

ISBN/EAN: 9783337145453

Printed in Europe, USA, Canada, Australia, Japan

Cover: Foto ©Andreas Hilbeck / pixelio.de

More available books at **www.hansebooks.com**

SUMMER EXCURSION ROUTES

AND

RATES.

DELAWARE, LACKAWANNA AND WESTERN
RAILROAD COMPANY.

1895.

PASSENGER DEPARTMENT,
26 Exchange Place, - - - - New York.

COOKE LOCOMOTIVE AND MACHINE COMPANY
PATERSON, NEW JERSEY.

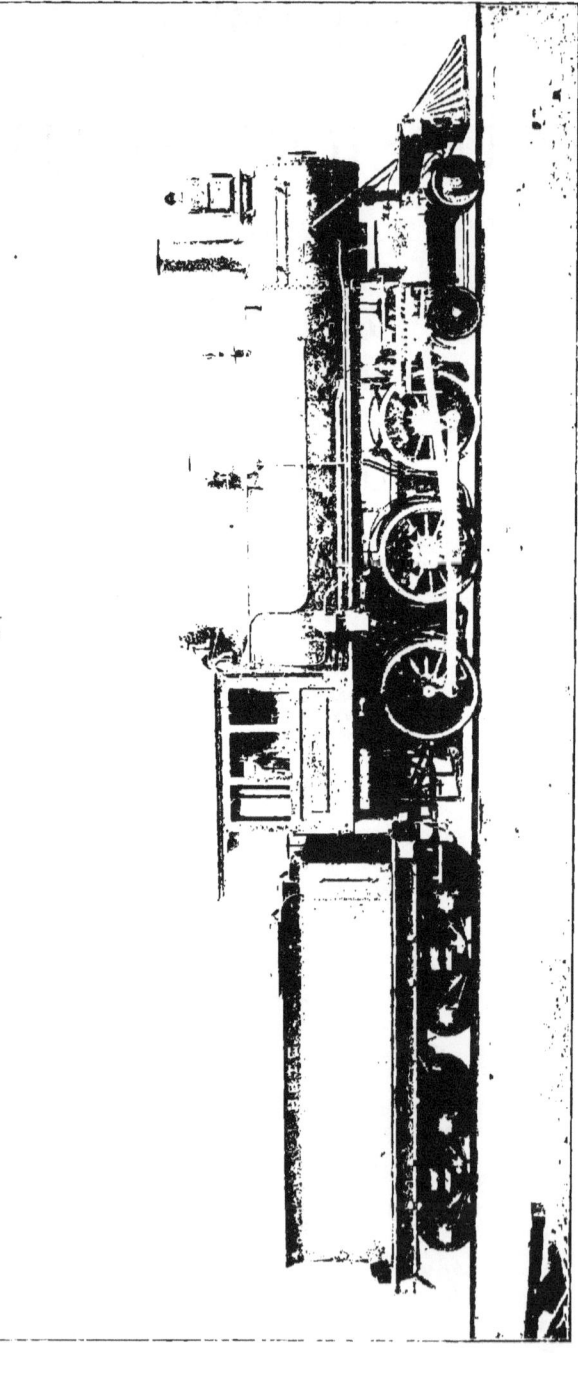

JNO. S. COOKE, PREST.
FRED. W. COOKE, VICE-PREST
WILLIAM BERDAN, SEC'Y & TREAS
CHAS. D. COOKE, SUPT.

SINGLE EXPANSION AND COMPOUND LOCOMOTIVES.

H. A. ALLEN, AGENT,
45 BROADWAY,
NEW YORK CITY.

☞ *Note page 181.*

GENERAL OFFICES OF
DELAWARE, LACKAWANNA AND WESTERN RAILROAD,
26 EXCHANGE PLACE, NEW YORK.

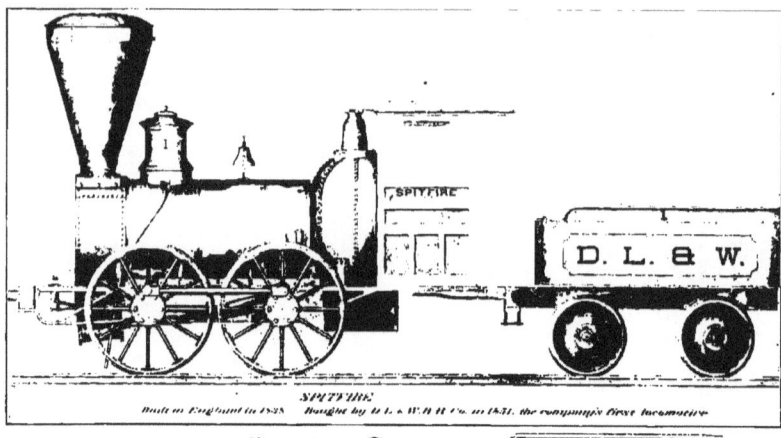

THE LACKAWANNA—THEN AND NOW.

Well! Is the Lackawanna getting any business?

Yours truly
Phil. Whitehead

SUMMER HOMES ON THE

Unadilla Valley Railway.

THE Unadilla Valley is one of the most beautiful Valleys in central New York. It is high in altitude and free from malaria, mosquitoes and insects. While the days are warm the nights are cool. The air is refreshing and exhilarating and equal to that of the Berkshire Hills in Massachusetts, and just the thing to build up exhausted and tired people. The country is freely watered with rivers, trout streams and mountain springs. The grass and verdure is of a deep rich green, and the valley is filled with song birds and wild flowers. The drives are numerous and the roads excellent.

The Summer service on the Unadilla Valley Railway will comprise trains most favorable to the needs of Summer Residents, coming from far distant points.

Richfield Springs, Cooperstown, Binghamton and Utica all of easy access, Utica distant eighteen miles.

The country lying along the line of the Unadilla Valley Railway, consists of some bottom land and then on the sides rolling hills and mountains.

There are numerous hamlets and villages at which board can be obtained at extremely reasonable rates.

The products of the country are mainly dairy products, this section of the country being one of the chief sources of the milk supply of the State, hence, first-class milk, cream, butter, cheese and all farm products can be easily obtained at very reasonable prices.

The Unadilla Valley Railway connects at New Berlin with the Ontario & Western Railroad, and at Bridgewater with the Delaware, Lackawanna & Western Railroad.

The Unadilla Valley is just the place for those who are seeking rest and health during the Summer months.

Forty miles of good boating on the river, and numerous ponds and lakes in the vicinity for fishing purposes.

TO MANUFACTURERS.

Look for sites on which to locate your manufacturing plant along the Unadilla Valley Railway. Abundant water power and cheap labor, coal cheap.

For shipping facilities and freight rates, communicate with

THE UNADILLA VALLEY RAILWAY CO.

80 BROADWAY,

NEW YORK CITY, N. Y.

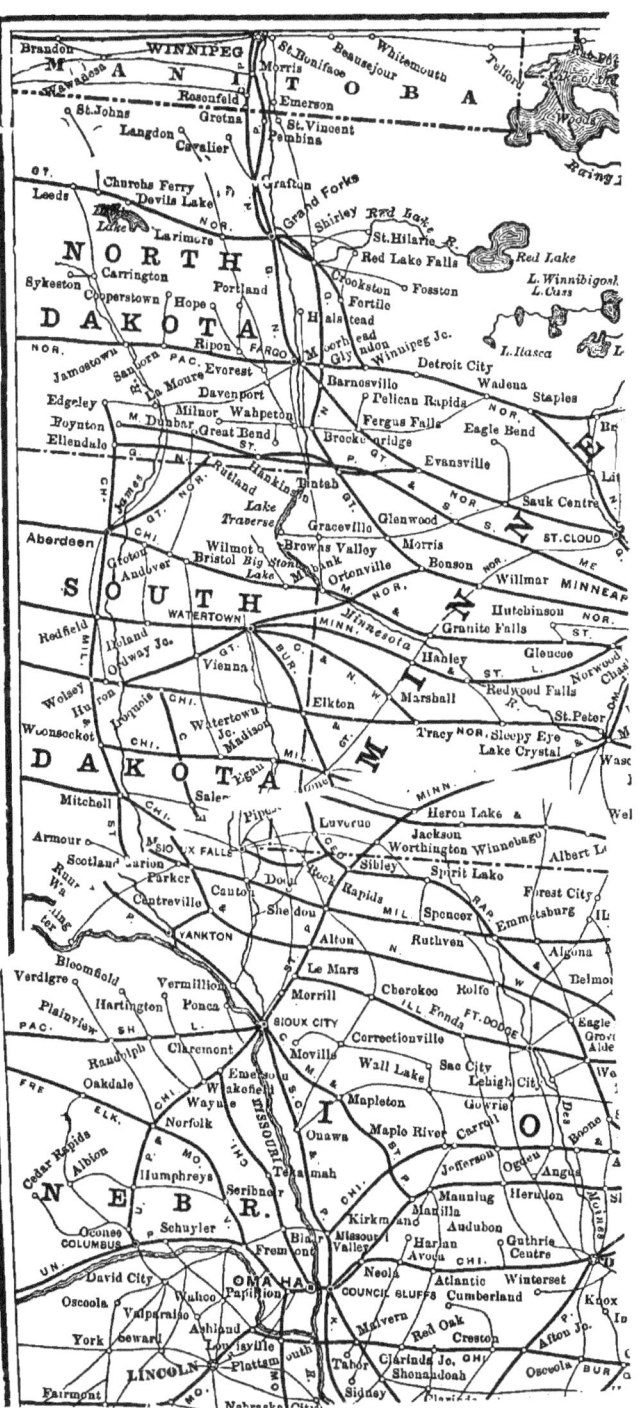

ROUTES AND RATES,		Pages 117-156
FAMILY TICKET AND COMMUTATION RATES,		" 164-165

Alford, Pa.,	77	Madison, N. J.,	30	ADVERTISEMENTS.		
Andover, N. J.,	46	Manunka Chunk, N. J.,	49	Am. Railway Supply Co.,		168
Atlanta, N. Y.,	99	Maplewood, N. J.,	25	Atlas Portland Cement,		180
Augusta, N. J.,	47	Marathon, N. Y.,	87			
Basking Ridge, N. J.,	28	Milburn, N. J.,	25	Bodega Espanola,		167
Bath, N. Y.,	96	Millington, N. J.,	28	Booss, F. & Bro.,		76
Baldwinsville, N. Y.,	90	Mine Brook, N. J.,	29	Boston & Lockport Block Co.		188
Berkeley Heights, N. J.,	27	Montclair, N. J.,	21	Bradley & Smith,		183
Bernardsville, N. J.,	29	Montville, N. J.,	38	Burt, Edwin C. & Co.,		107
Binghamton, N. Y.,	79-80	Morris Plains, N. J.,	33	Burnett Co.,		183
Bloomfield, N. J.,	21	Morristown, N. J.,	31-35			
Boonton, N. J.,	38	Moscow, Pa.,	61	Campbell & Thayer,		184
Branchville, N. J.,	47	Mountain Station, N. J.,	23	Castle Braid Co.,		187
Brick Church, N. J.,	22	Mountain View, N. J.,	37	Cayuga Lake House,		161
Bridgewater, N. Y.,	83	Mount Morris, N. Y.,	102-104	Century Fire Lloyds,		166
Bridgeville, N. J.,	49	Mount Pocono, Pa.,	57-59	Claremont & Co.,		185
Brisbin, N. Y.,	81	Mount Tabor, N. J.,	36	Continental Fire Lloyds,		167
Broadway, N. J.,	48	Mount Arlington, N. J.,	40	Cooke Locomotive & Machine		
Budd's Lake, N. J.,	45	Murray Hill, N. J.,	27	Co.,		4
Buffalo, N. Y.,	106-107	Newark, N. J.,	17			
Candor, N. Y.,	93	New Milford, Pa.,	78	Dame & Townsend,		163
Cedarville, N. Y.,	85	New Providence, N. J.,	29	Dickson M'f'g Co.,		173
Chatham, N. J.,	29	Newton, N. J.,	46	Dodge & Bliss,		174
Chester, N. J.,	40	Nicholson, Pa.,	77			
Chenango Bridge, N. Y.,	80	North Brookfield, N. Y.,	82	Eastman Kodak Co.,		169
Chenango Forks, N. Y.,	80	North Norwich, N. Y.,	81	Excelsior Paint & Roofing		
Clark's Summit, Pa.,	74	Norwich, N. Y.,	81	Co.,		184
Clifton, N. J.,	37	Orange, N. J.,	23			
Conklin, N. Y.,	79	Oswego, N. Y.,	91	Falk, Photographer,		2
Conklin Centre, N. Y.,	79	Owego, N. Y.,	93	Fall River Line,		170
Convent, N. J.,	31	Oxford, N. Y.,	81			
Cortland, N. Y.,	87	Oxford Furnace, N. J.,	48-49	Glen Island,		177
Coventry, N. Y.,	81	Paris, N. Y.,	82	Glenwood, The		163
Cresco, Pa.,	57	Passaic, N. J.,	37	Gold Car Heating Co.,		175
Dalton, Pa.,	74	Paterson, N. J.,	37	Gould Coupler Co.,		178
Dansville, N. Y.,	101-102	Peapack, N. J.,	29	Guarantee Co. of N. A.,		157
Delawanna, N. J.,	36	Pittston, Pa.,	67			
Delaware, N. J.,	49-50	Phillipsburg, N. J.,	48	Heft Lubricating Oil Co.,		175
Delaware Water Gap, Pa.,	50-54	Poolville, N. Y.,	82	House for Sale,		181
Denville, N. J.,	36	Portland, Pa.,	50	Hotel Athenæum,		162
Dover, N. J.,	38	Port Murray, N. J.,	48	Hotels Arlington & St. James		171
Earlville, N. Y.,	82	Port Oram, N. J.,	38-39	Hotel Breslin,		2
Easton, Pa.,	48	Pocono Summit, Pa.,	59-61			
East Orange, N. J.,	22	Preble, N. Y.,	88	Keating Wheel Co.,		182
Elmhurst, N. J.,	62	Richfield Springs, N. Y.,	85	Kittatinny, The		108
Elmira, N. Y.,	96-97	Rockaway, N. J.,	36	Knowles Steam Pump Co.,		167
Factoryville, Pa.,	74	Roseville Ave., N. J.,	20	Lake Keuka Park,		115
Far Hills, N. J.,	29	Sangerfield Centre, N. Y.,	82	Lappin Brake & Shoe Co.,		184
Fishing Points,	110	Sanquoit, N. Y.,	86	Liverpool, London & Globe,		76
Forest Park, Pa.,	56	Schooley's Mountain, N. J.,	47-48	Manning, Maxwell & Moore,		180
Franklin, N. J.,	47	Scranton, Pa.,	63-65	Mazzetti, Louis F.,		186
Fulton, N. Y.,	90	Sheldrake, N. Y.,	162	Meriden Britannia Co.,		75
Game Laws,	107-113	Sherburne, N. Y.,	81-82	Miller & Co.,		113
General Information,	17-18	Short Hills, N. J.,	26	Miller's Hotel, 3d page of cover		
Gillette, N. J.,	27	Sleeping and Parlor Cars,	13	Minett & Co.,		176
Gladstone, N. J.,	29	South Orange, N. J.,	23	Morris, Theo. W. & Co.,		184
Glenburn, Pa.,	74	Special Notice,	14	Mountain House,		162
Glen Ridge, N. J.,	21	Spragueville, Pa.,	56	Monarch Cycle M'f'g Co.,		109
Gouldsboro, Pa.,	61	Stanhope, N. J.,	45			
Great Bend, Pa.,	78-79	Stewartsville, N. J.,	48	National R'y Spring Co.,		157
Greene, N. Y.,	81	Sterling, N. J.,	27	N. Y. Belting & Packing Co.,		179
Greigsville, N. Y.,	104	Stop-over Privileges,	16	N. Y. State Mortgage Bank		
Grove Street (The Oranges),	22	Stroudsburg, Pa.,	54	and Savings Association,		188
Hackettstown, N. J.,	47	Succasunna, N. J.,	39			
Harrison, N. J.,	19	Summit, N. J.,	26	Pennsylvania Bolt & Nut Co.		185
Henryville, Pa.,	56	Syracuse, N. Y.,	89			
Highland Avenue, N. J.,	23	Tobyhanna, Pa.,	61	Richelieu & Ont. Nav. Co.		168
Hopatcong, N. J.,	40-44	Tully Lake Park, N. Y.,	88	River Farm House,		186
Hubbardsville, N. Y.,	82	Unadilla Forks, N. Y.,	83	Roebling's, John A. Sons Co.		166
Huntley, N. J.,	26	Utica, N. Y.,	86	Romer & Co.,		185
Ithaca, N. Y.,	93-95	Washington, N. J.,	48	Sanatorium, The,		114
Ironia, N. J.,	39	Waterloo, N. J.,	46	Silver Medal M'f'g Co.,		183
Introduction,	15	Waterville, N. Y.,	82	Spring House, Richfield Sp'gs		
Kingsland,	36	Watsessing, N. J.,	21	N. Y.,		170
Kingston, Pa.,	69	Wayland, N. Y.,	99	Stroud, James		179
Kingsleys, Pa.,	77	West Paterson, N. J.,	37			
Kenville, N. J.,	39	West Summit, N. J.,	27	The Hall Signal Co.,		1
Lackawanna & Montrose R.R.		West Winfield, N. Y.,	83	The Jackson & Woodin M'f'g		
(Alfred to Montrose),	78	Whitehall, N. Y.,	38	Co.,		174
Lafayette, N. J.,	47	Wilkesbarre, Pa.,	69	Turkish Baths,		185
Lamsons, N. Y.,	90	Willards, N. Y.,	80	U. S. Express Co., 2d pp. of cover		
La Plume, Pa.,	74	Wyoming, N. Y.,	25	Vose & Cliff Mfg Co.,		183
Lincoln Park, N. J.,	38	Wyoming Valley (The), Scranton, Pa., to Northumberland, Pa.,		Westcott Express Co., 4th page of cover		
Little Falls, N. J.,	37					
Lounsberry, N. Y.,	95		67-74	Wiscasset, The,		116
Lyndhurst, N. J.,	36					
Lyons, N. J.,	28					

PULLMAN VESTIBULED BUFFET PARLOR CAR.
ALL TRAINS ILLUMINATED BY THE PINTSCH SYSTEM.

AND

INFORMATION RELATIVE THERETO MAY BE OBTAINED OF

C. J. GUMMERSBACH, { EASTERN PASSENGER AGENT,
429 Broadway, New York.

M. L. SMITH, { DISTRICT PASSENGER AGENT,
328 Lackawanna Avenue, Scranton, Pa.

W. C. BRAYTON, { GENERAL AGENT PASSENGER DEPARTMENT,
Globe Block, Syracuse, N. Y.

HOWARD J. BALL, { GENERAL WESTERN PASSENGER AGENT,
11 Exchange Street, Elmira, N. Y.

FRED. P. FOX, { TRAVELLING PASSENGER AGENT, Elmira, N. Y.

ALSO OF THE FOLLOWING:

New York, (Barclay St. Depot)..........C. H. GOVE
" (Christopher St. Depot)...A. R. STILSON
" (429 Broadway)..........W. J. STEWART
" (14 Park Place)...............F. STILES
" (4th Ave., cor. 12th St....W. W. MEAKIM
" (942 Broadway)..........S. BEDELL
" (53 West 125th St.)..........N. F. GUYER
" (235 Columbus Ave.).......M. F. CLARK
Brooklyn, (338 Fulton St.)..............WM. WISERT
" (726 Fulton St.)......OSCAR SEYMOUR
" (106 Broadway)..........W. A. SMITH
Hoboken, N. J........................W. H. JEFFERDS
Paterson, "..........................F. M. BARR
Boonton, "..........................F. E. BLOXHAM
Newark, " (Depot)..............C. A. PALMER
" (182 Market St.)........F. T. FEAREY
Orange, "..........................W. T. ATNO
Summit, "..........................J. J. LANE
Chatham, "........................W. A. HELM
Madison, "........................C. R. HOPKINS
Morristown"......................W. R. M. FREGANS
Dover, "..........................A. M. McFALL
Stanhope, "......................M. VAN HORN
Waterloo, "......................W. N. GRAY
Newton, "........................Z. H. SNYDER
Hackettstown, N. J................W. M. EVERITT
Washington, "......................W. SHIELDS
" ..Ass't Ticket Ag't, H. S. GROFF
Oxford Furnace,".................W. J. AXFORD
Bridgeville, "....................R. H. KINNEY
Delaware, "....................HARRY PETERS
Portland, Pa.........................H. LOVE
Water Gap, Pa...................D. C. STAPLES
Stroudsburg, Pa..................A. C. LODER
Spragueville, "..................P. M. ARNOLD
Henryville, "....................H. W. SAYRE
Cresco, "......................W. D. YOTHERS
Mount Pocono, Pa................HARRY SMITH
Pocono Summit, Pa.............J. McCORMICK
Tobyhanna, "..................D. C YOTHERS
Gouldsboro, "...................S. S. HAGER
Moscow, "....................J. S. LATOUCHE
Elmhurst, "......................E. W. DAVIS
Scranton, " (Depot)............WM. H. COONS
" (326 Lack. Ave.)....M. L. SMITH
Clark's Summit, "...............W. P. LITTS
Glenburn, "...................JAS. EDWARDS
Dalton, "..........................A. BALL
Factoryville, "..................H. L. HARDING
Nicholson "......................E. D. BELL
Foster, "......................O. D. ROBERTS
Alford, "......................J. M. DECKER
Montrose, "...................H. J. McALPIN
New Milford, "..................D. W. HAGER
Great Bend, "..................C. C. SIMMONS
Conklin, N. Y...................F. P. BADGER

Binghamton, N. Y.................G. A. PRESTON
Pittston, Pa......................T. F. BURKE
Wyoming, Pa......................H. H. ANTRIM
Kingston, "...................J. M. NICHOLSON
Wilkes-Barre, Pa..................G. SMITH
Plymouth, "......................S. H. HICKS
Nanticoke, " (Depot),..........B. C. KISTLER
" (City)..............J. B. SCUREMAN
Shickshinny, "..................E. W. GARRISON
Berwick, "....................DUVAL DICKSON
Espy, "........................J. H. MILLER
Bloomsburg, "..................W. R. KOCHER
Rupert, "......................G. W. MEARS
Danville, "..................A. M. GEARHART
Northumberland, Pa................R. G. SCOTT
Greene, N. Y....................E. B. JACKSON
Oxford, "......................G. P. MEAD
Norwich, " (Depot)............W. S. WAGNER
Sherburne, N. Y..................H. H. TUCKER
Waterville, "..................C. H. GRAVES
Richfield Springs, N. Y.........C. C. MERRILL
Utica, N. Y. (City)...........J. H. MACGARRITY
Chenango Forks, N. Y.............C. C. MIX
Whitney's Point, "............L. N. ENGLISH
Marathon, "....................C. BURGESS
Cortland, N. Y. (Depot)..........W. E. WOOD
" (City)..................ROBT. BUSHBY
Homer, "......................J. H. STARIN
Syracuse, "....................R. M. SKEELE
" (Globe Block).......W. C. BRAYTON
Fulton, " (Depot)..............F. E. RICE
" (Village)..............F. E. RICE
Oswego, "....................W. B. PHELPS
Owego, "......................W. H. COREY
Ithaca, " (Depot)..............M. A. QUICK
" (City)................F. W. PHILLIPS
Waverly, "....................E. S. WHEELER
Elmira, "....................W. H. PETERS
Big Flats, "..................S. C. LEONARD
Corning, " (Depot)............H. E. ELWOOD
" (City)..................D. C. McKEE
Painted Post, N. Y...............D. M. SAYLES
Savona, "......................C. D. DAVIS
Bath, "........................G. H. PARKER
Kanona, "......................C. C. COOK
Wallace, "....................JAS. E. COOK
Cohocton, "....................J. C. CUFF
Atlanta, "......................E. W LENT
Wayland, "....................R. C. NEILL
Perkinsville, "..................E. SCHU
Dansville, "..................C. A. SNYDER
Mount Morris, "................J. A. MUNYON
Buffalo, N. Y. (Depot)........E. J. HUTCHINSON
" (11 Exchange St.).....G. H. STAGG
" (377 Main St.).......C. W. MILLER

PULLMAN VESTIBULED BUFFET SLEEPING CAR.
ALL TRAINS ILLUMINATED BY THE PINTSCH SYSTEM.

PULLMAN PARLOR AND SLEEPING CAR SERVICE.

Vestibuled Buffet Parlor Cars, daily except Sunday.
NEW YORK, HOBOKEN AND BUFFALO.

Train 3.
Leave New York.........................9.00 A. M.
" Hoboken................................9.15 A. M.
Arrive Buffalo.............................8 00 P. M.

Train 6.
Leave Buffalo.............................9.00 A. M.
Arrive Hoboken..........................7.50 P. M.
" New York.............................8.00 P. M.

Vestibuled Buffet Parlor Cars, daily except Sunday.
NEW YORK, HOBOKEN AND OSWEGO.

Train 3.
Leave New York.........................9.00 A. M.
" Hoboken................................9.15 A. M.
Arrive Oswego............................6.40 P. M.

Train 4.
Leave Oswego............................7.45 A. M.
Arrive Hoboken..........................5.07 P. M.
" New York.............................5.20 P. M

Vestibuled Buffet Parlor Cars, daily except Sunday.
NEW YORK, HOBOKEN AND RICHFIELD SPRINGS.

Train 3.
Leave New York.........................9.00 A. M.
" Hoboken................................9.15 A. M.
Arrive Richfield Springs................6 25 P. M.

Train 6.
Leave Richfield Springs................10.15 A. M.
Arrive Hoboken..........................7.50 P. M.
" New York.............................8.00 P. M.

NOTE.—This car will be placed in service June 24.

Vestibuled Buffet Parlor Cars, daily except Sunday.
NEW YORK, HOBOKEN AND ELMIRA.

Train 5.
Leave New York.........................1.00 P. M.
" Hoboken................................1.15 P. M.
Arrive Elmira..............................9.30 P. M.

Train 2.
Leave Elmira..............................6.00 A. M.
Arrive Hoboken..........................2.47 P. M.
" New York.............................3.00 P. M.

Buffet Parlor Cars, daily except Sunday.
NEW YORK, HOBOKEN AND PLYMOUTH.

Train 171.
Leave New York.........................4.00 P. M.
" Hoboken................................4.15 P. M.
Arrive Plymouth.........................9.40 P. M.

Train 172.
Leave Plymouth..........................7.10 A. M.
Arrive Hoboken..........................12.18 P. M.
" New York.............................12.30 P. M.

Vestibuled Buffet Sleeping Cars, daily.
NEW YORK, HOBOKEN AND BUFFALO.

Train 7.
Leave New York.........................7.30 P. M.
" Hoboken................................7 45 P. M.
Arrive Buffalo.............................7.15 A. M.

Train 10.
Leave Buffalo.............................4.30 P. M.
Arrive Hoboken..........................6.25 A. M.
" New York.............................6.40 A. M.

Train 8.
Leave Buffalo.............................7 30 P. M.
Arrive Hoboken..........................7.15 A. M.
" New York.............................7.30 A. M.

NOTE.—Passengers arriving at Hoboken on Train 10 may remain in car until 7.30 A. M.

Vestibuled Buffet Sleeping Cars, daily.
NEW YORK, HOBOKEN AND OSWEGO.

Train 9.
Leave New York.........................9.30 P. M.
" Hoboken................................9.45 P. M.
Arrive Oswego............................8.30 A. M.

Train 8.
Leave Oswego............................9.00 P. M.
Arrive Hoboken..........................7.18 A. M.
" New York.............................7.30 A. M.

Vestibuled Buffet Sleeping Cars, daily.
NEW YORK, HOBOKEN AND BUFFALO.

Train 9.
Leave New York.........................9.30 P. M.
" Hoboken................................9.45 P. M.
Arrive Buffalo.............................11.30 A. M.

Train 12.
Leave Buffalo.............................10.00 P. M.
Arrive Hoboken..........................9.28 A. M.
" New York.............................9.40 A. M.

Vestibuled Buffet Sleeping Cars, daily.
NEW YORK, HOBOKEN AND RICHFIELD SPRINGS.

Train 9.
Leave New York.........................9 30 P. M.
" Hoboken................................9 45 P. M.
Arrive Richfield Springs................8.05 A. M.

Train 8.
Leave Richfield Springs................9.15 P. M.
Arrive Hoboken..........................7.18 A. M.
" New York.............................7.30 A. M.

NOTE.—This car will be placed in service June 5.

Vestibuled Buffet Sleeping Cars, daily.
PHILADELPHIA AND BUFFALO.

Trains Penna. R. R. 54 and 570: D. L. & W. 7.
Leave Philadelphia, Broad St. Station..6 02 P. M.
Arrive Buffalo.............................7 15 A. M.

Trains D. L. & W. 12 and Penna. 567.
Leave Buffalo.............................10.00 P. M.
Arrive Philadelphia, Broad St. Station.10.00 A. M.

Pullman Parlor Cars, daily, except Sunday.

Stanhope Special.

Train 79.—LEAVE.
New York...4.20 P. M.
Hoboken....4.36 P. M.
Paterson....5.04 P. M.
Boonton.....5.30 P. M.
Dover........5.46 P. M.

Mt Arlington.5.57 P. M.
Hopatcong....6.01 P. M.
ARRIVE
Stanhope ....6.08 P. M.

Washington and New York Express.

Train 86.—LEAVE
Washington..7.02 A. M.
Hackettst'wn7.21 A. M.
Hopatcong..7.44 A. M.
Mt.Arlington 7.51 A. M.
Dover........8.02 A. M.

Boonton .....8.17 A. M.
Paterson.....8.40 A. M.
Hoboken.....9.05 A. M.
ARRIVE
New York...9.20 A. M.

SPECIAL NOTICE.

SUMMER EXCURSION TICKETS herein described are sold from June 1st to October 1st, and are good for return until October 31st, except when otherwise noted, and have all the privileges of first-class tickets, including stop-over at any point on the "LACKAWANNA," and on all lines permitting stop-over.

Should passengers desire to leave a train or boat, they should notify the conductor or other proper official, who will issue a stop-over check or endorse the ticket, if stop-over is allowed on that line.

Tickets reading *via* Fall River Line of Steamers are good for stop-over at Newport, R. I., in either direction, on application to Purser.

Tickets reading *via* Richelieu & Ontario Navigation Company's Steamers between Toronto or Alexandria Bay and Montreal do not include meals or berths going East; but are included going West from Montreal. Between Montreal and Quebec meals and berths are extra in both directions.

Tickets reading *via* New York Central & Hudson River Railroad, between Canandaigua or stations East, and Niagara Falls will be accepted for passage either *via* Lockport or Buffalo.

Through tickets *via* the New York Central & Hudson River or West Shore Railroads will be accepted for passage between Albany and New York by the Hudson River Day Line Steamers without extra charge.

Through tickets *via* the Hudson River Day Line Steamers will be accepted for passage on the New York Central & Hudson River or West Shore Railroads between Albany and New York on payment of $1.10.

Tickets reading *via* Delaware & Hudson Canal Co.'s Railroad will be accepted for passage between Plattsburgh and Fort Ticonderoga, on Lake Champlain Steamers.

Rail tickets between Albany and New York will be accepted for passage on People's (Night) Line of Steamers.

Children, between five and twelve years of age, half fare; over twelve, full fare.

One hundred and fifty pounds of baggage checked free on each full ticket, and seventy-five pounds on each half ticket.

Coupons between Richfield Springs and Cooperstown *via* Otsego Lake Steamboat and Stage Co. are good for passage only; baggage is charged extra.

As many of the Steamer and stage lines cease running, or make irregular trips about October 1st, passengers should consult the proper advertising matter on the subject.

Summer Excursion Tickets to local points mentioned herein are good for continuous passage only. Agents not supplied with regular tickets will use blank Excursion Tickets, Form 418, Limited to October 31.

Agents in New York, Brooklyn, Hoboken and Newark will use *Form "U" 418* to all stations (except Dansville, to which they will use Form 418, limited to October 31st).

INTRODUCTION.

THE DELAWARE, LACKAWANNA AND WESTERN RAILROAD COMPANY, in issuing its Summer Excursion Book for 1895, places before the travelling public, and particularly before the vacationists, holiday seekers, and those who are in search of a summer resort, a complete register of all the rural and urban spots in which the summer months may be advantageously spent, available in the States of New Jersey, Pennsylvania and New York, along their line, between the cities of New York and Buffalo.

A glance at the following pages will suffice to show that many of the most famous resorts in these States are directly on the Lackawanna Line, so that special allusion to them is unnecessary here.

A description of each place is given, much space being devoted to such among them as rank as summer resorts of national fame.

The illustrations herein contained are reproductions of photographs taken from scenes along the railroad, and are of a miscellaneous character.

A feature that will commend itself at once is the exhaustive list of *routes* and *rates* that is given, and which can be utilized in connection with tickets purchased *via* the Lackawanna road; and those in search of rest, recreation or sport, have only to glance over these pages, and from among the many mountain, lake and river resorts described, as well as those where wealth and fashion reign supreme, select a place to their taste. The Lackawanna penetrates a section of country so well diversified and so picturesque, that any person who has an appreciation of the Creator's handiwork, as displayed through almost the entire region traversed by this road, will be apt to reflect before making a choice.

Great care has been taken in the compilation of this book to guard against discrepancies, and it is offered to the public as a reliable guide and work replete with interesting reading.

The Company feels assured that the public will appreciate the effort that has here been put forward, and presents it to that public with the compliments of the Passenger Department.

Stop=over Privileges

On Summer Excursion Tickets.

NOTE —It should be understood that the stop-over privileges extended by the several lines (as noted below) require passengers to take such trains or boats as make stops regularly at the desired stopping-place. These stop-over privileges do not apply to tickets limited for continuous passages.

Line	Privilege
BOSTON & ALBANY R. R.	Stop-over allowed for 10 days on notice to conductor.
BOSTON & MAINE R. R.	Stop-over for 10 days allowed at any station (except between Salem or Reading and Boston) on notice to Conductor.
CANADIAN PACIFIC R'Y	Stop-over allowed on notice to conductor.
CANANDAIGUA LAKE STEAMBOAT CO.	No stop-over allowed.
CENTRAL VERMONT R. R.	Stop-over allowed at any station on notice to conductor.
CENTRAL R. R. OF NEW JERSEY	Stop-over allowed on notice to conductor, except on New York & Long Branch R. R.
CHAMPLAIN TRANSPORTATION CO. (STEAMER ON LAKE CHAMPLAIN)	Stop-over allowed on notice to purser.
CONCORD & MONTREAL R. R.	Stop-over allowed at any station on notice to conductor.
CONNECTICUT RIVER R. R.	Stop-over allowed at any station on notice to conductor.
COOPERSTOWN & CHARLOTTE VALLEY R. R.	Stop-over allowed at any station on notice to conductor.
DAY LINE STEAMERS (ON HUDSON RIVER)	Stop-over allowed on notice to purser.
DELAWARE & HUDSON CANAL CO. R. R.	Stop-over allowed at any station on notice to conductor.
DELAWARE, LACKAWANNA & WESTERN R. R.	Stop-over allowed at any station on notice to conductor.
FALL BROOK RAILWAY	Stop-over allowed at any station on notice to conductor.
FALL RIVER LINE (OLD COLONY S. B. LINE)	Stop-over allowed at Newport, R. I., in either direction, on notice to purser.
FITCHBURG R. R.	Stop-over allowed on notice to conductor.
GRAND TRUNK R'Y	Stop-over allowed at any station on notice to conductor.
HUDSON RIVER DAY LINE	Stop-over allowed on notice to purser.
KINGSTON & PEMBROKE R'Y	Stop-over allowed on notice to conductor.
KNOX & LINCOLN R. R.	Stop-over allowed on notice to conductor.
LAKE GEORGE STEAMBOAT CO.	Stop-over allowed on notice to purser.
LEHIGH VALLEY R. R.	Stop-over allowed at any station on notice to conductor.
MAINE CENTRAL R. R.	Stop-over allowed at any station on notice to conductor, except on excursion tickets which are limited to continuous passage in each direction.
MONTPELIER & WELLS RIVER R. R.	Stop-over allowed at any station on notice to conductor.
MT. WASHINGTON R. R.	No intermediate stops.
MUSKOKA & GEORGIAN BAY NAVIGATION CO.	Stop-over allowed.
NEW BEDFORD, MARTHA'S VINEYARD & NANTUCKET S. B. LINE	Stop-over allowed for 10 days on notice to purser.
NEW YORK CENTRAL & HUDSON RIVER R. R.	Stop-over allowed at any station on notice to conductor.
NEW YORK, NEW HAVEN & HARTFORD R. R.	Stop-over allowed on notice to conductor.
NEW YORK, PROVIDENCE & BOSTON R. R.	Stop-over allowed on notice to conductor.
NIAGARA NAVIGATION CO.	Stop-over allowed on notice to purser.
NORWICH LINE (NORWICH & N. Y. TRANSPORTATION LINE)	Steamers make no intermediate landing.
OLD COLONY R. R.	One stop-over allowed at any station on notice to conductor.
OLD COLONY STEAMBOAT LINE (FALL RIVER LINE)	Stop-over allowed at Newport, R. I., in either direction, on notice to purser.
OTTAWA RIVER NAVIGATION CO.	Stop-over allowed at Carillon, Grenville and Caledonia Springs—at other points on notice to purser.
PENNSYLVANIA R. R.	Stop-over allowed at any station on notice to conductor.
PEOPLE'S (NIGHT) LINE STEAMERS (ON HUDSON RIVER)	Steamers make no intermediate landing.
PHILADELPHIA & READING R. R.	Stop-over allowed at any station on notice to conductor.
PORTLAND, MT. DESERT & MACHIAS STEAMBOAT LINE	Stop-over allowed at any landing on notice to purser.
PORTLAND STEAM PACKET LINE	Steamers make no intermediate landings.
PROFILE & FRANCONIA NOTCH R. R.	Stop-over allowed at any station on notice to conductor.
PROVIDENCE LINE	Steamers make no intermediate landing.
PROVIDENCE & WORCESTER R. R.	No stop-over privileges.
QUEBEC CENTRAL R'Y	Stop-over allowed on through tickets, reading between Quebec and Sherbrooke, on notice to conductor.
RICHELIEU & ONTARIO NAVIGATION CO.	Stop-over allowed on notice to purser.
ROME, WATERTOWN & OGDENSBURG R. R.	Stop-over checks issued on notice to conductor.
ST. JOHNSBURY & LAKE CHAMPLAIN R. R.	Stop-over allowed on notice to conductor.
ST. LAWRENCE RIVER S. B. CO.	Stop-over allowed at any landing on notice to purser.
STEAMERS ON CAYUGA LAKE (CAYUGA LAKE STEAMBOAT)	Stop-over allowed at any landing on notice to captain.
STEAMERS ON SENECA LAKE (SENECA LAKE S. N. LINE)	Stop-over allowed at all landings.
STONINGTON LINE (PROVIDENCE & STONINGTON S. S. LINE)	Steamers make no intermediate landing.
THOUSAND ISLAND STEAMBOAT CO.	Stop-over allowed for 30 days.
VERMONT VALLEY R. R.	Stop-over allowed at any station on notice to conductor.
WESTERN NEW YORK & PENNSYLVANIA R. R.	One stop-over allowed on notice to conductor.
WEST SHORE R. R.	Stop-over allowed at any station on notice to conductor.
WHITEFIELD & JEFFERSON R. R.	Stop-over allowed at any station on notice to conductor.

GENERAL INFORMATION.

ON LEAVING New York City, the traveller by the DELAWARE, LACKAWANNA & WESTERN RAILROAD is carried across the Hudson by well-appointed ferry-boats, lighted with electricity, several of which are double-deckers with spacious upper and lower cabins.

The boats depart from the ferry at the foot of Barclay Street, making the trip across in twelve minutes, and from that at the foot of Christopher Street, which is directly across from Hoboken, in but five minutes.

The Company's new terminus at Hoboken is a model of artistic beauty. The station is Gothic in design, with long sloping roofs, and on the Northern side has a high, narrow tower, which adds greatly to its attractiveness. The general waiting-room is both large and airy. The natural-wood ceiling is supported by carved beams and arches, and the whole interior is of light wood, varnished and decorated. On the East side is the ticket office; on the South side is a room for ladies and a smoking room for gentlemen. On the North side are entrances for Hoboken patrons, as well as for those who cross from New York by the two ferries. A good restaurant, where a buffet lunch can be obtained, is provided in the waiting-room, and confectionery, fruit, etc., is obtainable at the counter adjoining.

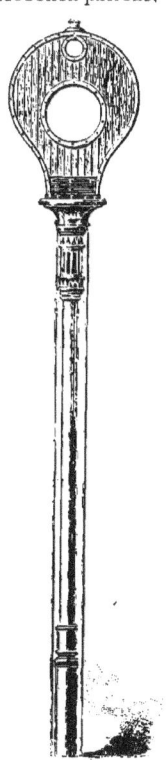

THE HALL BLOCK SIGNAL.

The baggage-room is on the north-west corner, and passengers and others will always receive prompt and polite attention and answers to inquiries from the employees in that department.

Experienced and well-posted ushers are stationed at the doors through which passengers pass to the trains. These men give the inquirer any information concerning the arrival and departure of trains, and, before the departure of each train, call out the names of all the stations along the route at which stoppage will be made.

The above-stairs portion of the station contains the headquarters of this railroad's branch of the Young Men's Christian Association, which are fitted up attractively. The room contains a rostrum and chairs enough to seat a large-sized audience. Meetings and entertainments are held at regular intervals, and much good results thereby to the employees. The conductors have a comfortably appointed room adjoining, and a furnished reception room. Baths, hot and cold, are provided. There is also a room in which all the men can meet for social intercourse, reading, playing games, etc.

The large train-shed contains nine tracks, all of which are kept occupied the greater part of the time by the incoming and outgoing trains.

It has been the policy of this Company to abandon regular train service on Sundays, and this has been found to work to the best advantage. By this policy the men are enabled to gain the rest which, it is believed, all men should have the Seventh Day, and they are better fitted to render more faithful service as a result. Only newspaper and milk trains are run on Sundays, and this cannot very well be avoided.

The motive power and rolling equipment of the Delaware, Lackawanna and Western are of the most approved types. The locomotives are built for speed, and with a view to hauling capacity. Spark arresters and extension fronts are being applied to all of those engines that were built prior to these innovations in modern mechanics, and all new engines are fitted with these appliances when built. In addition each engine is equipped with the "Blizzard" engine lamp for classification service.

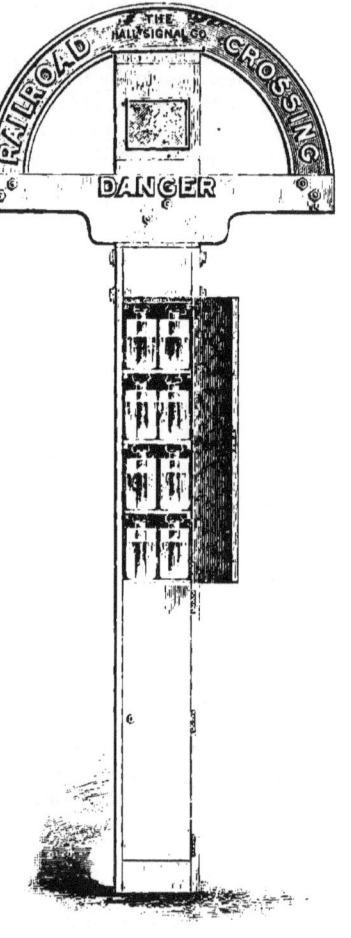

The Company is so rapidly replacing all its old passenger coaches with new cars, that scarcely any old rolling stock is now in use. These new coaches are mounted on trucks having steel-tired paper wheels.

The exteriors are painted in the Company's standard color, dark green, while the interiors are finished in polished mahogany, and have comfortable, high-backed seats, upholstered with maroon plush. The Company has adopted the Pintsch system of car lighting. Each car is fitted with globes containing four burners, from which a clear, white, brilliant light is obtained, which enables passengers to read in any part of a car without straining the sight. The illuminant is supplied from the plants at Hoboken and Buffalo, and is carried beneath the cars in tanks that are recharged when necessity requires.

It is the opinion of experienced travellers that no railroad in this country runs better equipped, or has more easy riding cars than these; and all trains are protected at the rear by two *utility* side tail lamps, well elevated, thus securing the longest possible range for the rear danger signal.

On all through express trains the modern vestibule attachment is used, and Pullman's best drawing-room parlor and sleeping-cars are run.

The Lackawanna is a double-track line to Buffalo, and is the shortest route running between New York and that city. The road-bed is heavily ballasted with gravel and sand, and is of unusual firmness. The heaviest steel rails are used to accommodate the additional weight of the constantly improving motive power and rolling stock.

By reason of these improvements travelling on this line is accompanied with all the elements of comfort and ease available, a result of skillful engineering and car building, and this is materially added to by the utilizing of anthracite coal in the locomotives, which affords greater immunity from the inconvenience caused by sparks, cinders, dust and smoke than the use of bituminous coal.

MORRIS AND ESSEX DIVISION.

FROM HOBOKEN the Morris and Essex Division extends westward. One line runs by way of Morristown, taking in the most beautiful and healthful resident-section of Northern New Jersey. The Boonton Branch diverges in a northerly direction after leaving the big Bergen tunnel at West End, touching at Paterson and Boonton, crossing the former line at Denville and again connecting with it at Dover, from which places both lines are operated as one westward to Washington, Warren County, N. J., seventy miles from Hoboken. The first station in New Jersey, beyond Hoboken, is

HARRISON. *Altitude, 29 ft.*
7 miles from New York ; Single ticket, 15 cts. ; Excursion ticket, 25 cts.

Formerly this place was called East Newark. It is situated in Hudson County, and borders on the Passaic River. Manufacturing industries hold sway here, and the town is better known thereby than otherwise. Across the Passaic River, which is spanned by a new iron girder railroad bridge, is

NEWARK. *Altitude, 38 ft.*
8 miles from New York ; Single ticket, 15 cts.; Excursion ticket, 25 cts.

This city is the commercial metropolis of New Jersey. It is situated on the west bank of the Passaic River, upon which craft of all kinds ply, and affords important communication with New York through Newark Bay and Staten Island Sound.

Newark is one of the oldest cities in the State. It covers a large area in Essex County, and ranks as one of the most important manufacturing centres of the United States. Its iron and leather industries are of great commercial importance.

The population is over one hundred and eighty thousand.

Broad Street, running north and south through the city, is one of the most attractive thoroughfares in the country, containing many great business houses, elegant residences, and churches. Washington Park and Military Park, with their numerous stately elms, are the pride of Newarkers. High Street is famous for the beauty of the architecture of its numerous costly residences.

The extreme northern, southern and western sections of the city are largely occupied by residences, and Newark lays just claim to having clean and well-maintained streets throughout.

The famous Passaic River course, where the National Association of Amateur Oarsmen occasionally settle their battles for supremacy, is situated here, and the course is known as one of the best used for rowing contests. It is decidedly picturesque on the Kearney side of the river, and at intervals, along both shores, the boat-houses of the various clubs are located.

All conveniences that any first-class city boasts of can be had here. These include gas, electric light, fine hotels and boarding-houses, good street car systems, theatres, athletic clubs and churches of every denomination. The drives in all directions are pleasing.

Newark, too, is a healthful and well-governed city. Its death rate is low, and epidemics seldom prevail. Several first-class papers supply the news daily.

The society of the city is most refined, and includes a number of the most famous families of New Jersey.

THE HALL BLOCK SIGNAL.

ROSEVILLE AVENUE. *Altitude, 143 ft.*

9 miles from New York ; Single ticket, 15 cts. ; Excursion ticket, 25 cts.

Formerly Roseville was a suburb of Newark, but the phenomenal growth of that city caused it to be included in its territory. It is wholly a resident section, and stands high and dry at the summit of the heaviest grade on the division. The houses are tastefully built, nearly all of them having gardens around them. Roseville Avenue is destined to become the most thickly settled part of the city, and residences are increasing with a rapidity worthy of a western boom. At this station the Bloomfield Branch leaves the main line. The first stop is at

WATSESSING. *Altitude, 135 ft.*
11 miles from New York ; Single ticket, 23 cts. ; Excursion ticket, 40 cts.

Here there is but a small settlement and a few farms. This is a congenial spot for quietude, and the residents have all the desirable elements of sociability. An important and progressive village just beyond it is

BLOOMFIELD. *Altitude 124 ft.*
12 miles from New York ; Single ticket, 25 cts. ; Excursion ticket, 45 cts.

The history of this town is associated with Revolutionary times, and it is among the best known places in the State. Although the enterprise of modern civilization has imprinted itself in every section, yet there are some old-fashioned houses and other landmarks which serve to remind one that Bloomfield was on record a century ago. At the head of the park stands the old church, a sacred pile, that for more than one hundred years has stood to the glory of God. For many years this has been the favorite resort of summer visitors. It is rich in its arboreal growth, has the fine roads, good society, and all the elements that arise from thrift and progressiveness. Bloomfield is the home of many prominent business men, and the residences, in many instances, are both sumptuous and costly.

Adjoining Bloomfield, and but one mile beyond it, is

GLEN RIDGE. *Altitude, 170 ft.*
13 miles from New York ; Single ticket, 27 cts. ; Excursion ticket, 47 cts.

It can be consistently said that this is one of New Jersey's beauty spots. Built, as it is, upon a hill, which commands a charming view of the surrounding country, an attractiveness is given it that favors but few places in this region. Ten years ago Glen Ridge was little more than a wooded slope. Wealth and enterprise have developed the available acres, and the work of improvement is still progressing. This is a village of handsome residences, grassy lawns, park-like estates, and fine roads. The residents, for the most part, are New Yorkers, and these have all the push that characterizes the wide-awake Gothamite.

Glen Ridge is a pleasant and a convenient spot in which to spend a summer. The last station on the branch is

MONTCLAIR. *Altitude, 239 ft.*
14 miles from New York ; Single ticket, 30 cts. ; Excursion ticket, 50 cts.

Montclair (often called the Athens of New Jersey), lying on the eastern slope of the Orange Mountains, is unsurpassed for beauty of situation and healthfulness in the vicinity of the metropolis.

The majority of the residences command magnificent views of New York harbor and the surrounding country.

The population is ten thousand, and the town is growing rapidly in a very substantial way. The public schools are excellent, and there is a military academy and several private schools.

The churches represent all the denominations. The water supply is excellent, and the town enjoys all modern improvements. Three newspapers record all local matters of interest.

Mountain Avenue, running at the base of the mountain from the Orange line to Upper Montclair (3½ miles), dotted by magnificent residences, is said to surpass any avenue or street in the vicinity of New York.

Montclair cannot be seen, to be appreciated, in an hour or two. One must penetrate its by-ways and shaded avenues to realize how much nature has done for this terraced hamlet.

About two-thirds of the roads are macadamized, and it will only be a matter of a few years when they will all be so.

This town may be recommended as desirable in every way, as a place of residence.

VERONA AND CALDWELL

are villages beyond Montclair, which are not on this line of railroad, but communication with them is attained by a stage route that connects with all Lackawanna trains at Montclair. The stage fare is 10 cents.

Mention is made of these places, as they are widely known and appreciated for their remarkable health-possessing qualities, and the picturesqueness of the surrounding country, together with their adaptability for summer residence.

Returning again to the main line, the next station beyond Roseville Avenue is

GROVE STREET, EAST ORANGE. *Altitude, 153 ft.*
10 miles from New York; Single ticket, 20 cts.; Excursion ticket, 30 cts.

A town of phenomenal growth and rich with pretty homes. The streets are uniformly laid out, paved, curbed, and have flagged sidewalks. A feature of the place is that the houses, for the most part, are built separately, and have spacious lawns, neat gardens, and beautiful shade. The streets, too, are lined with spreading shade trees. There are churches of all denominations within easy reach. The nearness to Newark and New York makes Grove Street a particularly desirable place of residence or temporary sojourn.

EAST ORANGE. *Altitude, 172 ft.*
10½ miles from New York; Single ticket, 25 cts.; Excursion ticket, 35 cts.

The same may be said of East Orange as has been said of Grove Street. In reality the former may be called the town proper, as many of the large stores that supply residents are located here. No more bustling little place exists on the line. It has all the elements of enterprise, including water, electric light, etc., schools, churches, social clubs, etc.

The Orange Athletic Club, known the country over, has fine grounds located here in the vicinity of the railroad station, and the drives which extend in all directions are as delightful as they are varied.

BRICK CHURCH. *Altitude, 180 ft.*
11 miles from New York; Single ticket, 25 cts; Excursion ticket, 40 cts.

Years ago, before the Oranges gained the enviable distinction they now possess as places of residence, an old brick church marked the place surrounding which this delightful town has been built. The name, therefore, for some reason, has clung to it. Years ago the name may have been appropriate, but to-day it has no special significance beyond that it recalls memories of times gone by. Brick Church may be said to be in the heart of the Oranges. There are but few luxuries obtainable in a large city not available here, and this town long since established for itself a reputation for being a most desirable one of residence. Here, situated on Prospect Street, is the beautiful home of the Orange Club, the principal social organization of the Oranges, and also the Orange Athletic Club House, which is both artistic in design and spacious.

ORANGE. *Altitude, 185 ft.*

12 miles from New York ; Single ticket, 25 cts.; Excursion ticket, 40 cts.

The city is located on a plain, almost level, and in all New Jersey no more delightful one can be found. Along the main avenue stores of all kinds do a thriving business. Electric and other street cars run to nearby points, so that great convenience in that respect is always at hand. The streets of the city are uniformly laid out and delightfully shaded. The private residences have spacious lawns about them, and many of the structures are marvels of architectural beauty. Electric lights and good water are among the luxuries. The city supports an opera house, and two or three newspapers. Churches of all denominations raise their spires in all parts of the town. The system of schools is as perfect as can be found anywhere. A charm about the city is the high mountain range that skirts the western boundary. The range is called Orange Mountains, and is a spur of the Blue Ridge. It runs toward the northeast, and slopes gracefully toward the valley in which the city is partly located. At the summit of the mountain is located Llewellyn Park, laid out with every elegance of taste and effect in artistic landscape gardening. It contains the homes of wealthy people, and is acknowledged to be the most magnificent spot in New Jersey. Near by, from Eagle Rock, a view of 25 miles around the country can be had. Thomas Edison, the "wizard of electricity," has a fine home in the park, as also had the late General McClellan. The side of the mountain is flecked with imposing residences and finely laid out grounds, among the oldest and finest being that of the Essex County Country Club, whose historic house and beautiful grounds make it one of the most charming country clubs in America.

HIGHLAND AVENUE. *Altitude, 182 ft.*

13 miles from New York ; Single ticket, 30 cts. ; Excursion ticket, 50 cts.

A few years ago this section of the Oranges was called "Valley Station," because the business portion lies in a valley. The name, in a sense, was misleading, because the side hills afford a most beautiful residence section. In addition to being a most desirable place in which to reside, Highland Avenue has a commercial importance. Its hat industry is very extensive, and the quality of the hats made ranks favorably with that of manufacture elsewhere. An incline railway near here conveys passengers to the summit of the Orange Mountains, and a ride on it is an enjoyable experience.

MOUNTAIN STATION. *Altitude, 156 ft.*

13½ miles from New York ; Single ticket, 35 cts. ; Excursion ticket, 55 cts.

There is a vast difference between this and its nearest neighbor. While Highland Avenue is really a very busy place, Mountain Station is the opposite. Essentially a town of homes it is picturesque in the extreme. Nature has been allowed to hold sway to a very large extent, and a feature that will impress the visitor most favorably is the magnificent shade that makes congenial the summer months. To the north the valley reaches out until the mountains are met, and is dotted with pretty residences. To the south the hill rises gradually from the railroad station, and residences with park-like grounds are to be seen in all directions, and extend along westward until they unite with

SOUTH ORANGE. *Altitude, 139 ft.*

14 miles from New York ; Single ticket, 40 cts.; Excursion ticket, 60 cts.

The Oranges terminate here after occupying five miles of territory. South Orange is an important place, because it is the terminus of a number of express and accommodation trains to and from New York. Like the other towns it is famous as a place of residence. Churches and schools are in plenty, and good local government

TENNIS COURT, SOUTH ORANGE FIELD CLUB.

LOOKING SOUTH, SOUTH ORANGE FIELD CLUB.

is a feature that recommends it. The drives about South Orange are romantic, and good roads are the rule. The "Field Club," an organization that needs no introduction, is favorably known wherever outdoor sports are discussed and indulged in. The club-house and beautifully laid out grounds, between Mountain Station and South Orange, are in plain view of passing trains, and here the wealth and beauty of the united Oranges meet in season to enjoy some of the best contests in the State.

The club-house is equipped with all the appurtenances of a first-class club, together with the necessary conveniences of one devoted so largely to field sports.

The grounds, twelve acres in extent, include a quarter mile bicycle-track, three baseball diamonds, eight tennis courts, two football fields, croquet grounds, quoit courts, trap shooting, etc.

From early summer till late in the fall, open tournaments are held in all out-door sports, in which the prominent amateur athletes of the country participate, and the bicycle and foot races, tennis and trap shooting contests, attract widespread attention.

A most interesting feature connected with the Field Club is the opportunity it affords to all its members for indulging in out-door sports and games. "Business men's" contests in baseball, tennis, quoits, etc., take place during the season, and only those are allowed to compete who have never acquired much skill in such sports. The prominent athletes have their opportunity in the open tournaments. Further, the children of members have exceptional facilities for innocent and healthy amusement in the grounds, and are afforded every protection by the keepers in charge.

The Field Club is essentially a family club, and is readily taken advantage of by all who are attracted to South Orange and its vicinity, and as a family summer resort it is very popular. In winter part of the grounds are flooded, and good skating is enjoyed.

MAPLEWOOD. *Altitude, 131 ft.*

16 miles from New York ; Single ticket, 45 cts. ; Excursion ticket, 65 cts.

A very pretty spot for persons who delight in beautiful scenery is Maplewood. Its location, at the base of the mountain, gives it a wild charm. As yet the village has not developed to any great size, but it has several pretty cottages situated on well-made streets, and here there is plenty of shade. The scenery about Maplewood is charming. It has excellent water, fine drives, and pure mountain air. For a summer vacation spot, it ranks among the most desirable places.

WYOMING. *Altitude, 160 ft.*

17 miles from New York ; Single ticket, 50 cts. ; Excursion ticket, 70 cts.

Wyoming is a charming little town, situated right on the side of the mountain. At this point the "first mountain" turns directly northward. Here are many beautiful homes, with spacious grounds, in the midst of a high-wooded slope, where all is wild and picturesque. The scenery from Wyoming is charming, and never grows tiresome. There is not an objectional feature in the town or neighborhood. It is essentially a home-spot, and persons who go there never regret it afterwards.

MILBURN. *Altitude, 148 ft.*

17 miles from New York ; Single ticket, 50 cts. ; Excursion ticket, 75 cts.

This is an old-fashioned town with quaint houses, whose style of architecture suggests a half-century or more ago. It even possesses the conventional mill-pond, which adds to its antiquated appearance. Milburn has always been a popular place for summer boarders. It is surrounded by farms, and has good boarding-houses in town. An excellent supply of water is one of the essential features of the place, and the well-cared-for roads are known all over the State. The terminus of the Milburn bicycle course is here, and in the season wheeling never ceases.

SHORT HILLS. *Altitude, 206 ft.*
18 miles from New York ; Single ticket, 55 cts. ; Excursion ticket, 80 cts.

Short Hills has one specialty to recommend it. As a place of residence it is charming. Situated in a large park, the residences, all of which are palatial, occupy plots, around which wind smooth, macadamized roads. There are no fences roundabout, and every house has a well appointed stable attached. The aim of the individual who established Short Hills has been carried out well. It is for homes only, and not a single place of business is connected with it. A few years ago this charming spot was but a wooded slope. Enough of the grand old forest trees have been preserved to afford a pleasing shade, that in summer almost hides the houses from view.

HUNTLY. *Altitude, 306 ft.*
20 miles from New York ; Single ticket, 55 cts.: Excursion ticket, 80 cts.

A little station on the mountain, established to accommodate the few people who reside there. A fine view of the valley can be had here, and on a clear day New York Bay is visible.

SUMMIT. *Altitude, 385 ft.*
21 miles from New York : Single ticket, 55 cts.; Excursion ticket, 80 cts.

There is no place on this line that can lay claim to more advantages than Summit. As its name implies it is situated on the brow of the second mountain, and is reached after the hard climb of a grade that begins at Milburn.

This village has developed solely on its own merits. Its growth has been strong and so far shows no signs of abating. Backing the development of Summit are men of wealth and thrift, and the houses that are in course of erection are attractively laid out, and its macadamized streets are of the finest and most elaborate kind. At present there are over fifty of them. Owing to its altitude Summit is a bracing spot in which to spend the summer. The air is always fresh and salubrious, and on that account persons afflicted with pulmonary troubles have made it their permanent home. In summer the population generally doubles. All the hotels and boarding-houses, of which there are many of the first class, are full, and the place presents a lively appearance. Many of the permanent residents rent their homes for the season, and there is often more demand for these than supply. Looking northward from Summit is a magnificent view of the Passaic Valley and Blue Ridge Mountain, and towards the southeast, Brooklyn, New York Bay and Staten Island can be seen. The drives through the valleys and over the mountains are magnificent.

Churches of the Episcopal, Methodist, Presbyterian, Baptist and Catholic faiths abound. The social centre is the Casino Club, to which is attached a theatre, bowling alley, etc. This centre is made up of the prominent men of the place and is well patronized. The fresh air home, so well known, and with which many benevolent women of Summit are identified, is situated on Stony Hill, south of Summit. The town is lighted with gas, and has a new and excellent sewerage system ; it is also supplied by the Commonwealth Water Company with pure water drawn from springs in the mountain.

At Summit the Passaic and Delaware Branch diverges toward the west and runs for 21 miles through a valley of unsurpassed beauty and loveliness. The first station is

CHILDREN'S FRESH AIR AND CONVALESCENT HOME AT SUMMIT, N. J.

WEST SUMMIT. *Altitude, 340 ft.*
22 miles from New York ; Single ticket, 65 cts.; Excursion ticket, 95 cts.

A small settlement of quiet homes. The surrounding country is given up to agricultural pursuits.

MURRAY HILL. *Altitude, 251 ft.*
23½ miles from New York ; Single ticket, 70 cts.; Excursion ticket, $1.00.

The ridge that skirts the village on the east is from whence the place is named. Several elegant homes of New Yorkers are situated here and the view is extensive and very fine. The country is fertile and is studded with many prosperous farms.

BERKELEY HEIGHTS. *Altitude, 226 ft.*
26 miles from New York ; Single ticket, 75 cts.; Excursion ticket, $1.10.

Until very recently this place was unimportant. A company having purchased a tract of land, has parcelled it out in building lots and laid out streets, and Berkeley Heights is soon destined to become a thriving spot.

GILLETTE. *Altitude, 213 ft.*
27 miles from New York ; Single ticket, 85 cts.; Excursion ticket, $1.15.

A quiet agricultural settlement surrounded by hills and containing charming patches of scenery. It is also a fine farming country and a healthful place for summer boarders.

STIRLING. *Altitude, 221 ft.*
28½ miles from New York ; Single ticket, 90 cts.; Excursion ticket, $1.20.

This place is associated with revolutionary history by having been named after Lord Stirling. Along the ridge of Long Hill are several pretty residences. The view

PASSAIC RIVER.

of the valley for miles east and west is one of the best in Morris County. Many of the residents find employment at a silk mill near by. Aside from this, agriculture is the principal pursuit.

MILLINGTON. Altitude, 274 ft.

30½ miles from New York ; Single ticket, 95 cts.; Excursion ticket, $1.25.

This is one of the most picturesque spots on the branch. The Passaic River winds around big bluffs and through fertile meadows here and gives a charm to the surroundings seldom met with in a region of this kind. Several persons have taken advantage of the picturesque surroundings to build handsome houses. The drives about Millington are interesting and the roads good.

LYONS. Altitude, 305 ft.

32 miles from New York ; Single ticket, $1.00 ; Excursion ticket, $1.30.

Lyons and neighborhood is devoted to agriculture. Though small and of little commercial importance, it is a splendid place wherein to spend a summer, as the surroundings are healthful and, here, farm life can be enjoyed without stint.

BASKING RIDGE. Altitude, 373 ft.

33½ miles from New York ; Single ticket $1.05 ; Excursion ticket, $1.40.

This is one of the most widely known antiquated towns in the State and may justly lay claim to be reckoned among the best. An old-fashioned style pervades this place which is full of odd buildings and quaint people. In the church-yards there are buried persons whose descendants reside in the vicinity and many of these headstones date back over 100 years. As a summer place of residence Basking Ridge will be found to be full of interest and very bracing.

BERNARDSVILLE. *Altitude, 366 ft.*
35 miles from New York; Single ticket, $1.10; Excursion ticket, $1.45.

This attractive place, situated as it is in the midst of the Somerset County Hills, is frequently alluded to as the "Alps" of New Jersey and the name is not misapplied. Bernardsville is famous as a health resort, and so popular has it become that several prominent families in New York own estates and spend their summers here. The estate of J. Coleman Drayton is acknowledged to be one of the finest in New Jersey. This entire section is charming, abounds in wild scenery, and is breezy and salubrious throughout the summer months. The mountain roads are hard and lead in all directions through pretty villages and a fine farming section. A summer spent here invariably creates a desire to repeat the experience.

Within the past two years the branch has been extended seven miles further, taking in the towns of

MINE BROOK. *Altitude 215 ft.*
37½ miles from New York: Single ticket, $1.20; Excursion ticket, $1.60.

FAR HILLS. *Altitude, 160 ft.*
39 miles from New York; Single ticket, $1.25; Excursion ticket, $1.65.

PEAPACK. *Altitude, 190 ft.*
41 miles from New York; Single ticket, $1.35; Excursion ticket, $1.80.

GLADSTONE. *Altitude, 230 ft.*
42½ miles from New York; Single ticket, $1.40; Excursion ticket, $1.85.

The general character of all these places is similar. The region, on account of the lack of railroad facilities until recently, is undeveloped. Peapack is quite a town. The Rockaway Valley railroad touches here on its way between Whitehouse and Mendham, and these two lines are destined to build up this spot. Gladstone is an old place with a new name, and is a town that has made great strides since it obtained railroad facilities. The region is well adapted to summer recreation, as the drives are good, and many interesting places are near by.

Returning to the main line the next station beyond Summit is

NEW PROVIDENCE. *Altitude, 271 ft.*
22 miles from New York; Single ticket, 60 cts.; Excursion ticket, 95 cts.

The village lies back about a half a mile from the station. It is a farming region and quite popular with city people, who find it a pleasant spot in which to spend the summer season.

CHATHAM. *Altitude, 231 ft.*
24 miles from New York; Single ticket, 65 cts.; Excursion ticket, $1.00.

This ancient town has always been held in high esteem by those who return every year to spend the summer. It has much to recommend it. The Passaic River flows through it, and affords good fishing and boating; the drives through the valley and over Long Hill are delightful. The Chatham Fish and Game Protection Association, which has recently erected a handsome Club House here, looks after the fish and game in the vicinity.

STANLEY, situated south of Chatham on the eastern slope of Long Hill, is a settlement of pretty homes, and, from its location, a grand and ever-changing panorama of the valley of the Passaic spreads out before the eyes. On account of the scenery from Long Hill, this locality has become popular.

DREW SEMINARY, MADISON, N. J.—ENTRANCE TO GROUNDS.

MADISON.   *Altitude, 245 ft.*
26 miles from New York ; Single ticket, 70 cts.; Excursion ticket, $1.10.

This enterprising town has for the past three years been prospering under a borough government. It has a Mayor and Town Council at the head of its affairs ; it also possesses excellent water and electric light systems, and all the comforts of a large city are available. Here, building is very active and it promises so to continue. Madison rejoices in four churches and the Webb Memorial Chapel, an imposing edifice, built and presented to the town by James A. Webb, Esq., a prominent and enterprising citizen. This place has been known as a health resort for a long time, and, on that account, may well be commended. It is noted for the number of its elegant residences, many of which are surrounded by large estates. Mr. H. McK. Twombley is now laying out, at enormous cost, over 200 acres as a park, and when the work has been finished it will prove one of the finest estates in New Jersey. The town itself is in a valley, and on both sides of the long sloping hills pretty homes are located. The view from these hills across the Passaic Valley is one of the features that captivates the seekers of suburban homes.

Drew Theological Seminary, in the immediate vicinity, is well known and is visited by persons from all parts. Good roads and picturesque drives make Madison a pleasant resort for city people during the summer months.

CONVENT. *Altitude, 379 ft.*
28 miles from New York ; Single ticket, 75 cts.; Excursion ticket, $1.15.

The Convent of St. Elizabeth, a large educational institution conducted by Sisters, is located in plain view of the railroad, and from this the station derives its name.

MORRISTOWN. *Altitude, 326 ft.*
30 miles from New York ; Single ticket, 80 cts.; Excursion ticket, $1.25.

This old town, so prominently associated with the history of the Revolutionary War, scarcely calls for any introduction here.

The place may justly lay claim to never having rested upon its past record. Ever since chosen as the headquarters of the Continental Army by Washington, its fame was established, and the associations of those stirring times of our nation's history are still cherished by the descendants of many of the gallant soldiers who took up arms and fought for their independence under the leadership of General Washington.

Not the pages of history alone point to Washington's association with Morristown, but his headquarters, situated on an eminence in the northern part of the city, have been preserved, and since they came into the possession of the State, more land has been added, which has been laid out in beautiful grassy lawns, and broad paths skirted by shade trees. Cannons that have, from time to time, been used in defence of the nation, and which were individually presented, are mounted and frown threateningly around the quaint old building. The national emblem is spread to the breeze daily, not only to indicate the spot, but also to show that the patriotism of our fathers is still ablaze in the breasts of their descendants. From the address of Hon. Theodore F. Randolph, on opening of this building to the public, July 4, 1875: "During the summer of 1873, this property, so long and widely known as the old headquarters of Washington, was offered for sale. A few gentlemen concluded to purchase it, and having done so, formed a society now known as the Washington Association of New Jersey, the principal object of which is to perpetuate this house with its great historic associations, and to gather within these walls so large and interesting a museum of articles connected with the Revolutionary and other history of the Colonies, that this old mansion, rendered immortal by the name of Washington, shall become a Mecca toward which all Americans will turn their steps and obtain, as from a fountain, inspiration to patriotic life and purpose. Under this roof have been gathered more characters known to the military history of the war of the Revolution than under any other roof in America—a fact not generally known. Here, the elegant and brilliant Alexander Hamilton lived during the long winter of 1779, and here he met and courted the lady he afterwards married, the daughter of General Schuyler. Here, too, were Green, the splendid fighting Quaker, as he was, and the great artillery officer Knox, the noble La Fayette, the stern Steuben, the polished Kosciusko, the brave Schuyler, gallant Light Horse Harry Lee, old Israel Putnam, mad Anthony Wayne, and that brave soldier, but rank traitor, Benedict Arnold. Here, too, from time to time, gathered prominent members of the Continental Congress and Statesmen of that day. This dwelling was also, for many months, the home of Martha, the wife of George Washington. Within these rooms, with quiet dignity and grace, she received her husband's guests. Never idle, she set a constant example of thrift and industry. In front of this house, in yonder meadow, lay

WASHINGTON'S HEADQUARTERS, MORRISTOWN, N. J.

P. S.—This Building is the old Ford Mansion about which so much is told in Lossing's Field Book and History of the Revolution.

encamped Washington's body guard—originally a selected troop of about one hundred Virginians. Day and night they kept watch and guard over these headquarters and the precious lives it contained. Many were the plans, and several were the attempts by the enemy to pierce to this old house and to the powder-mill in its rear, and thus at one blow destroy all hope of successful revolution. Had this house been once successfully attacked, and its inmates taken, America's Revolution would, in all probability, have been known to history as America's Rebellion. But, among these hills of Morris no Briton's foot ever trod in Revolutionary times save as a prisoner."

Fort Nonsence, where Washington's guns were planted, is at the summit of the highest hill in town. There a survey of the valley and surrounding country was made and a careful watch kept for the appearance of the enemy. The site of the old fort is marked by a slab bearing a suitable inscription. Morristown now has a population of nearly 10,000 and is governed by a Mayor and Common Council. Every convenience that other cities afford is available here. The avenues are broad, delightfully shaded, and well maintained. Some of the most magnificent residences in the country are located here, and they may be found in all parts of the city, on the neighboring hills, and in the suburbs. This entire region is a sanitarium, and no more healthful spot can be found. The population is made up largely of wealthy New Yorkers, and in summer it is the most sought-after resort within the same distance from New York. Manufacturing is not permitted within the city limits. The Green is a public park occupying an entire square. It is shaded by stately elms, and is divided into fine walks. An elegant soldiers' monument stands on the west side of the Green.

The drives for miles around are most beautiful. Pocahontas Lake is a pretty sheet of water within the city limits, and contains bass and pickerel. It affords good sport for the angler, and the catches are often large. Speedwell Lake is another pretty spot, situated about a mile outside of the city toward Morris Plains, and offers inducements to fishermen who wish to try their skill.

MENDHAM is seven miles from Morristown, and stages connect with all trains to carry passengers there. It has the distinction of being located in the heart of the mountains, and there is scarcely a cooler or more bracing spot in all New Jersey. It is renowned as a healthy spot, and also for the long extended view over valley and lower mountain. This place is nothing but an old-fashioned village, filled with quaint houses, honest people, fertile farms and perpetual happiness. If Mendham had first-class railroad facilities it would prove a dangerous rival to all other places in the State within the same distance from New York. In the warmer months it is filled with summer boarders, and its attractions are almost without limit.

MORRIS PLAINS. *Altitude 403 ft.*

33 miles from New York ; Single ticket, 90 cts. ; Excursion ticket, $1.35.

Many people regard this as being the most beautiful spot along this line. It derives its name from the fact that the town is built on a high plateau, surrounded on the north and west by mountains. Summer here is delightful, on account of the breeze having a clear sweep across the plain. The soil is sandy, and within an hour after a heavy shower is very often as dry as though there had been no rainfall. For this reason the entire section is remarkably healthful. The roads are splendidly kept up, and driving is a luxury. A mile back from the station an imposing building stands ; this is the State Hospital for the Insane. Morris Plains is composed nearly entirely of fine buildings, owned and occupied by well-to-do citizens. There is a small lake within the village limits, where boating and fishing can be enjoyed.

34 DELAWARE, LACKAWANNA & WESTERN R. R.

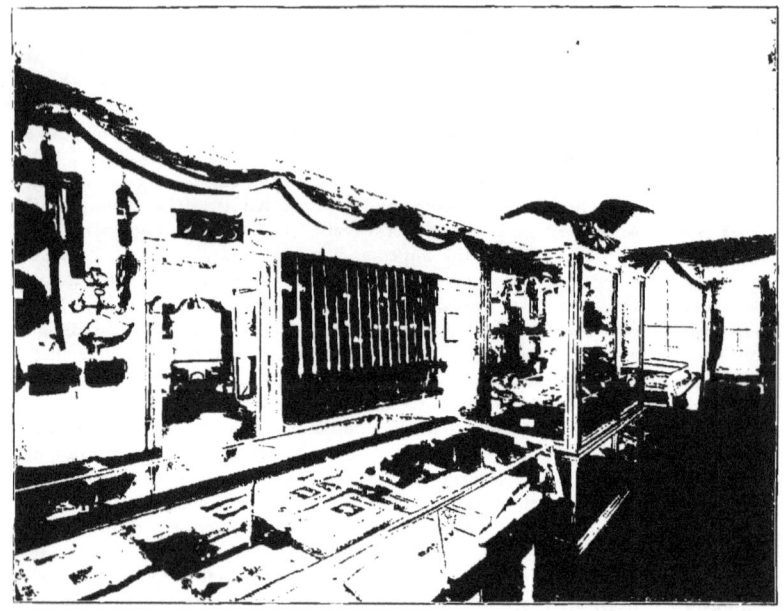

INTERIOR, WASHINGTON'S HEADQUARTERS.

INTERIOR, WASHINGTON'S HEADQUARTERS.

INTERIOR, WASHINGTON'S HEADQUARTERS.

INTERIOR, WASHINGTON'S HEADQUARTERS.

MOUNT TABOR. *Altitude, 531 ft.*
36 miles from New York; Single ticket, $1.00; Excursion ticket, $1.40.

Mount Tabor has become famous on account of the annual gathering of the Methodists, who hold their camp meeting exercises here, and enjoy a quiet sociability in accord with their religious precepts. It is one of a number of picturesque peaks that jut out from the Blue Ridge Mountains. The mountain slope is dotted here and there with pretty cottages owned by members of the Methodist faith, and occupied by them nearly all summer. Life here is calm and enjoyable, and the place is restricted against all nuisances and disorder.

DENVILLE. *Altitude, 520 ft.*
37 miles from New York; Single ticket, $1.00; Excursion ticket, $1.50.

This is a quiet farming district, of few inhabitants, and for a person of an agricultural turn of mind it may well be recommended, for here all its attendant luxuries, such as fresh eggs, milk, etc., can be had. A short branch road connects here with Boonton, and the run between these points occupies but fifteen minutes.

ROCKAWAY. *Altitude, 556 ft.*
39 miles from New York; Single ticket, $1.05; Excursion ticket, $1.60.

A good deal of life is to be found in this bustling little village of manufacturing industries. Rockaway is prettily situated, partly in a valley and partly on a side hill. The Rockaway River flows through it, lending to the picturesqueness of the place. The village boasts of several good stores, and in summer is a favorite spot in which people can spend a summer vacation.

The attention of the reader is now directed to the Boonton Branch, which meets the Morris and Essex division at Dover, the next station beyond Rockaway, where both lines continue westward as one.

After leaving Hoboken, the first station west of the Hackensack River, is

KINGSLAND. *Altitude 25 ft.*
8 miles from New York; Single ticket, 25 cts.; Excursion ticket, 35 cts.

Noted principally for being the place at which the Company's machine shops are located. The village is thrifty, and of steady growth. It contains many farms, and some pretty cottages.

LYNDHURST. *Altitude 34 ft.*
9 miles from New York; Single ticket, 30 cts.; Excursion ticket, 40 cts.

The country about here is attractive, and the pretty village that is growing about the railroad testifies to its healthy popularity. A very pleasant summer can be spent here in driving and roaming about the country.

DELAWANNA. *Altitude, 53 ft.*
10 miles from New York; Single ticket, 35 cts.; Excursion ticket, 45 cts.

A quiet spot, of great beauty, and few inhabitants, bordering on the Passaic River, which at this point assumes a picturesqueness that at once charms the newcomer. Boating, bathing and fishing are among the pleasures peculiar to this place.

PASSAIC. *Altitude, 97 ft.*
11 miles from New York; Single ticket, 40 cts.; Excursion ticket, 55 cts.

Passaic is one of the three important cities on the branch. It contains a population of over 20,000, and is a thriving city, where enterprise carries everything before it towards prosperity. The city contains many miles of broad, well-shaded streets, and is famous for the large number of its elegant residences. No city in New Jersey has enjoyed a more wondrous and continuous growth. Here are churches of all denominations, a theatre, athletic clubs, etc. Although Passaic is a city, it attracts hundreds of city people each recurring summer.

CLIFTON. *Altitude, 121 ft.*
13 miles from New York; Single ticket, 45 cts.; Excursion ticket, 65 cts.

The village of Clifton lies to the eastward of the railroad, and is as pretty and well laid out as any in the State. It is noted for the number and variety of its shade trees, and the quiet character of its inhabitants.

PATERSON. *Altitude, 188 ft.*
15 miles from New York; Single ticket, 50 cts.; Excursion ticket, 70 cts.

Paterson is called the "Lyons of America," on account of its immense silk industries. It is one of the largest cities in New Jersey, and in the importance of its industries probably ranks second; principal among these is the building of locomotives. The Delaware, Lackawanna & Western Railroad runs along the western section of the city, and plays an important part in its commercial welfare. A tour of the manufactories is not only interesting but instructive. The high falls of the Passaic, famous throughout the country, are also worthy of a visit on account of the great beauty of Nature's handiwork.

WEST PATERSON. *Altitude, 188 ft.*
16 miles from New York; Single ticket, 50 cts.; Excursion ticket, 70 cts.

A suburb of Paterson, just outside the city limits.

LITTLE FALLS. *Altitude, 187 ft.*
19 miles from New York; Single ticket, 65 cts.; Excursion ticket, 80 cts.

This pretty little village, the honors of which are divided between manufacturing and agricultural pursuits, can be cheerfully recomended as a place of resort, at once pleasing and refined. Here all the comforts of country life await the stranger, and the fertile farms that dot the valley supply vegetables, milk and eggs in abundance. Little Falls turns out a great amount of carpeting every year, and the falls here are the attraction of the manufacturer. The angler, too, can enjoy himself, and, if fortune favors, may find good luck in casting his line in the Passaic; black bass fishing is not only good at this point, but the place is also known as being one of the very best along the river. The angling grounds are above the falls.

MOUNTAIN VIEW. *Altitude, 175 ft.*
21 miles from New York; Single ticket, 70 cts.; Excursion ticket, 90 cts.

The name of this spot originates from the fact that it is in full view of the Blue Ridge mountains. It is a farming country whose chief attraction is pure air, beautiful scenery and good drives.

LINCOLN PARK. *Altitude, 174 ft.*
23 miles from New York; Single ticket, 75 cts.; Excursion ticket. 95 cts.

WHITEHALL. *Altitude, 221 ft.*
26 miles from New York; Single ticket, 80 cts.; Excursion ticket, $1.05.

MONTVILLE. *Altitude, 309 ft.*
28 miles from New York; Single ticket, 85 cts.; Excursion ticket, $1.15.

These three villages have the same character as Mountain View, and are all desirable places in which to spend the summer months.

BOONTON. *Altitude, 411 ft.*
30 miles from New York; Single ticket, 80 cts.; Excursion ticket. $1.25.

Boonton is among the oldest towns in the State. It is beautifully situated on a mountain side, and commands a view extending over 15 miles across the Passaic Valley. In fact the valley scenery from Boonton captivates strangers who come into the town, and it would be difficult to find anything more magnificent. There is a wild grandeur about the Rockaway River as it flows down the mountain through the town and then breaks into foaming cascades as it tumbles along the ravine, winding in many directions in descending to the valley. The Rockaway River at Boonton affords wild views that are seldom equalled within the limits of civilization. Boonton was at one time a great iron manufacturing centre, but of late years this industry has fallen into decay. As a place of residence it is superb, the society is good, the surroundings are salubrious, and the air is permeated with the odor of pine from the mountains. As a summer resort this town is almost too well known to need recommendation, and the city people who spend the hot months here do not seem to be able to get back again soon enough.

DENVILLE, where the Boonton Branch tracks cross the M. & E. Division, is 35 miles from New York by this line. After a run of four miles around the base of a high mountain both lines meet at

DOVER. *Altitude, 573 ft.*
39 miles from New York, or 42 miles by the M. & E. Division; Single ticket, $1.10; Excursion ticket, $1.75.

On entering Dover one finds a busy centre surrounded by high hills and delightful scenery. The large shops of the Delaware, Lackawanna & Western are located here, and a small army of men are kept at work the year round building new cars and repairing the old. Several other manufacturing industries are also here and are thriving. Dover is a great mining center, the adjacent mountains being filled with a fine deposit of iron. The U. S. Government powder works are located at Picatinny and are one of the attractions to visitors. The city has fine schools, churches of all denominations, and an opera house. The mountain drives in this section are peculiarly inviting. The Rockaway River and Morris Canal both flow through the city. In summer Dover is one of the liveliest cities in New Jersey.

PORT ORAM. *Altitude, 642 ft.*
44 miles from New York; Single ticket, $1.15; Excursion ticket, $1.80.

A quiet little farming hamlet which derived its name from being a station on the Morris Canal.

SUMMER EXCURSION ROUTES AND RATES.

ROCKAWAY RIVER, BOONTON, N. J.

BOONTON FALLS, N. J.

After leaving Port Oram the Chester Branch runs eleven miles westward through a country famous for its rugged mountain peaks, green valleys and brisk streams. This entire section of Morris County ranks among the most healthful portion of New Jersey. There is no limit to the pastoral beauty of the scenery north, and the advantages Port Oram has for vacation enjoyment are numerous. The fertile farms offer every inducement to lovers of rest and quiet, and the hotels and boarding-houses cater especially for city boarders. In fact, each of the villages overflow with city people during the summer months. The water is pure and of good quality, the drives delightful, and the air remarkably bracing. The villages on the Chester Branch are

KENVIL (formerly McCAINSVILLE). *Altitude, 712 ft.*

47 miles from New York; Single ticket, $1.25; Excursion ticket, $1.95.

SUCCASUNNA. *Altitude, 724 ft.*

48 miles from New York; Single ticket, $1.30; Excursion ticket, $2.00.

IRONIA. *Altitude, 699 ft.*

50 miles from New York; Single ticket, $1.35; Excursion ticket, $2 05.

HORTON. *Altitude, 693 ft.*

52 miles from New York; Single ticket, $1.40; Excursion ticket, $2.10.

CHESTER. *Altitude, 682 ft.*

55 miles from New York; Single ticket, $1.50; Excursion ticket, $2.25.

Returning to the main line, the next station is

MT. ARLINGTON. *Altitude, 995 ft.*

47 miles from New York; Single ticket, $1.25; Excursion ticket, $1.95.

Mount Arlington is the station from which Lake Hopatcong is reached by wagon or stage, and was established by enterprising citizens of Lake Hopatcong as a convenience in reaching trains. From this station are special stages to Hotel Breslin.

HOPATCONG STATION (Lake Hopatcong.) *Altitude, 926 ft.*

46 miles *via* Boonton, or 49 miles *via* M. & E. Division; Single ticket, $1.30; Excursion ticket, $2.05.

On alighting from the train the prospective sojourner expects to have his craving for a glimpse at this silver pool in the mountains satisfied at once. But in this he is mistaken. Instead, a little steamboat of the Lake Hopatcong Steamboat Co.—" A Reasoner," " G. L. Bryant," and " Fannie "—awaits him at the landing, adjoining the station on the Morris Canal, and runs by a rather unusual and interesting route to all important points on the lake to deliver passengers.

One of the novelties of the trip is a pleasant ride of a mile up the canal to the lock. On reaching the latter point the boat is " locked in " and raised up several feet; and when the surface is reached, Lake Hopatcong, with its clear green water, irregular shores and numerous rock-bound, wooded islands, presents itself with such suddenness as to completely enrapture all who are contemplating a loiter of more or less lengthy duration on its sloping shores. And at the Lake Landing, one hundred and fifty feet north of the station, are also other steamers—the latter belonging to the Hopatcong Steamboat Company—which carry passengers to all points on the Lake. The boats of the Hopatcong Line are comfortably appointed side-wheelers, and at the present comprise the "Hopatcong," the "Musconetcong," and a steam launch, the "Nariticong." In addition to these, a new steamer has been launched

The lake itself is partly located in Morris and partly in Sussex County. Its altitude is 926 feet above the sea level, and 36 feet above the Delaware River, 35 miles westward. The water, which rises from crystal springs, is transparently green, very deep, and teems with game fish. Black bass and pickerel of enormous size are caught every season, and catfish of good weight are also taken. Hopatcong is the rendezvous of expert fishermen and fisherwomen, and it is the rare sport thus provided that attracts many an angler here each season. Howard P. Frothingham, Esq., Mayor of the borough of Mount Arlington, himself an enthusiastic fisherman, is the fish warden for Lake Hopatcong. He enjoys his office, because, as a true sportsman, he likes to see game fish protected. Woe be to those caught by him fishing out of season, or in season, for that matter, using nets, fikes or any other unlawful means of trapping the fish. Persistent effort on his part has driven these scalawags out of his jurisdiction, so that legitimate fishermen who go to Hopatcong can count on having good sport and happy catches for their trouble.

In this limited space it would be impossible to describe and do justice to the famed beauties of this lake. It so closely resembles Lake George that it is frequently alluded to as the " Lake George of New Jersey." This allusion is justified, although

SUMMER EXCURSION ROUTES AND RATES. 41

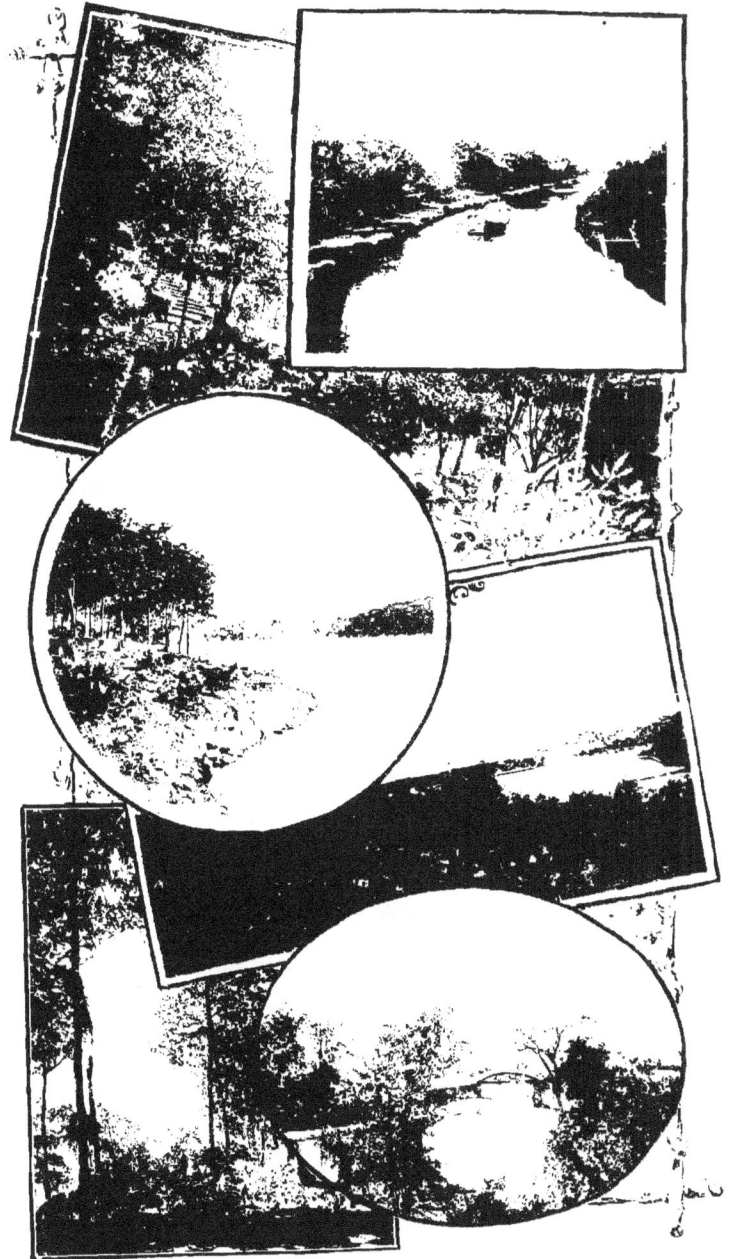

PHOTO-CHROME ENG. CO., 162 LEONARD ST., N. Y.

SCENES IN AND ABOUT LAKE HOPATCONG.

42 DELAWARE, LACKAWANNA & WESTERN R. R.

PHOTO-CHROME ENG. CO., 160 LEONARD ST., N. Y.

SCENES IN AND ABOUT LAKE HOPATCONG.

BRIDGE ON THE MORRIS CANAL, LAKE HOPATCONG, N. J.

Lake George is so much larger as to make the comparison hardly fair. Lake Hopatcong, however, has an advantage of fully 600 feet in altitude over its rival, and in the beauty of its scenery its equality is unquestioned.

Indian tradition is closely associated with both lakes, although Hopatcong never had a Cooper to weave that subtle charm about it that will always cling to the "Horicon," as a result of the ingeniously constructed plots and charming description of Central New York given by the famous writer of "The Leatherstocking Tales."

There is such a variety to the ever-changing scenery of Lake Hopatcong, or "Hopachung," as the red men called it when they settled on its shores. When the water is ruffled by the slightest breeze, its depth appears to lessen, and at sunset, when the surface becomes mirror-like, the shadows of the mountains seem to sink fathoms into the sparkling depths.

About the middle of June, the influx of visitors commences, and from that time until September one round of gaiety succeeds another. The hotels and boarding-houses are full, the lake becomes dotted here and there with pleasure craft of all descriptions, from the frail canoe with sail and paddle to the costly steam launches. The Hotel Breslin, at Mount Arlington, is the largest hostelry on the lake. It is the abode of fashion and culture. The grounds surrounding it are terraced, and handsomely laid out with blossoming shrubs and flowers. The view from the long piazza over the lake comprises many pretty patches of scenery.

The Hotel Breslin will, this season, be under the management of Mr. J. H. King, of the Plant System Hotels of Florida, of which the celebrated Tampa Bay Hotel is one.

For camping out this place excels all others. The wooded shores offer the finest kind of seclusion; the bathing is good, and fishing adds materially to the pleasures of camp life. Not the least interesting feature of an evening on the lake is to watch the camp fires gleaming here and there along the opposite shores, and listen to the frequent camp cries of "rival" parties blending with song and musical accompaniment.

The little hamlet of Mount Arlington is a collection of neat cottages bordering on the lake, and on the hill above it. One of these, the cottage of Miss Lotta

BRIDGE ON THE MORRIS CANAL, LAKE HOPATCONG, N. J.

Crabtree, the actress, deserves particular mention, because its interior is not only gorgeous in its appointment, but in the extent of its artistic arrangements it has been praised by every connoisseur in decorative art.

The walks and rambles are as numerous as they are beautiful, and while out on a tramp anyone fond of exercise is likely to run across an extraordinary number of people, and wonder whence these folks came. Anyhow, everyone there is out for pleasure or rest and each makes the best of his opportunity.

A peculiar freak of nature here is Floating Island, at the southern extremity of the lake, near Shippenpont. The island never appears over one foot above the surface of the water, and is covered with tamarack, spruce and wild flowers of a curious growth in great variety.

Raccoon Island is on the eastern boundary of Henderson's Cove and is covered with a heavy growth of timber. From the fact that human bones have been unearthed on the island, it is supposed that the Indians buried their dead there.

Halsey Island opposite Nolan's Point is artificial. Many years ago the Canal Company, backed by proper authority, flooded the lake and this caused the water to rise to a sufficient height to flood part of the main land peninsulas, thus forming several islands of which this is the largest.

The River Styx, an arm of the lake that empties into it back of the mountain, is quieter than any place around. It is a romantic spot, and on account of the solitude that prevails is a favorite abode for such birds as herons, which stand in the water on one leg, heedless of all that surrounds them.

Henderson's Cove is probably the most beautiful spot on the lake; it is made so by the rugged bluffs that overhang it, which are covered by a hardy growth of oak and hemlock. Trips by boat to the cove are one of the fascinating pleasures of life here.

The lake finds its outlet by the Musconetcong River, which flows an irregular course and empties into the Delaware, 40 miles distant. At times the Canal Company utilizes the water as a means for feeding the Canal, and at such times the lake surface recedes two feet or more.

STANHOPE. *Altitude, 871 ft.*

48 miles from New York; Single ticket, $1.40; Excursion ticket, $2.10.

Stanhope has become known, not on account of its iron-smelting industries, but by reason of its general thrift. It has several churches and schools; has stores of all kinds, and rejoices in one weekly paper. Passengers alight here to be staged through the mountains to

AT ANCHOR, BUDD'S LAKE, N. J.

BUDD'S LAKE. *Altitude, 933 ft.*

Distance from Stanhope, 3 miles.

"Restless and sparkling, its silvery sheen,
Reflects the bold hills in a setting of green."

This pretty sheet of water, almost circular in shape, boasts of being one of the most delightful lakes near New York. It is the resort of many people who love to enjoy the summer season surrounded by pleasant associates in an atmosphere of pure, health-giving air. The beauties of Budd's Lake are always enjoyable, and there is no monotony in a sojourn there. The man who likes fishing, here may gratify his whim by dropping in his line and hauling out vigorous black bass or pickerel. Both these voracious varieties are ready to meet the angler half-way and take the alluring bait. The wonderful stillness of the water, especially at eventide, attracts the holiday maker, and boating is much indulged in. The conventional hammock can find no more delightful place to swing in than above the ruffled wavelets as, under the influence of a cool morning breeze, they ripple on the pebbly shore. Everybody comes here in happy expectancy, and, unless hypercritical and difficult to please, is not disappointed, except, perhaps, at the too short summer which gives way to breezy autumn when the inevitable "good-bye" to the mountains has to be spoken. The sportsman can linger longer and get well repaid for his pains. He may have enjoyed himself thoroughly and been fortunate with rod or gun, but the inducement of bagging a few ducks from the lake, where they congregate every fall, often proves an attraction too strong to be resisted.

WATERLOO. *Altitude, 716 ft.*
52 miles from New York; Single ticket, $1.50; Excursion ticket, $2.25.

Here, at the gateway of the rugged hills of Sussex County, begins the Sussex Railroad. The road is 26 miles long, and traverses a very picturesque country. It is wild, full of little lakes, ponds and silvery streams, that furnish excellent fishing. On account of the mountainous character of the neighborhood, game of all sorts abounds. The partridge is frequently seen along the highways, and, during the fall—

> " Up from the stubble gets the quail,
> I hear the partridge drumming."

Bears, too, are not strangers in Sussex, and scarcely a season goes by that some one does not have to recount the destruction of one or more of these furry creatures. The summer sojourner, of course, is not as eager to kill bears as to roam about at will and avoid them. There is no danger, however, of meeting bruin in the summer months, as it is only in winter that he ventures within the bounds of civilization to forage for his provisions, and, satisfied by stealing a pig or two, he returns quietly to his lair.

As there are innumerable farms and plenty of good hotels and boarding-houses, the region through which the Sussex Railroad runs is particularly inviting to summer vacationists. In fact, any person who appreciates a mountain summer, with pleasant surroundings, can make no mistake in giving any of the places mentioned a season's trial. On leaving Waterloo, the first station is

ANDOVER. *Altitude, 635 ft.*
58 miles from New York; Single ticket, $1.75; Excursion ticket, $2.65.

NEWTON. *Altitude, 599 ft.*
63 miles from New York; Single ticket, $1.90 ; Excursion ticket, $2.95.

NEWTON, the county seat of Sussex, is considered one of the prettiest, as well as most prosperous, towns in North Jersey. The altitude ranges from 580 to 800 feet above mean tide at New York. The population is about 3,500, and the locality one of the healthiest in the state. The town has two shoe-factories, employing over 500 persons, besides other manufactories. Its streets are lighted by arc electric lights, and water is to be introduced during the coming year. Gas is also at command for lighting and heating. The principal streets are macadamized, and the sidewalks are flag and granolithic. As the nights are invariably cool, the daily range of 15° to 25° brings refreshing sleep, and mosquitoes are rarely seen. It has two newspapers, which are known far and wide as compendiums of local news. With prompt and convenient train service, there is no more desirable place in the Jersey Highlands. Business men traveling between town and city are favored by trips in the cool of the day, the average running time being two hours, and on some trains without change of cars. New York morning papers reach the town at 8.30 A. M. The drives in the neighborhood are noted for their beauty, and the proximity to Swartswood, Culvers, Hopatcong, and other lakes, render a summer residence a matter of comfort as well as pleasure. There is a Sunday train to and from New York.

SUMMER EXCURSION ROUTES AND RATES. 47

THE ISLAND, SWARTSWOOD LAKE, N. J.

LAFAYETTE. *Altitude, 554 ft.*
68 miles from New York; Single ticket, $2.05; Excursion ticket, $3.25.

AUGUSTA. *Altitude, 495 ft.*
71 miles from New York; Single ticket, $2.20; Excursion ticket, $3.45.

BRANCHVILLE. *Altitude, 576 ft.*
73 miles from New York; Single ticket, $2.25; Excursion ticket, $3.50.

FRANKLIN. *Altitude, 552 ft.*
76 miles from New York; Single ticket, $2.35; Excursion ticket, $3 60.

Returning again to the main line the next station is

HACKETTSTOWN. *Altitude, 564 ft.*
57 miles from New York; Single ticket, $1.65; Excursion ticket, $2.45.

This is one of the oldest towns in New Jersey. It is situated in the midst of pleasant surroundings, and is an enterprising village of pretty homes and well shaded streets. It has a Mayor and Council and its municipal government is good. The Hackettstown Collegiate Institute, known throughout the country as a prominent seat of learning, is situated here. During the summer season the town is very active on account of the influx of the city people who come to obtain recreation and wholesome air.

SCHOOLEY'S MOUNTAIN.

Like an immense forest, lying some distance back from the town, is Schooley's Mountain, a resort almost too well known to require detailed description. The mountain, when viewed from a distance, resembles a long plateau, so even is its summit, and it is covered with a rich growth of forest trees. Nature has been so unusually kind to this romantic spot that many wealthy gentlemen have selected it as their summer home. Among these are Alfred Sully, Esq., the well-known railroad magnate, and Mr. E. D. Stokes. The Sully abode is palatial in its appointments, and the grounds are laid out in bright flower-beds, arbors and shrubbery. Mr. Sully takes great pride in his valuable assortment of grapes, and has one of the choicest graperies in the State. The air on the mountain is cool and bracing and is favorable for all pulmonary affections and asthma. There are no mosquitoes here, and slumber at night should always be between a pair of warm blankets. Heath House is the most prominent summer hotel on the mountain and is filled every season with the best class of city guests.

PORT MURRAY. *Altitude, 585 ft.*

63 miles from New York ; Single ticket, $1.85 ; Special ticket, $1.70 ; Excursion ticket, $2.75.

WASHINGTON. *Altitude, 503 ft.*

67 miles from New York ; Single ticket, $1.90 ; Special ticket, $1.70; Excursion ticket, $2.85.

This is the most important city in Warren County and is noted for the number of its manufactories, principal among which are the piano and organ industries. The town is located at the base of Pohatcong Mountain and the valley is one of wonderful beauty and fertility. The city is noted for its fine hotels and summer boarding houses and for that reason is well patronized by out of town folks.

BROADWAY. *Altitude 373 ft.*

72 miles from New York ; Single ticket, $2.05 ; Special ticket, $1.85 ; Excursion ticket, $3.05.

STEWARTSVILLE. *Altitude, 372 ft.*

76 miles from New York ; Single ticket, $2.05 ; Special ticket, $2.00 ; Excursion ticket, $3.20.

PHILLIPSBURG. *Altitude, 218 ft.*

82 miles from New York ; Single ticket, $2.05 ; Excursion ticket, $3.25.

This city, one of the largest in the State and an important railroad centre, is the last in New Jersey on the line of this road. It is situated on the Delaware River. In mentioning Phillipsburg it is sufficient to indorse it as a city where all conveniences afforded by other places of its size can be had. The manufacturing industries are important and represent vast wealth. But, after all, this place ranks more as a railroad centre than otherwise.

EASTON, PA. *Altitude, 218 ft.*

81 miles from New York ; Single ticket, $2.10 ; Excursion ticket, $3.30.

Easton is situated just across the Delaware River from Phillipsburg, and is connected by a long bridge. This city, being among the largest in Pennsylvania, needs no description here ; in limited space justice could not be done to it.

Returning again to the main line, which continues westward from Washington, the first station beyond is

OXFORD FURNACE. *Altitude, 436 ft.*

71 miles from New York ; Single ticket, $2.05 ; Special ticket, $1.85 ; Excursion ticket, $3.05.

If this little town were referred to as a small edition of Sheffield, it should not be considered as inappropriate. The iron industry is all that is recognized here.

The Oxford Steel and Iron Company controls the immense plant that turns out nails famous the country over. Nearly all the inhabitants depend on this industry for a living. The town was founded by a Scranton family, and its great success is principally due to their energy. Blairstown, the home of the Hon. John I. Blair, one of New Jersey's iron kings, is within a few miles of here, and is well worth a visit.

BRIDGEVILLE. *Altitude, 486 ft.*

75 miles from New York ; Single ticket, $2.15 ; Special ticket, $1.95 ; Excursion ticket, $3.20.

Just across the little Pequest River, on the three-arch stone viaduct bridge, is this quiet town. The attraction here is fishing, and the waters that furnish it are the Pequest River, Beaver Brook, and several small ponds. Among the natural attractions is Jenny Jump Mountain, close by. The region hereabouts is one of delightful simplicity, and profitable farming is largely conducted.

MANUNKA CHUNK, N. J.
Junction of Belvidere Division Pennsylvania R. R. for Trenton, Philadelphia and the South.

MANUNKA CHUNK. *Altitude, 511 ft.*

77 miles from New York ; Single ticket, $2.20 ; Special ticket, $2.00 ; Excursion ticket, $3.30.

At this point the road connects with the Belvidere Division of the Pennsylvania Railroad for Philadelphia, Baltimore, Washington, and all points south and southwest. The place is small, and agricultural pursuits are the principal industry.

DELAWARE. *Altitude, 290 ft.*

80 miles from New York ; Single ticket, $2.25 ; Special ticket, $2.05 ; Excursion ticket, $3.40.

Delaware is located among the hills of northern New Jersey, and but a short distance from the Delaware River. The surrounding country is hilly, almost

DELAWARE WATER GAP FROM THE SOUTH.

mountainous. Numerous roads lead to places of varied interest, affording delightful drives. Several picturesque and romantic spots in the vicinity invite the rambler, while the river is a source of entertainment for the boatman and fisherman. The Gap, and other attractions within easy reach, are the objects of frequent picnics and excursions during the season. In summer the population generally doubles. A number of good boarding houses are located in the vicinity, and Delaware is quite a popular summer resort.

PORTLAND, PA. *Altitude, 292 ft.*

83 miles from New York ; Single ticket, $2.35 ; Special ticket, $2.15 ; Excursion ticket, $3.50.

This pretty little village is reached by crossing the Delaware River on a 1,200-foot bridge. The river view afforded from trains at this point is very fine. Portland has several commercial industries and is an important town in this region.

DELAWARE WATER GAP. *Altitude 390 ft.*

88 miles from New York ; Single ticket, $2.55 ; Special ticket, $2.35 ; Excursion ticket, $3.70.

Of all the resorts along the line of the Lackawanna, none is more strikingly beautiful than this great handiwork of Nature. Its praises have been sung for generations, and one never wearies of them. From the time that the Redskin ruled the domain the popularity of this grand chasm through the mountains was established, and each year the demand for hotel accommodation continues to increase. There is a peculiar rugged picturesqueness about the scenery that attracts the attention of the observer, and holds it until it is so firmly imprinted on the mind as never to be forgotten. Residents love to tarry by the clear water of the grand old Delaware, and enjoy the pleasures of boating and fishing, and the transient visitor is willing to

MT. TAMMANY, MT. BLOCKADE AND MT. MINSI, WATER GAP.

journey any distance, if it is only to spend a day here. Many excursions are run to Water Gap from different points during the summer months, and so popular have these become that they are booked for months in advance at the Company's passenger department offices.

A critical review of this region, and the Delaware River, cannot fail to be of interest to the readers.

The Delaware River rises 200 miles northward, in two lateral branches, flowing from the western slope of the Catskill Mountains, 2,000 feet above the sea level. The western branch passes through a lake near its source, retaining, for a wonder, its quaint aboriginal name "Utsayantha." This is described as a circular sheet of transparent water covering an area of 70 acres and having an elevation of 1,888 feet ; a mirror of beauty in the wooded wilderness, so secluded that few save the red men have ever gazed upon its serene solitude. In its course the river hugs the base of the grand old mountains, older in date of upheaval than the snow-clad "Alps," which once formed a barrier to its passage, and rolled back the flood of waters, submerging for a long time the lesser hills and swelling plains that now, clad in verdure, adorn its borders.

The character of the rocks in this portion of the Blue Ridge is that of gray and red sandstone and conglomerates, containing white quartz pebbles of large size. The escarpment at the point of dislodgement is more bold on the New Jersey portion of the mountain, the means of the angle for the entire elevation of 1,600 feet being about 70 degrees, while projecting cliffs, as seen from the gorge, exhibit sections of perpendicular descent. On the Pennsylvania mountain the general slope from the summit to the river is less precipitous ; a mass of talus having been detached from the crest by the frost of winter, and pouring like lava down its sides, has covered the surface to the depth of many feet, concealing the rugged projections that characterize the face of the opposite mountain.

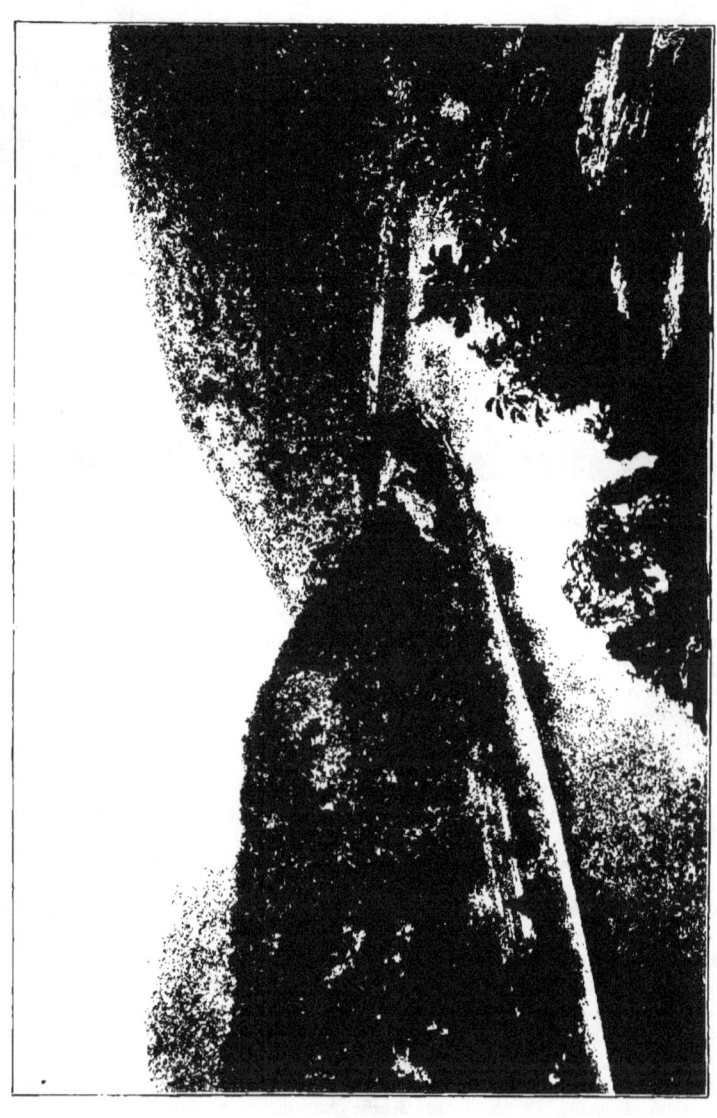

DELAWARE WATER GAP.

From both the summits—Mount Tammany in New Jersey and Mount Minsi in Pennsylvania—views of great extent and beauty are obtained, but it is difficult to do them justice by mere description; they must be seen to be fully appreciated. One overlooks an extent of country to the south as far as eye can reach; a scene of vast breadth, comprising mountains and hills, villages and farmhouses, cultivated fields, groves of woodland and primitive forests—the river on its sinuous journey filling up the picture. It was upon the summit of Minsi, that, over a quarter of a century ago, a romantic young lady lost her way, and was exposed for a greater part of a night on the ledge of a cliff, to which she had fallen, and from which with much

DELAWARE WATER GAP FROM NEW JERSEY SHORE.

difficulty she was rescued. On the way to Mount Minsi to the settled portion of the Gap, a fine view is obtained from

PROSPECT ROCK.—This bare platform, though much below the summit, enables the visitor to enjoy one of the finest pieces of scenery on the Delaware. The view up the river extends beyond the islands to the distant hills and mountain, through which the river winds its tortuous course and glides smoothly along the base of the precipice from which you are gazing. Near Prospect Rock is

WATER GAP.

THE HUNTER'S SPRING.—A wild, secluded spot where many a Lenape huntsman as well as those of modern times, have been refreshed, and have lain in wait for the deer as they came panting for the cooling waters. It is at the head of a wild ravine and the source of Eureka Creek, which tumbles over the rocky bed in its rapid descent to the river, and in which are found Moss Cataract and Rebecca's Bath. Near by is

THE LOVER'S LEAP.—This is the artist's favorite spot and is made memorable as the scene where the Indian Princess " Winona " and her lover took their fatal leap.

CALDENO CREEK.—This is a noted spot. It has its rise high up the side of Mount Minsi. Dashing and foaming in its descent, it flows at length into the valley, and after gladdening the inmates of several farm houses, changes its course and runs close by the ruins of an old saw mill, which at one time it made busy as the machinery was put in motion by the plashing of the water over a big wheel. From the old mill the stream flows across a green meadow and again loses itself in an entanglement of forest, from which it again emerges at Moss Cataract, dashes over its mossy bed, fills Diana's bath afresh, gives a leap over the falls of its own name and hastens on to lose its identity in the broad waters of the Delaware.

TABLE ROCK AND COOPER'S CLIFF.—Both are situated on an extended rocky platform of about 300 feet in elevation, overlooking the river and the cultivated hills in the distance. The confused mixture of forest and hills, and the cultivated land below the cliff on which one stands, forms a beautiful foreground to the finely developed proportions of the gorge in the distance.

SUNSET HILL rises only a few rods to the northeast of the apparently undisturbed stratification of Table Rock, and is a confused, disjointed, irregular mass of rock from base to apex.

We have given a tolerably fair idea of the general character of the scenery and views at Water Gap, but its attractions, if they begin, certainly do not end there. There are numerous walks besides those we have named, and drives which we have not mentioned at all—long drives to the beautiful falls of Winona and Bushkill, and short drives to romantic places with commonplace names: Fox Hill, the Knob, Lake of the Mountain and a dozen others. Stroudsburg is but four miles distant.

The air about here is pure and appetizing, and while the days are not hot nor humid, the nights are so delightfully cool that sleep of the kind that rests and invigorates is assured. The Water Gap is famous for its fine hotels, where the best service in the land is bestowed without stint. The drinking water, from Caldeno Creek is very pure.

STROUDSBURG, PA. *Altitude, 400 ft.*

92 miles from New York: Single ticket, $2.70; Special ticket, $2.50; Excursion ticket, $3.85.

This old town is delightfully situated on Broadhead's Creek and is the capital of Monroe County. It is the first town of importance the road touches in Pennsylvania. It was founded by Col. Stroud, after whom it is named, and occupies the old site of Fort Hamilton. The place, which has a population of 2,000 inhabitants, is remarkable for its beauty as well as for the beauty of the surrounding country. Among the delightful bits of scenery named from the town are the Blue Ridge mountains lying to the south and Pocono Mountain to the north. At the point where Broadhead's Creek flows through the town, two other streams converge—McMichael's and Pocono Creek. Stroudsburg has many interesting historical associations. The watering places in the vicinity always prove attractive to summer visitors. Among them are Lake Pokonoming, Porter and Perch; and Bushkill, Buttermilk, Sawkill, Marshall's and Saw Creek Falls. Trains running westward begin a gradual ascent. The grade is steep and the powerful engines have to do their best in order to draw their load to the summit of Pocono Mountain. From this station passengers will take stages for Forest Park.

ALWAYS READY.

STEAMBOAT "KITTATINNY,"

Trip to Water Gap and return requires half an hour. Fare, 25 cents.

ROW BOATS

With or without oarsmen.
Bait and Fishing Tackle Supplied.

ALBERT C. GRAVES,
Boatman.

FOREST PARK.

BUSHKILL, PIKE COUNTY, PENNSYLVANIA.

15 miles from Stroudsburg.

It comprises about sixteen thousand acres of land, diversified by mountain and valley, lakes and streams.

Its mountain streams, fed by bubbling springs, are the lurking places of countless trout, and the lakes are the abiding places of the gamy black bass and the sun-loving perch.

In the forest, much of which is in primeval state, deer and bear, partridge and pheasant, grouse, quail, woodcock, foxes, rabbits and squirrel abound.

SPRAGUEVILLE. *Altitude, 524 ft.*

96 miles from New York ; Single ticket, $2.85 ; Special ticket, $2.65 ; Excursion ticket, $4.05.

Spragueville is an attractive village surrounded by many hills, which give it a picturesque appearance. It is the summer home of several wealthy persons whose residences are costly and beautiful. Like its larger neighbor, Stroudsburg, it is located on Broadhead's Creek, which at this point is decidedly pretty ; it is famous for the fine trout fishing it affords. The Analomink streams, both celebrated for their trout, are near the village. The drives are magnificent for miles around and this kind of pleasure, coupled with equestrianism and pedestrianism, keeps tourists busy enjoying themselves.

HENRYVILLE. *Altitude 784 ft.*

100 miles from New York ; Single ticket, $2.95 ; Special ticket, $2.75 ; Excursion ticket, $4.20.

Running out a few miles on the D., L. & W., anxious to spend all day Saturday taking fine brook trout, beauties that run up to 1¾ lbs. in weight, we should go to Henryville, in Monroe County, Pa., and there find a little town prettily situated on the mountain side. At the depot a spanking team of farm horses and a good springy buckboard await us with which to take a drive over the mountain to Parkside. Here one is surrounded by some of the most prolific brook trout streams in America—East and West Branch, Broadhead, Cranberry, Heller, Paradise and Devil's Hole—all famous. Parkside, on the banks of the Analomink, is a beautiful little rural retreat, not more than three hour's ride from New York. The Park House is situated in the centre of a beautifully laid out ground, with the river at one side and the mountains on the other. The altitude of the place gives it perfect freedom from mosquitoes and malaria, and in summer the temperature is delightfully cool.

The ride over the hills from the depot will give you an appetite alone worth the trip. And the food! Food that is clean and fresh, food that is free of a city smell, food that has a natural ring to it—butter, cream, eggs, milk, vegetables, and all sorts of things produced right from the farm. We will lounge about the farm Friday evening, smoking our pipes or cigars and listening to the yarns about the big fish we will have to battle with in the morning ; then retire for the night. There is no trouble about going to sleep, and when we awake, a refreshing breakfast awaits us, after which we will go forth and flail the wooded streams, coming in with good creels of fine-sized fish. Sunday resting about the farm we partake of delicious fruit, and breathe the invigorating mountain air until night falls again, and once more we seek the restful couch. The early morning train may be taken on Monday, and—the city reached only too soon. The points of interest within easy riding or driving distance are the Water Gap, Red Rock Glen, Prospect Ledge, Silver Cascade, Pocono Summit, Point Lookout and one or two others of less fame.

PHOTO. BY T. E. DILLON, SCRANTON, PA.
ON THE LACKAWANNA AT CAPOUSE.

CRESCO. Altitude, 1,203 ft.

105 miles from New York ; Single ticket, $3.15 ; Special ticket, $2.95 ; Excursion ticket, $4.45.

Cresco is situated in the highlands of Monroe County close to where the waters of the Delaware River flow. It can be safely asserted that the forests and streams here give more pleasure than the average sportsman can find time to indulge in ; a region of woodland and water, it attracts them every season, and has attained for itself a well-deserved reputation.

MOUNT POCONO. Altitude, 1,824 ft.

111 miles from New York ; Single ticket, $3.35 ; Special ticket, $3.15 ; Excursion ticket, $4.65.

The visitor realizes that he is now very near the highest point of the mountains, because the panoramic view that spreads before his gaze calls attention to the fact. These mountains cross the northeasterly counties of the State and are spurs of that same great chain that traverses the Atlantic Coast section from the Catskills in New York State to the Black Mountains in North Carolina. The scenery in the Pennsylvania portion of the range is unrivalled, and in the way of sport with rod and gun is not surpassed by any other State. In standing at the top of Pocono Mountain which is 2,000 feet above tide-water, two entire counties are unfolded to the view, as well as the Water Gap and Delaware River. The air at this great height is strong and bracing, and, as it is introduced to the relief of the overworked seeker of health and

Big Fill-In, Mt. Pocono, Pa.

PHOTO, BY T. E. DILLON, SCRANTON, PA.
A LONG WHILE BETWEEN BITES.

happiness, it blows through the mountain pines which impart to it a resinous odor calculated to stimulate the appetite.

Persons afflicted with hay fever and asthma should come here to get cured. Another feature that recommends this region is its absolute freedom from the mosquito pest. As the thermometer rarely rises above 80 degrees in the hottest weather, outdoor life is always agreeable. At night log fires on the hearth, warm wraps and blankets on beds are in order.

In recent years the tendency has been to develope new mountain resorts. The success of Mount Pocono is fully assured, and persons who are satisfied with its healthfulness, its accessibility and adaptability to sport with rod and gun, have erected first-class hotels and cottages right in the heart of the wilderness.

Among the numerous drives that have become popular are those to Pocono Knob, Buckhill, Paradise Falls and Devil's Hole. Here are charming walks leading in all directions through the forest, which nature has strewn with rhododendrons and other shrubs.

POCONO SUMMIT. *Altitude, 1,961 ft.*

114 miles from New York: Single ticket, $3.45; Special ticket, $3.25;
Excursion ticket, $4.75.

This paradise of the sportsman does not differ in character from Mount Pocono. The doors of the few hotels are open to welcome the season's guests, and every facility for comfort and enjoyment will be offered. The engineers of western-bound trains

View from Bluff, Overlooking Tunnel, Scranton, Pa.

THE WISCASSET AND WATER GAP FROM WISCASSET HEIGHTS.

are always glad when they reach the summit that they may take matters a little easier in the descent that follows.

TOBYHANNA. *Altitude, 1,929 ft.*
118 miles from New York; Single ticket; $3.60; Special ticket, $3.40; Excursion ticket, $4.95.

Tobyhanna is a mountain village of about 800 inhabitants, and is prettily situated on the western slope of Pocono, about equal distance from Stroudsburg and Scranton. Several industries are established here and the outlook is promising. The air being pure, cool and bracing, the place is becoming famous as a resort for people affected with pulmonary diseases.

GOULDSBORO. *Altitude, 1,970 ft.*
124 miles from New York; Single ticket, $3.80; Special ticket, $3.60; Excursion ticket, $5.15.

A small town named after the late Mr. Jay Gould, who, in the early part of his life, established a tannery here. It is a pleasant, healthy spot, and is growing in favor as a summer resort.

MOSCOW. *Altitude, 1,887 ft.*
132 miles from New York; Single ticket, $4.10; Special ticket, $3.90; Excursion ticket, $5.50.

This is quite a thriving town and one of the prettiest west of the mountains. It is also a fine agricultural region, and in summer is gay with the cheery voice of happy vacationists. The walks and drives about here are among the most attractive features.

ELMHURST. *Altitude, 1,400 ft.*
135 miles from New York; Single ticket, $4.20; Special ticket, $4.00;
Excursion ticket; $5.60.

A quiet colony of refined people, that has become noted as an excellent place to spend a vacation. It is healthful, and the scenery in the neighborhood is very attractive.

PHOTO. BY T. R. DILLON, SCRANTON, PA.
ELMHURST TO SCRANTON, PA.

Elmhurst, nine miles from Scranton toward New York, has in the last few years come into deserved prominence as a place of resort. It is noted for its pure water, pure air, and beautiful scenery.

Hotel Elmhurst is replete with every modern improvement, including gas and electric bells in every room, and is supplied with pure spring water, with thorough plumbing and drainage. The broad porches command an extended view of mountain, lake and woodland. The hotel grounds comprise four acres and contain croquet and lawn tennis courts, and are made doubly attractive by the flowers and shrubbery and well-kept and verdant lawns.

Elmhurst is brought into close communication with Scranton by the Nay Aug Falls and Elmhurst boulevard, just completed, which provides a magnificent driveway second to none in this country, between Scranton and Elmhurst. From the heart of the city the road emerges into beautiful Nay Aug Park and after spanning Nay Aug gorge with a steel bridge 350 feet long and 125 feet above the water, winds around the mountain peaks in graceful curves and with easy grades, disclosing at every turn grand and far reaching mountain views, which place this beautiful drive without a peer for scenic effect.

SCRANTON. *Altitude, 740 ft.*
145 miles from New York; Single ticket, $4.55; Special ticket, $4.35; Excursion ticket, $6.00.

Scranton is the capital of Lackawanna County, Pa. Its coal and iron industries have placed it in the foremost rank of manufacturing cities. Millions of people annu-

PHOTO. BY T. E. DILLON, SCRANTON, PA.
ELMHURST TO SCRANTON, PA.

ally pay tribute to the output of coal from the Scranton region, and the steel rails that thread this continent from ocean to ocean, and from the Canadian border to the Gulf, are to a very large extent produced right in the rolling mills within plain view of the Lackawanna trains as they speed by.

Scranton is also a metropolis of northeastern Pennsylvania, the third city of the State; it has a population of 100,000. Being located in the famous Lackawanna-Wyoming Valley, and on the Lackawanna River, it occupies a succession of hills and eminences, important among which is Hyde Park Hill, from which a magnificent view of the city and surrounding country may be obtained.

The city is supplied with good water and claims to be one of the best lighted places in the country. The hotels are good and well maintained. There are churches of all denominations, literary societies, clubs, both athletic and otherwise, and excel-

PHOTO. BY T. E. DILLON, SCRANTON, PA.
VIEW NEAR SCRANTON, PA.

NORTHERN APPROACH TO PARADISE TUNNEL.

PHOTO. BY T. E. DILLON, SCRANTON, PA

MOSES TAYLOR HOSPITAL, SCRANTON, PA.

lent street-car facilities. Several railways connect here, making it an important railroad centre as well as manufacturing town. Not the least interesting feature of the city is a visit to the rolling mills and giant coal breakers, which, when the busy season is at its height, crush and prepare for shipment fifty-five thousand tons a day. A visit to the subterranean coal galleries in the mines will prove an entertaining experience and one well worth the trouble.

Despite the immense amount of manufacturing done here the city, unlike many others, is not permeated with smoke and gases, as might be expected. On the contrary the air is pure, and the city is a very pleasant place to visit or remain in at any season of the year. In fact, Scranton contains as many magnificent residences and public buildings as any city of its size in the United States, and this bears the best testimony to its healthfulness that can be given.

Among the resorts within short distance are Mauch-Chunk, with its great switchback and gravity road to Honesdale. Numerous lakes in the surrounding mountains afford good fishing, black bass and pickerel being plentiful.

IN THE WYOMING VALLEY.
PHOTO. BY T. R. DILLON, SCRANTON, PA.

IN THE WYOMING VALLEY.

THE BLOOMSBURG DIVISION.

FOLLOWING the Susquehanna River along the greater part of the division, the view from the train is particularly fascinating. This portion of the Wyoming Valley abounds in historic interest as well as in some of the wildest scenery that can be found on the line. For the latter reason it has grown rapidly in favor as a region for summer resort.

The first station beyond Scranton is:

BELLEVUE. *Altitude, 723 ft.*

146½ miles from New York; Single ticket, $4.60; Special ticket, $4.35; Excursion ticket, $6.05.

TAYLORVILLE. *Altitude, 723 ft.*

148 miles from New York; Single ticket, $4.65; Special ticket, $4.35; Excursion ticket, $6.10.

LACKAWANNA. *Altitude, 637 ft.*

151½ miles from New York; Single ticket, $4.75; Special ticket, $4.35; Excursion ticket, $6.30.

DURYEA.

152½ miles from New York; Single ticket, $4.80; Special ticket, $4.35; Excursion ticket, $6.35.

PITTSTON. *Altitude, 572 ft.*

154 miles from New York; Single ticket, $4.85; Special ticket, $4.35; Excursion ticket, $6.40.

At this point the railroad crosses the Susquehanna River. Among the many interesting places are Campbell's Ledge, a high and picturesque bluff, which, in early history, was used by the Indians as a point of observation from which they kept themselves posted as to what was going on around them.

SUSQUEHANNA AVENUE. *Altitude, 579 ft.*

155 miles from New York; Single ticket, $4.90; Special ticket, $4.35; Excursion ticket, $6.50.

"AMONG THE DUSTY DIAMONDS (300 FEET) UNDERNEATH THE GROUND."
AT MOUNT LOOKOUT COLLIERY, WYOMING, PA.

WEST PITTSTON. *Altitude, 579 ft.*

155½ miles from New York; Single ticket, $4.90; Special ticket, $4 35;
Excursion ticket, $6.50.

WYOMING. *Altitude, 588 ft.*

157½ miles from New York; Single ticket, $4.95; Special ticket, $4.35;
Excursion ticket, $6.60.

This town became noted as early as 1778, through being the scene of a massacre by Indians, now better known as the Wyoming Massacre. The spot where the butchery occurred is an interesting place to visit.

Here is situated the celebrated Methodist Episcopal Seminary, which was originally erected in 1844 at the modest cost of $5,000. This great institution flourished until 1853, when the original building was burned, but soon after another and far handsomer building took its place. The popularity of Wyoming Seminary as a Christian School and Educational Establishment has so extended that it now comprises some half a dozen or more buildings.

MALTBY. *Altitude, 558 ft.*

159½ miles from New York; Single ticket, $5.50; Special ticket, $4.35;
Excursion ticket, $6.65.

PHOTO. BY T. E. DILLON, SCRANTON, PA.

ON THE LACKAWANNA.

BENNET. *Altitude, 553 ft.*

161 miles from New York; Single ticket, $5.00; Special ticket, $4.35;
Excursion ticket, $6.70.

At Bennet's connection is made with the Harvey's Lake branch of the Lehigh Valley. Harvey's Lake is a pretty sheet of water, high up in the mountains, which has long been famous as a resort for excursionists and sportsmen.

KINGSTON. *Altitude, 562 ft.*

162 miles from New York; Single ticket, $5.00; Special ticket, $4.35;
Excursion ticket, $6.80.

At Kingston, connection is made with Wilkes-Barre, one mile distant. A line of electric cars operate between the two places. The Delaware, Lackawanna & Western's workshops occupy a large plot of ground here and contribute largely to the prosperity of the town. Coal operations also are extensively carried on, and the company's largest coal breaker is in use here. Wyoming Seminary is in the immediate neighborhood.

WILKES-BARRE. *Altitude, 550 ft.*

165 miles from New York; Single ticket, $5.00; Special ticket, $4.35;
Excursion ticket, $6.85.

Wilkes-Barre is one of the most prosperous cities of Pennsylvania. It is beautifully situated in the Wyoming Valley, and owes its prosperity to the rich and extensive anthracite coal fields in the vicinity. One of the great veins is thirty feet in thickness.

On account of the supply of coal, so close at hand, many industries have sprung up here and capital has been heavily invested. The citizens have been generous in their outlay of money, and in consequence the city has been improved, being made much more attractive than nature could possibly make it. The society is refined, and as a summer resort the city offers many inducements.

PHOTO. BY T. E. DILLON, SCRANTON, PA.

SUSQUEHANNA AT SHICKSHINNY.

PLYMOUTH. *Altitude, 535 ft.*

165 miles from New York; Single ticket, $5.05; Special ticket, $4.45; Excursion ticket. $6.90.

AVONDALE. *Altitude, 530 ft.*

167½ miles from New York; Single ticket, $5.10; Special ticket, $4.50; Excursion ticket, $7.00.

NANTICOKE. *Altitude, 538 ft.*

168½ miles from New York; Single ticket, $5.15; Special ticket, $4.55; Excursion ticket, $7.05.

Connection is made here with the Pennsylvania Railroad.

SUMMER EXCURSION ROUTES AND RATES. 71

HUNLOCKS. *Altitude, 531 ft.*
172½ miles from New York; Single ticket, $5.25; Special ticket, $4.70; Excursion ticket, $7.25.

SHICKSHINNY. *Altitude, 521 ft.*
178 miles from New York; Single ticket, $5.25; Special ticket, $4.85; Excursion ticket, $7.45.

This place is much better than its sing-song name would imply. It is situated in the midst of wild mountain scenery and is as romantic a spot as exists in the valley.

PHOTO. BY T. R. DILLON, SCRANTON, PA.
THE SUSQUEHANNA, NEAR SHICKSHINNY.

Besides the grand scenery, the fishing in the Susquehanna here is good, and black bass is plentiful. Shickshinny is located at the extreme southern outcrop of the Wyoming coal basin.

HICK'S FERRY. *Altitude, 521 ft.*
183½ miles from New York; Single ticket, $5.30; Special ticket, $5.00; Excursion ticket, $7.65.

BEACH HAVEN. *Altitude, 530 ft*
186 miles from New York; S:ng'e ticket, $5.30; Special ticket, $5.10; Excursion ticket, $7.75.

BERWICK. *Altitude, 501 ft.*

189 miles from New York; Single ticket, $5.30; Special ticket, $5.15;
Excursion ticket, $7 85.

Berwick is quite a manufacturing town, and here the extensive plant of the Jackson and Woodin Car works is located. The manufacture of iron piping is largely carried on in the town.

BRIAR CREEK. *Altitude, 502 ft.*

192 miles from New York; Single ticket, $5.30; Special ticket, $5.25;
Excursion ticket, $8 00.

WILLOW GROVE. *Altitude, 516 ft.*

193½ miles from New York; Single ticket, $5.30, Special ticket, $5.25;
Excursion ticket, $8.10.

LIME RIDGE. *Altitude, 509 ft.*

195½ miles from New York; Single ticket, $5.30; Special ticket, $5.25;
Excursion ticket, $8 15.

ESPY. *Altitude, 490 ft.*

199 miles from New York; Single ticket, $5.30; Special ticket, $5.25;
Excursion ticket, $8.30.

BLOOMSBURG. *Altitude, 489 ft.*

201 miles from New York; Single ticket, $5 35; Special ticket, $5.25;
Excursion ticket, $8.35.

The Lackawanna connects here with the Bloomsburg and Sullivan road. Bloomsburg is a prosperous place, and is the capital of Columbia County. The State Normal School occupies a commanding site in town. The angler will find excellent fishing here.

Bloomsburg, conceded to be the most progressive and prosperous town along the Susquehanna, is one of the prettiest in the State, and owing to the large number of manufactories established within a few years is rapidly increasing in importance. Beautiful scenery, good fishing and fine roads commend it to the attention of the tourist. The Bloomsburg and Sullivan R. R. here connects with the D. L. & W. and affords easy access to the famous fishing and hunting grounds of Sullivan County, "The Adirondacks of Pennsylvania." The educational advantages of Bloomsburg are of the best, and the buildings of one of the largest Normal schools in the country, situated on the hill above the town, attract the eye from every direction. The floral establishment of J. L. Dillon, one of the most extensive in the country, is one of the sights of the place. Tourists will find Bloomsburg a desirable place to visit.

RUPERT. *Altitude, 482 ft.*

203 miles from New York; Single ticket, $5.35; Special ticket, $5.25;
Excursion ticket, $8.45.

At this point connection is made with the Philadelphia and Reading's Catawissa Division, and the road crosses Fishing Creek. The summer tourist and fisherman alike will find Rupert a nice place to spend the outing season.

PHOTO. BY T. E. DILLON, SCRANTON, PA.
CARNATION FIELD (CONTAINING 75,000 PLANTS) OF J. L. DILLON, OF BLOOMSBURG, PA.

CATAWISSA. *Altitude, 473 ft.*

204½ miles from New York; Single ticket, $5.35; Special ticket, $5.25; Excursion ticket, $8.50.

DANVILLE. *Altitude, 457 ft.*

213 miles from New York; Single ticket, $5.65; Special ticket, $5.51. Excursion ticket, $8.85.

At one time Danville was famous for the extent of its iron industry, but continued labor strikes have reduced the output almost to nil.

CHULASKY. *Altitude, 455 ft.*

216 miles from New York ; Single ticket, $5.80 ; Special ticket, $5.60 ; Excursion ticket, $9.00.

CAMERON. *Altitude, 458 ft.*

218 miles from New York ; Single ticket, $5.90 ; Special ticket, $5.65 ; Excursion ticket, $9.10.

NORTHUMBERLAND. *Altitude, 452 ft.*

225 miles from New York: Single ticket, $6.05; Special ticket, $5.71; Excursion ticket, $9.12.

Northumberland is the terminus of the division. Connection is here made with the Northern Central road (Pennsylvania system).

CLARK'S SUMMIT. *Altitude, 1,242 ft.*

152 miles from New York; Single ticket, $4.80; Special ticket, $4.60; Excursion ticket, $6.30.

Clark's Summit is the highest point between Scranton and Great Bend, and the road here runs through a series of deep cuts and over heavy grades. The country is magnificent, and abounds in fine farms. The attractions are many and varied, and several beautiful lakes and streams repay the sportsmen who visit them with catches of fish.

GLENBURN. *Altitude, 1,260 ft.*

155 miles from New York: Single ticket, $4.90; Special ticket, $4.70; Excursion ticket, $6.45.

DALTON. *Altitude, 986 ft.*

156 miles from New York: Single ticket, $4.95; Special ticket, $4.75; Excursion ticket, $5.50.

Dalton is to Scranton what many of those beautiful country towns in New Jersey are to New York, viz: The country residence place of many of the most prominent business and professional men of that active and thriving city. The beautiful drives, the invigorating air and the many and varied changes of scenery render this and the other villages in close proximity to it the most popular places for obtaining rest and comfort during the heated season of any along the line of the road.

LA PLUME. *Altitude, 877 ft.*

158 miles from New York; Single ticket, $5.00; Special ticket, $4.80; Excursion ticket, $6.60.

FACTORYVILLE. *Altitude, 890 ft.*

160 miles from New York; Single ticket, $5.10; Special ticket, $4.90; Excursion ticket, $6.65.

This growing town is principally noted for its fine dairy produce and farms. The mountain attractions are numerous and the drives pretty. A short stay here will well repay.

LAKE WINOLA.—Four and a half miles from Factoryville, one of the most beautiful and largest sheets of water in Northern Pennsylvania, fed entirely by springs, and clear as crystal. It is surrounded by beautiful groves, and noted for its fine summer cottages, boating, bathing, fishing. Here are superb black bass, and pickerel in abundance, that attracts the angler from far and near. Its altitude is 1,100 feet. The air is cool and bracing—free from malaria. There are many beautiful drives in the neighborhood, and the scenery is unsurpassed. A more delightful place cannot be found in the State to spend the hot summer months.

A large hotel, that will accommodate 400 people, is situated on the bluff, 80 feet above the lake, and from which a fine view of the surrounding country is obtainable. Commodious stages run from every important train from Factoryville to the Lake.

SUMMER EXCURSION ROUTES AND RATES.

Trade Mark for everything except Spoons, Forks, Knives, etc.

5th Ave. Front, Madison Sq., West.

Meriden Britannia Company's
Gold and Silver Plate

HAS ALL THE ARTISTIC CHARACTER OF THE BEST SOLID WARE AT A FRACTION OF THE COST.

And it wears. Otherwise we would not have the largest business in our line in the world.

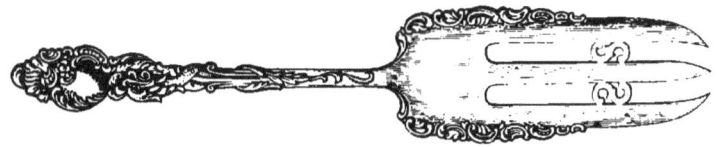

COLUMBIA COLD MEAT FORK.

Exclusive designs in Meat Platters, Entree Dishes, Chafing Dishes, Tea Ware, etc., Silver-plate on nickel silver base and silver soldered.

We have just issued a small book entitled: "A Historical Sketch of Madison Square," which may be had by customers on application.

Trade Mark for Spoons, Forks, Knives, etc.

Manufactured by
Meriden Britannia Co.,
MADISON SQUARE,
New York.

208 5th Ave.,   1128-1130 Broadway.

Factories: { Meriden, Conn., and Hamilton, Ont.

Broadway Front.

F. BOOSS & BRO.

ESTABLISHED 1853.

FINE FURS

Gold Medal,
Paris, 1878.

42d SEASON.

Highest Award,
Centennial, 1876.

SPECIALTIES IN

SEAL SKIN GARMENTS

And Newest Designs in Capes and Collarettes.

Also a fine line of Scarfs, Muffs, and Novelties of every description; Gentlemen's Fur Coats, Caps, Gloves and Collars; Coachmen's Capes and Sleigh Robes of all descriptions. Fur trimming in all its varieties, to which we invite special attention.

Shipping Furs Bought at the Highest Market Prices.

F. BOOSS & BRO.,
449 BROADWAY, 26 MERCER ST., NEW YORK CITY.

Grand Street "L" Station. TELEPHONE 388 SPRING.

CATALOGUES MAILED ON APPLICATION.

LIVERPOOL &

LONDON & GLOBE

INSURANCE CO.

FIRE LOSSES PAID IN U. S. EXCEED

$63,000,000.

45 William St., New York City.

PHOTO, BY T. E. DILLON, SCRANTON, PA.

NEAR NATICOKE.

NICHOLSON. *Altitude, 765 ft.*

166 miles from New York ; Single ticket, $5.30 ; Special ticket, $5.00 ;
Excursion ticket, $6.70.

After passing through a tunnel over 2,000 feet long this pretty little place is brought into view. Tunkhannock and Martin Creeks form a junction below the village, and furnish good water power for the several manufacturing industries. Nicholson became known through the tanning industry, and the depletion of the forest about here is due to the incessant destruction of trees for tan bark.

FOSTER. *Altitude, 893 ft.*

172 miles from New York ; Single ticket, $5.50 ; Special ticket, $5.00;
Excursion ticket, $7.15.

KINGSLEY'S *Altitude, 981 ft.*

175 miles from New York ; Single ticket, $5.60 ; Special ticket, $5.00 ;
Excursion ticket, $7.30.

ALFORD. *Altitude, 1,053 ft.*

180 miles from New York ; Single ticket, $5.75 ; Special ticket, $5.00 ;
Excursion ticket, $7.45.

LACKAWANNA & MONTROSE R. R.

This little road, which connects with the main line at Alford, has but three stations. The country through which it runs is both healthful and picturesque, and is well adapted for summer homes. The stations are

HART LAKE. *Altitude, 1,592 ft.*
184 miles from New York ; Single ticket, $5.95 ; Special ticket, $5.20 ;
Excursion ticket, $7.85.

TIFFANY'S. *Altitude, 1,619 ft.*
184½ miles from New York ; Single ticket, $6.05 ; Special ticket, $5 30 ;
Excursion ticket, $8.05.

Population, 2,000 ### MONTROSE. *Altitude, 1,800 ft.*
195½ miles from New York ; Single ticket, $6.15 ; Special ticket, $5.40;
Excursion ticket, $8.20.

The terminal of the newly constructed and picturesque Montrose and Lackawanna R. R. is situated in the very centre and highest point of a moderately hilly and finely cultivated region, equal in area to forty miles square, surrounded on all sides by the hills of the tortuous Susquehanna River, and the mountain ranges of the Lackawanna. The outlook to these distant hills and mountains, and into seven or eight counties of Pennsylvania and New York, over the intervening region of forests, orchards, cultivated fields and pleasant agricultural homes, presents in every direction views of rural beauty and picturesque loveliness.

A natural lake of about fifty acres lies at the foot of the hills on one side, while gently sloping down the other lies the village with its imposing court-house and fine school building; its seven churches; its attractive village hotels, stores, and its many pretty homes, some of which are thrown open to the accommodation of summer guests.

Charming drives lead to natural lakes and streams lying but a few miles distant in every direction, and these afford excellent fishing. The water is pure and the air is full of exhilarating life-giving ozone. Here we have no mosquitoes, no fogs, no malaria, no sleepless nights. Montrose is within one hour of Binghamton and Scranton, six hours from New York and seven from Philadelphia.

This place is destined to become a famous and popular summer resort.

NEW MILFORD. *Altitude, 1,087 ft.*
186 miles from New York; Single ticket, $5.95; Special ticket, $5.00;
Excursion ticket, $7.50.

New Milford is in the heart of the tannery region, and a beautiful country. The scenery is picturesque, and varies from the fertile valley to the high, tree-clad mountain. The great number of lakes and streams in the mountains make it the favorite resort of fishermen. The village is a thriving one and supports several industries,

GREAT BEND. *Altitude, 860 ft.*
193 miles from New York; Single ticket, $6.05; Special ticket, $5.00;
Excursion ticket, $7.75.

The spot is beautifully situated on a level plain surrounded by a framework of mountains, and the Susquehanna River flows through it. A mineral spring, whose

SUMMER EXCURSION ROUTES AND RATES. 79

PHOTO. BY T. E. DILLON, SCRANTON, PA.
"WHEN EVENING SHADOWS FALL." SUSQUEHANNA RIVER.

waters contain many virtues, is also one of the beneficial features of the place. The scenery about here, and the village itself, attract a great many visitors. The Company has established shops and a round-house here. Great Bend possesses numerous industries that give the place considerable commercial importance.

CONKLIN, N. Y. Altitude, 852 ft.
198 miles from New York; Single ticket, $6.10; Special ticket, $5.00;
Excursion ticket, $7.85.

CONKLIN CENTER. Altitude, 864 ft.
201 miles from New York; Single ticket, $6.15; Special ticket, $5.00;
Excursion ticket, $7.90.

BINGHAMTON. Altitude, 843 ft.
207 miles from New York; Single ticket, $6.15; Special ticket, $5.00;
Excursion ticket, $8.00.

Binghamton is too well known to require any detailed description here. It will be sufficient to say that it enjoys the distinction of being as beautiful a city as the Empire State can boast. The city enjoys good water and the great manufacturing industries that have sprung up are due as much to this as to anything else. These industries first brought the railroad here, and so many lines centre in the city that it is fast taking rank among the great railroad centres of this country. The Chenango and Susquehanna Rivers flow through the city and give it a pleasing picturesqueness. Elegant residences and fine streets attract visitors, and a tour of the different districts meets with appreciation and approval.

At Binghamton is located the National Home for Indigent Commercial Travelers, their wives and children; a benevolent enterprise which has the hearty support of the commercial travelers of this country and their employers. The Home will cost when completed, $125,000. The corner-stone was laid October 9, 1894, by the Grand Master of Masons of the State of New York, with impressive ceremonies, in the presence of Governor Flower of New York, Governor Pattison of Pennsylvania, and many other distinguished people and a large number of organizations, civic and military. The Home is located on one of the handsomest sites in this country, a picturesque hillside near the city.

The Susquehanna Valley House is pleasantly situated on the river side and is in charge of a committee of ladies who direct it as an institution for destitute orphan children in the city and vicinity. Churches of all denominations, good schools, libraries and clubs and several widely known newspapers form a few of the attractions which make the city eligible to would-be residents.

At Binghamton the Utica, and Syracuse, Binghamton and New York Divisions branch to the north; the former terminating at Utica, with a branch running from Richfield Springs Junction to Richfield Springs, and the latter running direct to Oswego, on Lake Ontario.

The Utica Division.

CHENANGO BRIDGE.

213 miles from New York; Single ticket, $6.25; Special ticket, $5.00; Excursion ticket, $8.25.

CHENANGO FORKS. *Altitude, 893 ft.*

215 miles from New York; Single ticket, $6.25; Special ticket, $5.00; Excursion ticket, $8.60.

The Syracuse, Binghamton and New York Division branches from the Utica Division here. The "Forks" is an agricultural district, where dairying is extensively carried on, and considerable cheese is manufactured.

WILLARDS.

220 miles from New York; Single ticket, $6.25; Special ticket, $5.00; Excursion ticket, $8.65.

SUMMER EXCURSION ROUTES AND RATES. 80a

COMMERCIAL TRAVELERS' HOME, BINGHAMTON, N. Y

LIVINGSTON MIDDLEDITCH CO.,
PRINTING,
149 to 153 Leonard St.,
NEW YORK.
TELEPHONE, "186 FRANKLIN."

Lake Keuka,
Eight hundred feet above Sea Level.

STEUBEN COUNTY, NEW YORK.

Absolutely free from Malaria, Miasma, Hay Fever and Mosquitoes.

THE FAVORITE FISHING GROUNDS OF THE LATE SETH GREEN.

Salmon Trout, Black Bass, Pickerel.

EXCELLENT HOTEL ACCOMMODATIONS

FOR OVER ONE THOUSAND GUESTS AT VARIOUS LOCATIONS AND PRICES,

COMPRISING

HOTELS AND ADJACENT COTTAGES, AND BOARDING HOUSES.

NUMEROUS EXCELLENT MEDICINAL SPRINGS.

Nine hours ride from New York, Philadelphia, Baltimore, Washington and Boston, via Delaware, Lackawanna & Western, and Bath & Hammondsport Railways, on the direct route to Niagara Falls. The finest steamboats and the lowest rates of fare to be found upon any of the inland lakes of this country. Steamboats make sixteen trips per day, the entire length of the lake, 22 miles.

Lake Keuka is in the heart of the great grape growing and champagne manufacturing districts of the United States. Its scenery is unsurpassed.

Excellent locations are set apart for excursion parties, including groves and play grounds.

For full particulars on all questions, address

THE LAKE KEUKA NAVIGATION CO.,
HAMMONDSPORT.

NEW YORK.

GREENE. *Altitude, 937 ft.*

227 miles from New York; Single ticket, $6.25; Special ticket, $5.00; Excursion ticket, $8.80.

The railroad now enters the charming valley of the Chenango. This thriving village is prettily situated at the base of high hills, and the surroundings are charming. Many industries, as well as good schools, thrive here, and churches are numerous, and a weekly newspaper is also issued.

BRISBIN.

229 miles from New York; Single ticket, $6.25; Special ticket, $5.00; Excursion ticket, $8.85.

COVENTRY.

236 miles from New York; Single ticket, $6.25; Special ticket, $5.20; Excursion ticket, $8.90.

Coventry is but a small village, and has all the characteristics of a good agricultural section.

OXFORD. *Altitude, 980 ft.*

240 miles from New York; Single ticket, $6.25; Special ticket, $5.00; Excursion ticket, $9.00.

Oxford is a fine old town that boasts a century's growth, and is surrounded by hills, possessing springs which, by log conduits, supply the town with an abundance of pure water. The Chenango River, affording some choice scenery, flows through the valley, and around the base of the mountains. Nearly all the farms make a specialty of dairy produce. The cheese factories consume a very large portion of the milk supply of the district. The factories here are numerous and successful. Oxford possesses churches of all denominations, one or two schools, and one academy.

NORWICH. *Altitude, 1,014 ft.*

249 miles from New York; Single ticket, $6.50; Special ticket, $5.00; Excursion ticket, $9.00.

This is one of the most flourishing towns in Southern New York, having the advantages of water power on the Chenango River, and of ready markets north and south. The industries aare miscellaneous and abundant. Dairying is by no means the most important of them. As a resort, Norwich has long been famous. Six miles from the town, and along a good road, is Chenango Lake, a romantic sheet of water, possessing charming scenery and plenty of game fish. The Chenango River also is inviting to anglers. All the desirable features of civilization and good society exist in the village, and to this condition its thrift and prosperity may be attributed.

NORTH NORWICH.

255 miles from New York; Single ticket, $6.50; Special ticket, $5.00; Excursion ticket, $9.35.

SHERBURNE. *Altitude, 1,040 ft.*

258 miles from New York; Single ticket, $6.50; Special ticket, $5.00; Excursion ticket, $9.70.

Nature here is in her element, and one fond of the natural may be constantly kept on the move. Among the attractions are Madison Pond, eight miles distant, a magnificent and transparent sheet of water where fish abound; Mad Brook, one mile distant, and a resort full of romantic beauty; a waterfall of sixty feet into a chasm, the sides of which rise one hundred feet on either side; a sulphur spring is to be found at the foot of these falls. Unrivalled scenery awaits the tourist from Pratt's and Hunt's mountains. The town is full of commercial enterprises, schools, churches, lodges, etc., and is surrounded by a remarkably fine agricultural region.

EARLVILLE. *Altitude, 1,107 ft.*
263 miles from New York; Single ticket, $6.60; Special ticket, $5.00.

Situated on the east branch of the Chenango River, on the line of Chenango and Madison counties, this pretty village offers unusual inducements to the summer tourist. It is in the midst of picturesque surroundings, fertile farms and charming drives. The railroad station is one mile away. Hamilton, with its well-established Colgate University, is six miles away.

POOLVILLE. *Altitude, 1,100 ft.*
267 miles from New York; Single ticket, $6.75; Special ticket, $5.00.

HUBBARDSVILLE. *Altitude, 1,211 ft.*
272 miles from New York; Single ticket, $6.75; Special ticket, $5.00.

Situated on the east branch of the Chenango River, Hubbardsville is noted for the cultivation of hops and for dairy produce that form an important branch of its industry. The village lies at the head of the Chenango Valley. This is also the station for East Hamilton, half a mile distant.

NORTH BROOKFIELD. *Altitude, 1,182 ft.*
275 miles from New York; Single ticket, $6.85; Special ticket, $5.00.

This town of less than a thousand inhabitants is as busy a one for its size as the State can boast. It possesses saw mills, flour mills, wagon and sleigh manufactories, and quantities of hay, hops, cereals, and dairy products are shipped from here daily. It is located on the east branch of the Chenango River.

SANGERFIELD CENTER. *Altitude, 1,190 ft.*
280 miles from New York; Single ticket, $6.95; Special ticket, $5.00.

WATERVILLE. *Altitude, 1,246 ft.*
280 miles from New York; Single ticket, $7.00; Special ticket, $5.00.

The town is situated on Oriskany Creek, in Oneida County. It is famous for its beautiful location, its fine society, churches and schools, and the extent of its manufacturing and dairy interests.

MARSHALL.
284 miles from New York; Single ticket, $7.10; Special ticket, $5.00.

PARIS. *Altitude, 1,422 ft.*
285 miles from New York; Single ticket, $7.10; Special ticket, $5.00.

ALONG THE RICHFIELD BRANCH.

On reaching RICHFIELD JUNCTION, which is four miles west of Paris, the Richfield Branch begins. It is 22 miles long, and the traveler's happiest thought is to arrive at Richfield Springs, one of our famous and most delightful watering places. Along this line a number of pretty little towns may be found, and the general character of the country is charming and interesting. The first station is

BRIDGEWATER. *Altitude, 1,184 ft.*

294 miles from New York; Single ticket, $7.35; Special ticket, $5.15.

At this point connection is made for points on the line of the Unadilla Valley Railway—viz: "River Forks," which is the station for "Unadilla Forks," Leonardsville, West Edmeston, Sweets, South Edmeston, New Berlin and points further south in the Unadilla Valley down to its junction with the Susquehanna River by means of the Ontario & Western Railroad (New Berlin Branch).

The Unadilla Valley is famed for the salubrity of its climate; although the days are warm the nights are always cool, and the broad Valley dotted here and there with blooded cattle grazing peacefully presents a scene of extreme beauty. Drouth is never known here, and the grass and foliage always maintain a beautiful green during the Summer season very similar to the green of Erin's Isle.

The beautiful Unadilla River flows the entire length of the Valley, winding about in and out among oziers and willows with peaceful current.

The whole Valley, about forty (40) miles in length, is an attractive place for summer residences.

There are no mosquitoes or other insect pests, and The Unadilla Valley Railway Company purposes inaugurating an especially good service for Summer residents.

Butternut Falls, between Leonardsville and West Edmeston, is a beautiful spot containing a magnificent cascade and fine picnic grounds.

All of the little hamlets on this line are beautiful little spots, and New Berlin, in the middle of the Valley, is an attractive pleasant spot of historic interest for the Summer tourists, on account of its accessibility to Cooperstown and other well known resorts.

The drives hereabouts are endless and beautiful.

UNADILLA FORKS. *Altitude, 1,194 ft.*

295 miles from New York, Single ticket, $7.35; Special ticket, $5.15.

WEST WINFIELD. *Altitude, 1,183 ft.*

297 miles from New York; Single ticket, $7.40; Special ticket, $5.25.

This is a prosperous village of about 700 inhabitants, pleasantly situated in a valley which is considerably above the Mohawk River. The place thrives on account of its large manufacturing interests, and the industry and high moral standing of the community at large. Its agricultural and dairy interests are of great importance. Several churches, schools, and one academy are maintained, and a weekly paper is published here. A branch of the Unadilla River flows through the village and furnishes power for the factories.

Genesee Valley at Dansville, N. Y.

EAST WINFIELD. *Altitude, 1,194 ft.*
299 miles from New York; Single ticket, $7.45; Special ticket, $5.30.

CEDARVILLE.
301 miles from New York; Single ticket, $7.50; Special ticket, $5.35.

The town, like its neighbors, the Winfields, is situated in Herkimer County, and is about two miles from the railroad station. Its location, at the head of a creek that flows into the Mohawk, lends it a romantic appearance. The Unadilla River rises two miles east, and affords excellent sport for anglers. Cheese-making is the principal industry. Several natural caves and springs may be found at Litchfield Hill, two miles away.

MILLER'S MILLS. *Altitude, 1,353 ft.*
303 miles from New York ; Single ticket, $7.55 ; Special ticket, $5.40.

SOUTH COLUMBIA. *Altitude, 1,454 ft.*
308 miles from New York ; Single ticket, $7.70 ; Special ticket, $5.55.

RICHFIELD SPRINGS. *Altitude, 1,750 ft.*
311 miles from New York ; Single ticket, $7.80 ; Special ticket, $5.65 ;
Excursion ticket, $10.75.

By steady advancement Richfield Springs has come to rank as one of the first watering-places in the country. The village has been fitted by nature as an ideal summer resort. With its elevation of 1,750 feet above the sea, nestled among the mountains of Otsego County, near the centre of New York State, it has every natural advantage to make it a charming place in which to spend the summer.

The summer season railroad connections make this spot of easy access from New York, as Pullman parlor car trains run to and fro every night and morning. The trip by the Delaware, Lackawanna and Western Railroad is through picturesque scenery, thus making a day journey desirable. Connections are made from Washington and Philadelphia, so as to render this the most desirable route from the south and southwest to Richfield Springs. Otsego Stage and Steamboat Company make direct connection with through trains on the Delaware, Lackawanna and Western Railroad for Cooperstown during the summer season.

The scenery in and about Richfield Springs is charming. The wooded hills and cultivated plains spread a landscape which is truly inspiring to look upon, and wonderfully invigorating to pass through.

Not the least important feature at this place is the number of drives through a picturesque country, upon well-cared-for roads, which enhance the pleasure, and make the pastime very popular with the guests. Among others are the following : To Mount Otsego, Otsego Lake, Cooperstown, the Mohawk Valley, Richard Croker's beautiful Stock Farm, Henderson Home ; the one most popular of all is around Canadarago Lake, a distance of twelve miles over a road as smooth as a floor. Canadarago Lake is a delightful place for boating and fishing. A pleasure steamer plies daily for public or private accommodation. The main dock is but one mile from the village.

The erection of one of the most complete bathing establishments in the world, a few years since, has made the place famous as a water cure and bathing resort. The celebrated White Sulphur Spring supplies the new bathing establishment with mineral water, which is used for baths as well as for beverage, with almost incredible results in healing and restoring the feeble and infirm. Several prominent medical societies have met here during the past few years, and their resolutions concerning the baths have always been commendatory.

The hotels and boarding-houses are good and numerous, and several may be found along the shores of Canadarago Lake. Churches of various denominations flourish, and the Springs boast of a daily paper.

Returning again to the Utica Division, the first station beyond Richfield Junction is

CLAYVILLE. *Altitude, 1,129 ft.*

291 miles from New York ; Single ticket, $7.25 ; Special ticket, $5.00.

SAUQUOIT.

293 miles from New York ; Single ticket, $7.30 ; Special ticket, $5.00.

The village is situated on Sauquoit Creek, or River, a swift stream of crystal water, which has been found well adapted for brewing purposes and dyeing, as well as other uses. There are cotton, paper, saw and flouring mills here, and one or two cheese factories.

CHADWICKS. *Altitude, 756 ft.*

295 miles from New York ; Single ticket, $7.35 ; Special ticket, $5.00.

WASHINGTON MILLS. *Altitude, 634 ft.*

297 miles from New York ; Single ticket, $7.40 ; Special ticket, $5.00.

NEW HARTFORD. *Altitude, 563 ft.*

298 miles from New York ; Single ticket, $7.45 ; Special ticket, $5.00.

UTICA. *Altitude, 410 ft.*

302 miles from New York ; Single ticket, $7.70 ; Special ticket, $5.00.

This substantially built city ranks among the largest and most prosperous in the Empire State. It is famous for the number of its cotton mills, some of which are the largest in the world. Various industries are carried on here on a large scale. Utica is among the greatest of our manufacturing cities.

Every convenience and commercial interest to be found in any first-class city exists here. It is particularly noted for the number of its fine churches, schools, and public buildings, and possesses besides many elegant residences and beautiful streets. A palatial Masonic Home has recently been erected here.

Syracuse, Binghamton and New York, and Oswego and Syracuse Divisions.

BARKER. *Altitude, 933 ft.*
221 miles from New York ; Single ticket, $6.45 ; Special ticket, $5.15 ;
Excursion ticket, $8.95.

WHITNEY'S POINT. *Altitude, 953 ft.*
228 miles from New York ; Single ticket, $6.55 ; Special ticket, $5.25 ;
Excursion ticket, $9.15.

LISLE. *Altitude, 960 ft.*
230 miles from New York ; Single ticket, $6.50 ; Special ticket, $5.30 ;
Excursion ticket, $9.20.

KILLAWOG. *Altitude, 998 ft.*
234 miles from New York ; Single ticket, $6.70 ; Special ticket, $5.35;
Excursion ticket, $9.35.

MARATHON. *Altitude, 1,038 ft.*
237 miles from New York; Single ticket, $6.80; Special ticket, $5.45;
Excursion ticket, $9.50.

This thriving incorporated town, with many advantages enjoyed by larger places, is situated in Cortland County. Established in the midst of an agricultural region, it is blessed with an abundance of farm and fruit produce, besides which it possesses numerous factories and mills. Good hotels, churches and schools abound.

MESSENGERVILLE.
241 miles from New York; Single ticket, $6.90; Special ticket, $5.55;
Excursion ticket, $9.65.

BLODGETT'S MILLS. *Altitude, 1,079 ft.*
247 miles from New York; Single ticket, $7.00; Special ticket, $5.70;
Excursion ticket, $9.90.

CORTLAND. *Altitude, 1,111 ft.*
250 miles from New York; Single ticket, $7.05; Special ticket, $5.80;
Excursion ticket, $10.00.

Cortland is a busy town, located on a beautiful river with a troublesome name, the Tioughnioga, which furnishes water power to many of the mills. A number of factories and foundries are to be found here, but wagon-making is the chief industry. The production of butter and cheese is also extensively carried on. The town is liberally supplied with churches, public and private schools; not the least among the latter is the State Normal School. Several newspapers thrive, and the best hotels are open all the year round.

HOMER. *Altitude, 1,136 ft.*
253 miles from New York; Single ticket, $7.05; Special ticket, $5.85; Excursion ticket, $10.00.

Situated 33 miles south of Syracuse, 253 miles from New York, is one of the earliest settled towns in Cortland County. Its population is about 4,000. Main, a long, broad street, is bordered upon each side with rows of beautiful shade trees, has broad well-paved walks, is lighted by electricity, and has an electric street railway over it. Each side is well built up, there being three hotels, two national banks, several large and handsome brick business blocks, four churches, and a large, fine new academy employing fourteen teachers. It has a gravelly soil, filled with the purest water, and has a pure, healthful and bracing air, a place free from malaria or mosquitos. It has telephones, telegraph, express, many enterprising manufacturing establishments, several flour mills, extensive water works, and well-equipped fire department; in short, has all that goes to make up the requirements of a progressive, active, thriving village, healthful and pleasant for summer residents or for those seeking a permanent home, when all the surroundings that go to make a home attractive and satisfactory are ever present and always gratifying.

LITTLE YORK. *Altitude, 1,159 ft.*
257 miles from New York; Single ticket, $7.10; Special ticket, $5.95; Excursion ticket, $10.00.

PREBLE. *Altitude, 1,193 ft.*
260 miles from New York; Single ticket, $7.10; Special ticket, $6.05; Excursion ticket, $10.00.

This place was named after Commodore Preble, of naval renown. It is noted for the number of its dairies, and the excellence of its butter and cheese. Here the Tioughnioga River flows by. The neighborhood is celebrated for its noble mountains, some of which stand 1,700 feet above sea level, and for the numerous lakes which afford splendid fishing. They are Hoag, Crooked, Green, Goodell and Little York lakes, and each is a beautiful sheet of water, teeming with fish. The valley is two miles wide at Preble, and the drives through it are delightful.

TULLY. *Altitude, 1,248 ft.*
265 miles from New York; Single ticket, $7.15; Special ticket, $6.06; Excursion ticket, $10.00.

TULLY LAKE PARK.

This popular summer resort lies one and a half miles south of Tully, and borders on Big Lake, which is a mile long and a quarter of a mile wide. This lake is one of a chain of seven lakes whose picturesqueness and beauty rival those of Killarney. These lakes are stocked with pickerel, bass and perch, and the fishing is excellent throughout the entire summer.

Tully Lake Park was organized and is managed upon the plan of the Thousand Island Park at Clayton. It has thirty cottages built and owned by residents of Syracuse and New York City. Besides this, there is a hotel large enough to accommodate one hundred guests.

During the months of July and August the Central New York Assembly holds its annual sessions on the shore of Big Lake, opposite the Park. The Assembly is patterned after the famous Chautauqua, and many speakers of national renown have been engaged for the coming season.

Tully Lake Park is famed for its high altitude, and is essentially a place where persons seeking rest and harmless recreation will find themselves thoroughly satisfied and at home.

APULIA. *Altitude, 1,240 ft.*

267 miles from New York; Single ticket, $7.15; Special ticket, $6.06; Excursion ticket, $10.00.

ONATIVIA.

272 miles from New York; Single ticket, $7.20; Special ticket, $6.06; Excursion ticket, $10.00.

JAMESVILLE. *Altitude, 585 ft.*

280 miles from New York; Single ticket, $7.20; Special ticket, $6.06; Excursion ticket, $10.00.

The size of the four above-named towns is limited, each having the general characteristics of others in this section. They are centres of agricultural districts with a fertile soil, a healthy climate, scenery of more than ordinary attraction, and with an industrious and thriving population. The entire region is worthy of attention, and a trip through here will well repay the tourist for his exertion.

SYRACUSE. *Altitude, 398 ft.*

287 miles from New York; Single ticket, $7.25; Special ticket, $6.06; Excursion ticket, $10.00.

The capital of Onondaga County, Syracuse is beautifully situated on Onondaga Lake, around which the great salt mines are centered. Syracuse is as famous as Droitwich for its salt, and its annual shipments are enormous. It is one of the chief cities on the Erie Canal, to which it furnishes a large amount of commerce. The iron, beer, pottery, brick, glass and cutlery industries also play an important part in the city's prosperity.

There are a great many churches and schools here, and no one with inclination toward religion or education need be without them. The Lackawanna Railroad finds Syracuse one of its largest distributing points for coal. The company here delivers upwards of half a million tons annually, part of which is transhipped by canals and connecting railroads.

Taking it as a city and business centre, Syracuse is among the most important in the United States.

LAKE SIDE. *Altitude, 398 ft.*

291 miles from New York, Single ticket, $7.35; Special ticket, $6.15; Excursion ticket, $10.00.

PLEASANT BEACH. *Altitude, 372 ft.*

292 miles from New York,

MAPLE BAY.

293 miles from New York.

STILES. *Altitude, 380 ft.*
294 miles from New York; Single ticket, $7.45; Special ticket, $6.25; Excursion ticket, $10.00.

BALDWINSVILLE. *Altitude, 389 ft.*
299 miles from New York; Single ticket, $7.50; Special ticket, $6.30; Excursion ticket, $10.00.

This old town, originally called Columbia, and then Baldwin's Bridge, until the Post Office department compromised on the present name, represents one of the most intelligent communities in Central New York. It possesses many churches and schools, and a good paper, which supplies the townspeople with the news. Baldwinsville was settled in 1797 by Dr. James C. Baldwin, and it derives its name from him. This is one of the pleasantest spots in Onondaga County, and is located on the Seneca River, which furnishes several mills and factories with power. A fine grade of cheese is made here, and the neighborhood is justly celebrated for its good dairies and agricultural products. Fishing in Mass Lake is excellent.

LAMSONS. *Altitude, 394 ft.*
304 miles from New York; Single ticket, $7.60; Special ticket. $6.40; Excursion ticket, $10.00.

Lamsons is given up to tanneries and a few other mills, and plays no very important part as a village. The village of Phenix is three and a half miles distant, and is a very pretty place. It lies on the east bank of the Oswego River, and on the Oswego and Syracuse Canal. The population is over 2,000, and the village contains several churches, good schools and hotels.

SOUTH GRANBY. *Altitude, 370 ft.*
306 miles from New York; Single ticket, $7.65; Special ticket, $6.45; Excursion ticket, $10.00.

FULTON. *Altitude, 386 ft.*
311 miles from New York; Single ticket, $7.75; Special ticket, $6.50; Excursion ticket, $10.00.

An important town in Oswego County, with a population of over 10,000. It is situated on the Oswego River, twelve miles from its mouth, and has magnificent water power. Milling is the chief industry, and over 1,500 barrels of grain a day are milled. Next in importance come the cheese and dairy interests, which are also large. It is estimated that the annual shipment of these is over 500 tons. Besides these, several tanneries, saw mills and foundries flourish here.

Fulton is an excellent place of residence, and possesses many churches of all denominations, public and private schools, and two or more weekly papers. Lake Neahtawanta is close to the railroad station, and the Oswego County fair grounds are near by.

NORTH FULTON. *Altitude, 379 ft.*
312 miles from New York; Single ticket, $7.75; Special ticket, $6.50; Excursion ticket, $10.00.

MINETTO. *Altitude, 327 ft.*
317 miles from New York; Single ticket, $7.90; Special ticket, $6.50; Excursion ticket, $10.00.

BURTE POINT, OSWEGO, N. Y.

OSWEGO. *Altitude, 297 ft.*

322 miles from New York; Single ticket, $7.95; Special ticket, $6.50;
Excursion ticket, $10.00.

Oswego is the terminus of the division, and a pretty city it is. Situated right on the shore of Lake Ontario, which appears like a mighty ocean, Oswego is the city of "silver gloss starch," and as such it is known on account of the immense quantity of this commodity that it manufactures annually. The Oswego River divides the city and affords elegant residence sites on both shores. The lake front is also a popular place for private dwellings. Considering that the canal, lake and several lines of railroad furnish shipping facilities, it is not to be wondered at that Oswego is a prosperous and growing city. It has fine commercial institutions, banks, public buildings, and almost unlimited manufacturing industries. As a place of residence it has the appearance of an elegant and refined suburb, and the breezes from the lake render it delightfully cool and invigorating. In summer, the temperature, at the hottest, rarely exceeds 70°.

The celebrated Deep Rock Spring is situated here, and, for the accommodation of tourists and invalids, a fine hotel has been erected upon it.

As far back as 1732 the Assembly at Albany appropriated moneys and appointed agents and interpreters to look after the sustaining of the trading post called Oswego. The French and English had severe engagements for its possession, as many as twenty thousand troops being massed here at one time. Some gallant attacks on the forts occurred, and many lives were sacrificed. In 1814 the British appeared off Oswego, and, landing a land force, captured the city after a desperate struggle, taking some of its prominent citizens prisoners of war, the last of whom have but recently been laid to rest. Fort Ontario, now garrisoned by a company of the 9th Infantry, stands in a commanding position on a high bank on the east side of the river. The view of Lake Ontario from the ramparts is expansive and beautiful. The Life Saving Station nestles at the foot of the fort bank. An English lady, writing to friends in the British Empire in 1848, thus describes the climate at Oswego : "When winter had once set in Oswego became a perfect Siberia. At length spring returned with its flowers, and converted our Siberia into an uncultivated Eden, rich in all the majestic charms of sublime scenery and primeval beauty and fertility. If ever the fond illusions of poets and philosophers, that Atlantis, that new Arcadia, that safe and serene Utopia, where ideal quiet and happiness have so often charmed theory, if ever this dream of social bliss, in some new planted region is to be realized, this unrivaled scene of grandeur and fertility bids fairest to be the place of its abode. Here the climate is serene and equal, the vigorous winters that brace the frame and call forth the power of mind and body to prepare for its approach are succeeded by a spring so rapid, the exuberance of vernal bloom bursts forth so suddenly, after disappearance of those deep snows which cherish and fructify the earth, that the change seems like a magical delusion.''

The plant of the Standard Oil Co.'s Shook factory, the Diamond Match Factory, the Oswego Starch Factory, and the Oswego Shade Cloth Company are among the largest institutions of their kind in the world. Malt, boilers and engines are manufactured in large quantities, and shipped to all parts of the globe. Millions of feet of Canadian lumber are received during the season of navigation. A new electric road has been constructed from the heart of the city to a beautiful summer retreat, three miles west of the city, running on the lake side of the boulevard; the view, as the summit of the boulevard hill is reached, and the descent begins, baffles description.

THE BUFFALO DIVISION.

The tourist is now cordially invited to start afresh at Binghamton, where the Buffalo Division commences, and continue the journey westward. The first station is

LESTERSHIRE. *Altitude, 848 ft.*

210 miles from New York; Single ticket, $6.20; Special ticket, $5.10; Excursion ticket, $8.10.

Of this place it may be said, that if humanity goes about barefoot, it is not because there is insufficient foot-wear in town. Here the manufacture of boots and shoes is more than equal to all the other industries combined.

WILLOW POINT. *Altitude, 848 ft.*

212 miles from New York; Single ticket, $6.30; Special ticket, $5.15; Excursion ticket, $8.25.

VESTAL. *Altitude, 828 ft.*

215 miles from New York; Single ticket, $6.30; Special ticket, $5.25; Excursion ticket, $8.40.

APALACHIN. *Altitude, 819 ft.*

221 miles from New York; Single ticket, $6.50; Special ticket, $5.40; Excursion ticket, $8.60.

OWEGO. *Altitude, 819 ft.*
228 miles from New York; Single ticket, $6.60; Special ticket, $5.50;
Excursion ticket, $8.85.

Owego is the capital of Tioga County, and is a pretty town made up of refined people. It is surrounded by fine farming country, and here agriculture is extensively carried on. The Susquehanna River flows through the town, and a number of creeks that flow into it keep the land well watered. A few factories and mills find occupation for many people, and the dairies and cheese factories afford a good outlet for the farm produce. Owego possesses many churches of all kinds, as well as schools, etc., and several crisp newspapers.

This place was once the home of Nathaniel Parker Willis, the poet, and it is believed that he gained much of the inspiration from which were born many of the delightful verses that made him famous all over the world for a quarter of a century from the romantic hills and valleys that surround the town.

THE CAYUGA DIVISION.

At Owego this division begins and runs northward to Ithaca, thirty-four miles. The first station is

CATTATONK. *Altitude, 859 ft.*
234 miles from New York; Single ticket, $6.75; Special ticket, $5.65;
Excursion ticket, $9.15.

A small settlement on Cattatonk Creek, where agriculture takes precedence over everything.

CANDOR. *Altitude, 900 ft.*
239 miles from New York; Single ticket, $6.90; Special ticket, $5.80;
Excursion ticket, $9.45.

Candor is a flourishing little town of about 2,000 inhabitants, and is situated on Cattatonk Creek. It is famous for the number of its manufacturing industries. Churches of all denominations are here established, as well as a first-class newspaper. The town has grown rapidly, and shows a decided spirit of enterprise. This is the station for Spencer Springs.

WILLSEYVILLE. *Altitude, 953 ft.*
243 miles from New York; Single ticket, $7.05; Special ticket, $5.95;
Excursion ticket, $9.75.

CAROLINE. *Altitude, 980 ft.*
250 miles from New York; Single ticket, $7.30; Special ticket, $6.20;
Excursion ticket, $10.25.

ITHACA. *Altitude, 307 ft.*
262 miles from New York; Single ticket, $7.50; Special ticket, $6.50;
Excursion ticket, $10.50.

In all probability nature has been more lavish with her gifts in the vicinity of Ithaca than in any other one place in the Empire State. A great lake, a magnificent

 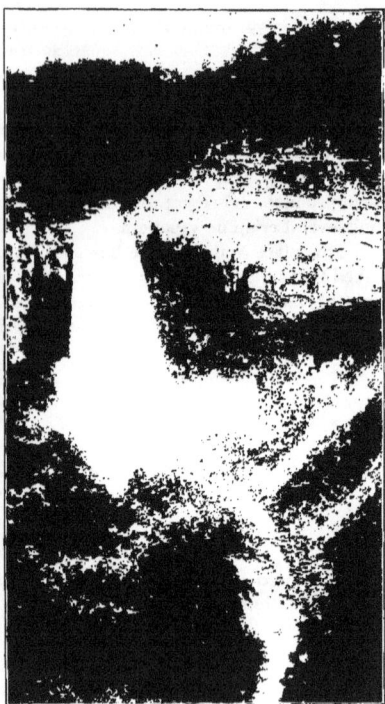

ITHACA FALLS, HEIGHT, 160 FT.
ITHACA, N. Y.

TAUGHANNOCK FALLS, HEIGHT, 215 FT.
ITHACA, N. Y.

region where health and happiness abide, and where the eyes of mankind can feast until the soul is content and the mind is benumbed with bewilderment.

Ithaca has been called the "region of cascades," and the name is certainly appropriate to the surroundings. It would seem as though the hand of nature has busied itself to an unusual extent in carving out of the rocks the irregular crevices through which the silvery streams of crystal water plunge and turn until they reach their natural level. In addition may be found a great many ravines which have a peculiar interest attached to them. These delightful works of nature seem to partake of a form of phenomena, and are all the more interesting on that account. There are 96 falls by actual count which vary in height from 5 feet to 340 feet. One mile from the village is Ithaca Falls, 160 feet high, or 7 feet less than Niagara. The width of the fall is 150 feet. Nine miles from Ithaca are the world-famed Taughannock Falls that glory in being 48 feet higher than Niagara.

All the falls are not directly within the town boundary, but there are fifteen close by, the height of each of which is over 100 feet. It is generally conceded that Cascadilla and Fall Creeks furnish the most enchanting of all the waterfall scenery. Taughannock Falls is the highest in the State, being 215 feet, while the rock rises 145 feet above it. The falls and surrounding scenery are almost unapproachable for magnificence.

Ithaca is situated at the head of Cayuga Lake, and has a population of 12,000. It is principally famous as the seat of Cornell University, founded by Ezra Cornell, whose idea is best expressed by his own words: "I would found an institution where any person can find instruction in any study." The University has turned out many a learned scholar, and is too well known to require a detailed description here.

Cayuga Lake is one of the finest inland lakes that make Central New York so famous as a summer resort. It is forty miles long and reposes between high hills that stretch along its entire length, and far beyond to the south. It is, also, one of the most magnificent lakes in this country, being clear and of great depth; it abounds in most entrancing scenery. Lake fishing, which is always a delightful pastime, is here indulged in every season by many enthusiastic fishermen who invariably catch sufficient lake trout, bass, etc.; to convince them that old Cayuga Lake is the veritable Mecca of anglers.

THE BUFFALO DIVISION.
(Continued.)

After passing Owego the next station is

LOUNSBERRY. *Altitude, 807 ft.*
232 miles from New York; Single ticket, $6.70; Special ticket, $5.55;
Excursion ticket, $9.00.

This is a small town, pleasantly situated, and is desirable as a resort for city people who enjoy quiet and good air. The valley along this section is famous for the cultivation of tobacco, and it is a common sight to gaze upon plants growing upwards of six feet high. The industry of drying and curing the "weed" is both large and profitable.

NICHOLS. *Altitude, 789 ft.*
236 miles from New York ; Single ticket, $6.75 ; Special ticket, $5.60 ;
Excursion ticket, $9.00.

LITCHFIELD. *Altitude, 797 ft.*
242 miles from New York ; Single ticket, $6.85 ; Special ticket, $5.70 ;
Excursion ticket, $9.40.

WAVERLY. *Altitude, 833 ft.*
246 miles from New York ; Single ticket, $6.95 ; Special ticket, $5.75 ;
Excursion ticket, $9.60.

This town has its principal importance in being a junction point with the Lehigh Valley and New York, Lake Erie and Western Railroads. At Athens, four miles distant, the immense plant of the Union Bridge Works is located.

WILLIWANNA. *Altitude, 801 ft.*
250 miles from New York ; Single ticket, $7.00 ; Special ticket, $5.85 ;
Excursion ticket, $9.75.

LOWMANVILLE. *Altitude, 828 ft.*
257 miles from New York ; Single ticket, $7.15 ; Special ticket, $5.90 ;
Excursion ticket, $10.00.

ELMIRA. *Altitude, 857 ft.*
264 miles from New York ; Single ticket, $7.25 ; Special ticket, $6.00 ;
Excursion ticket, $10.25.

Situated in the broad and fertile valley of the Chemung, surrounded by well-wooded hills rising from four to six hundred feet, this city presents many attractions to those who are seeking pleasure, health, or even business.

WILLOW VISTA, ELMIRA, N. Y

Here are gathered about 35,000 people, among whom are many of State and national reputation. The streets are shaded by grand old trees ; the homes are comfortable and attractive, and well-kept lawns on every side are evidences of thrift and culture.

Elmira is a city of churches ; among the most notable of all the denominations is the Congregational Park Church, under the pastorship of the Rev. Thos. K. Beecher. The First Baptist church is also new, and of modern architecture.

The New York State Reformatory, situated on a broad plateau at the foot of the western hills, is of much interest as illustrative of real reformation among the younger class of criminals. In itself, both in architecture and location, it is a striking building, and well repays one for a few hours' visit.

Of parks there are four. The most important is "Eldridge Park," in the northern portion of the city ; it contains about 40 acres, with a natural lake of crystal water, half a mile in circumference ; many miles of fine drives and walks ; also pavilions, summer houses, a bear pit, and all requisites of first class pleasure grounds, which it is, not only for the people of Elmira, but for many cities of the surrounding country.

Here are about 20 miles of electric car roads running to and from all parts, as well as to the thriving village of Horseheads, six miles north.

In the northwestern part of the city is the Elmira College, for Women. This educational institution is among the first in the land. Its location is high and healthy, and its grounds spacious. On East Hill, at an elevation of 200 feet, stands the Gleason Sanitarium, where invalids may find skilled medical care, or the pleasure seeker a quiet summer home.

The charming valley, at this point, is largely devoted to the culture of tobacco, and large crops are annually raised ; and also vegetables of the finest quality. The " hill country " is given up to dairying and churning, and its butter is gaining an enviable reputation for quality.

The Chemung, an Indian word which means "big horn," is a shallow stream, with a succession of rapids and long, still pools, known as " The Eddys." Above

AT WORK.

the city are some particularly fine bits of scenery, as the hills are very abrupt and wooded to the water's edge. Splendid camping spots are to be found, near which run good springs of clear water, and much of this best of summer pastime is indulged in along the picturesque banks. Black bass fishing is also good. A fair number of manufactories are located here, and various industries are represented. Much material is shipped annually to all points of the surrounding country.

NORTH ELMIRA. *Altitude, 861 ft.*
268 miles from New York ; Single ticket, $7.30 ; Special ticket, $6.10 ;
Excursion ticket, $10.45.

BIG FLATS. *Altitude, 917 ft.*
274 miles from New York ; Single ticket, $7.40 ; Special ticket, $6.15 ;
Excursion ticket, $10.65.

CORNING. *Altitude, 931 ft.*
280 miles from New York ; Single ticket, $7.50; Special ticket, $6.25 ;
Excursion ticket, $10.90.

This city has gained fame for the extent of its glass manufacture, and for the excellence of the glass it produces. It is the Junction of the Fall Brook Railway.

ALONG THE CHEMUNG RIVER, ELMIRA, N. Y.

PAINTED POST. *Altitude, 969 ft.*
283 miles from New York; Single ticket, $7.50; Special ticket, $6.30.

COOPERS. *Altitude, 969 ft.*
286 miles from New York; Single ticket, $7.55; Special ticket, $6.35.

CURTIS. *Altitude, 995 ft.*
289 miles from New York; Single ticket, $7.55; Special ticket, $6.40.

CAMPBELLS. *Altitude, 1,014 ft.*
291 miles from New York; Single ticket, $7.55; Special ticket, $6.45.

SAVONA. *Altitude, 1,059 ft.*
298 miles from New York; Single ticket, $7.60; Special ticket, $6.55.

BATH. *Altitude, 1,102 ft.*
301 miles from New York; Single ticket, $7.60; Special ticket, $6.60.

This fine and prosperous little town is situated in the beautiful Cohocton Valley. It has a population of about 4,000 people, and is the county seat of Steuben. The

SUMMER EXCURSION ROUTES AND RATES. 99

State Soldiers' Home for veterans is located here, and is an institution of which the citizens are proud. At Bath connection is made with the Bath and Hammondsport Railroad for Hammondsport, and other points on Keuka Lake.

KANONA. *Altitude, 1,145 ft.*
304 miles from New York ; Single ticket, $7.65 ; Special ticket, $6.70.

AVOCA. *Altitude, 1,194 ft.*
308 miles from New York ; Single ticket, $7.65 ; Special ticket, $6.75.

WALLACE. *Altitude, 1,233 ft.*
311 miles from New York ; Single ticket, $7.65 ; Special ticket, $6.80.

COHOCTON. *Altitude, 1,288 ft.*
316 miles from New York ; Single ticket, $7.68 ; Special ticket, $6.90.

ATLANTA. *Altitude, 1,319 ft.*
320 miles from New York ; Single ticket, $7.68 ; Special ticket, $6.95.

This village is also in the Cohocton Valley. Formerly called Bloods, it was thought that it might prove more prosperous, and grow fully as well, if given a more pleasing name. Atlanta is a shipping point for an abundant supply of grapes which are grown around the village of Naples.

WAYLAND. *Altitude, 1,361 ft.*
326 miles from New York ; Single ticket, $7.68 ; Special ticket, $7.00.

We are now at the highest point on the Buffalo Division, and the magnificent view of the valley, with its rich and prosperous farms stretching for miles, invites the tourist to feast upon, if, but for a moment, the grandeur of the landscape. It is not only on account of the fact that Wayland offers this graceful picture in the large album of Nature that it ranks as a prosperous and interesting neighborhood, but also because husbandry flourishes and is necessarily foremost. Here vacationists will find pure air, plenty of milk, eggs and vegetable produce, together with clear, wholesome water. Wayland excels in all these. The Portland Cement Company has a large factory here, which gives the town just enough life to make it agreeable.

IN THE GENESEE VALLEY.

It is doubtful if the Empire State, famous for the number of its fertile valleys, can offer any other that presents so many charming characteristics as the Genesee. It is a series of magnificent farms, as fertile as any the world produces; it possesses winding rivers and rapid streams that dance in and out of patches of woodland, meeting each other in unexpected ways. The fruit alone that is grown annually in this valley is sufficient to supply almost all the markets of the State; and, as a grain-growing country, it produces more for its size than any other valley in the world. In the spring the air is heavy with the odor of blossoms, and in the fall the red and golden fruit hangs in clusters in the orchards

THE GENESEE VALLEY. IN AND AROUND DANSVILLE, N. Y.

PERKINSVILLE. *Altitude, 1,358 ft.*
328 miles from New York; Single ticket, $7.75; Special ticket, $7.00.

DANSVILLE. *Altitude, 960 ft.*
333 miles from New York; Single ticket, $8.00; Special ticket, $7.00;
Excursion ticket, $13.30.

The approach to Dansville, from either direction, is through a country abounding in picturesque scenery, which apparently culminates in the surroundings of this hill-

MILL CREEK BRIDGE, (118 FT.) DANSVILLE, N. Y.

encircled town. Lying 400 feet below the railroad, it is enclosed on three sides by an ampitheatre of hills which, on either hand, stretch far away, and are lost on the distant horizon. Like a vast living panorama, hundreds of square miles of valley and hill are spread out before the traveler, who is both surprised and delighted with the beauty of a picture of surpassing loveliness, rarely equalled in this or any foreign land. Nature is here more gently picturesque than rugged or grand. Although the hills rise upwards of a thousand feet, they are dotted almost to their summits with farms, vineyards and grain fields, which alternate with masses of evergreen and stretches of timber land.

On nearer acquaintance many hidden attractions are discovered by the artist and the lover of the beautiful—wild, rocky ravines, with precipitous sides and crystal cascades, deep gorges set with pine and hemlock, numerous mountain streams and tangled undergrowth, where the silence of the forest is broken only by the song of the bird or the whirr of the partridge. Stony Brook Glen, similar in its rocky formation and waterfalls to Watkins Glen, a favorite resort, is two miles from the town; winding roads lead over the hills in every direction, and provide charming walks and drives without number. On the eastern hill-slopes are vineyards covering hundreds of acres, which are increasing yearly. This, in itself, speaks volumes for the healthfulness of the climate, for where grapes thrive miasmatic conditions are unknown. In the fertile garden valley a deep alluvial deposit furnishes rich soil for raising nursery stock—the chief industry of the town—in which many have invested capital; and so favorable are all the conditions of growth that in two years trees attain a size and strength that require three years in other nursery centres. This is the home of the famous Genesee white winter wheat, so successfully raised here in large quantities, and the grain fields at every season form an attractive feature of the landscape.

The region within which Dansville is situated is salubrious. It is exempt from malaria, and the vital statistics justify its claim to favorable distinction in respect to diseases caused or prolonged by environment. This is probably due to its elevation above sea-level, swift running streams, dry, porous soil, evergreen forest growth, a climate equable and genial on account of its altitude, and more especially to the exceptional dryness and purity of the air. The Meteorological Bureau Reports, and the weather maps of the Smithsonian Institute, show that the narrow strip of Western New York State, forming the northerly divide of the Alleghany chain draining into Lake Ontario, enjoys much less humidity than the surrounding country; indeed, not until one approaches the pine forests of Northern Michigan, or the equally inhospitable dry plains west of the Mississippi River, can there be found any such low average. It is only this small section, within a region of twelve hundred miles of the Atlantic coast line, that this can be said. These combined influences make it a desirable place of residence or resort. And here on the eastern hill-slope, standing as a vision of hope and promise to thousands, is the Jackson Sanatorium, one of the largest and most complete health institutions in the world. Many are attracted yearly to this favored spot, not less by nature's ample provision of pure air and beautiful scenery, than by the opportunities afforded for recovery and recuperation under the care of skilled physicians.

The mountain spring which supplies the Jackson Sanatorium with water ranks as one of the most famous among home and foreign spas. Dansville has a population of over 4,000. Two railroads, gas and electric lighting, telegraph and telephone, eight mails daily, eight churches, union school, an efficient fire department, good water power, chair, broom-handle, fruit-basket and reaper factories; extensive flour and health-food interests; planing and foundry plants, paper and pulp mills; three weekly newspapers and three monthly journals.

Electric street railroads are now in course of construction, and these will shortly be opened to traffic.

No change of cars is required between New York and Dansville, and the trip may be made in 9 hours. Time from Buffalo, two hours. Pullman cars are connected with all trains.

Those who have had the good opportunity to ride over the Lackawanna road by daylight, and are not prejudiced, agree that the view of the Genesee Valley, as seen from a car window, is not rivalled by any other landscape in this country. A glimpse of the valley is obtained at

GROVELAND. *Altitude, 448 ft.*

341 miles from New York; Single ticket, $8.10; Special ticket, $7.00.

MOUNT MORRIS. *Altitude, 585 ft.*

348 miles from New York; Single ticket, $8.15; Special ticket, $7.00.

This delightful village is situated on a tableland, and commands an uninterrupted view of the valley. To the west may be seen the High Banks, noted in history for

The Sanatorium, Dansville, N. Y.

the ravages of the red men whom General Sullivan was at one time commissioned to exterminate. The railroad crosses the Genesee River here. Mount Morris is a famous resort of the inhabitants of Buffalo, and in summer they collect here in great numbers. A huntsman's club has been formed, and is conducted with regulations similar to the Meadowbrook and other kindred clubs. The periodical " runs " are among the most exciting scenes that enter into the season's gayeties.

Bass fishing in the Genesee River is excellent, and attracts many. From Mount Morris to Geneseo, the capital of Livingston County, the drives over excellent roads are pleasing. This feature, above all the other worthy considerations, forms a decided attraction.

Extensive salt works are established here, and they form a principle feature of commerce. At Mount Morris connection is made with Western New York and Pennsylvania.

LEICESTER. *Altitude, 660 ft.*
351 miles from New York; Single ticket, $8.25; Special ticket, $7.10.

GREIGSVILLE. *Altitude, 742 ft.*
354 miles from New York; Single ticket, $8.30; Special ticket, $7.20.

Greigsville is noted for its salt industry. One mine is 1,200 feet in depth, and the salt is taken out in enormous quantities. The amount of labor distributed can be imagined, when the figures relating to the out-put foot up to 800 tons per day. The village is surrounded by a magnificent farming country, and is a pleasant region in which to spend a summer.

CRAIG'S. *Altitude, 864 ft.*
357 miles from New York; Single ticket, $8.35; Special ticket, $7.30.

LINWOOD. *Altitude, 937 ft.*
360 miles from New York; Single ticket, $8.35; Special ticket, $7.40.

BUFFALO, ROCHESTER AND PITTSBURGH JUNCTION.
363 miles from New York; Single ticket, $8.40; Special ticket, $7.55.

This, as its name implies, is a junction point with the Buffalo, Rochester & Pittsburgh Railroad. There are two salt shafts, 800 feet in depth, located here and getting ready to begin operations.

EAST BETHANY. *Altitude, 1,006 ft.*
369 miles from New York; Single ticket, $8.45; Special ticket, $7.65.

EAST ALEXANDER. *Altitude, 944 ft.*
374 miles from New York; Single ticket, $8.50; Special ticket, $7.70.

ALEXANDER. *Altitude, 933 ft.*
376 miles from New York; Single ticket, $8.50; Special ticket, $7.75.

Genesee Valley from the Sanatorium, Dansville, N. Y.

DELAWARE, LACKAWANNA & WESTERN R. R.

CADY. *Altitude, 945 ft.*

379 miles from New York; Single ticket, $8.60; Special ticket, $7.80.

DARIEN. *Altitude, 931 ft.*

382 miles from New York; Single ticket, $8.65; Special ticket, $7.90.

FARGO. *Altitude, 836 ft.*

387 miles from New York; Single ticket, $8.80; Special ticket, $8.00.

ALDEN. *Altitude, 858 ft.*

389 miles from New York; Single ticket, $8.90; Special ticket, $8.00.

WEST ALDEN. *Altitude, 820 ft.*

391 miles from New York; Single ticket, $8.95; Special ticket, $8.00.

LOONEYVILLE. *Altitude, 768 ft.*

393 miles from New York; Single ticket, $9.00; Special ticket, $8.00.

EAST LANCASTER. *Altitude, 738 ft.*

395 miles from New York; Single ticket, $9.05; Special ticket, $8.00.

LANCASTER. *Altitude, 699 ft.*

398 miles from New York; Single ticket, $9.10; Special ticket, $8.00.

EAST BUFFALO. *Altitude, 622 ft.*

404 miles from New York; Single ticket, $9.25; Special ticket, $8.00.

At East Buffalo are located the extensive car shops of this railroad, where new cars are constructed and old cars rebuilt to be re-commissioned. The enormous coal chutes belonging to the Company are one mile long and have a storage capacity of 150,000 tons. A large yard and cattle pen are also among the Company's possessions at East Buffalo.

A busy little place, called DEPEW, after Chauncey M. Depew, Esq., is close by, and promises to become famous as the greatest car manufacturing town in the United States.

BUFFALO. *Altitude, 582 ft.*

410 miles from New York; Single ticket, $9.25; Special ticket, $8.00.

This great city is the terminus of the road. It is the largest railroad centre in the State, and among the greatest of the entire nation. It has been said that a person can start at a given point in the large yards, and walk a hundred miles on the tops of freight cars. No exaggeration is indulged in, however, when the statement is made that cars from every railroad of any importance in the land are constantly represented on some one of the vast network of rails laid within the city limits.

Buffalo plays an active part as a distributing point for grain and lumber, the latter trade coming largely from Canada. The wharves along Lake Erie present a busy aspect at all times, and a day can be well spent among the shipping.

The wealth of the city is one of its most startling features, and millionaires are not by any means a rarity. The population aggregates about 265,000, which enables Buffalo to rank as the third city in the State.

With a water front of two and a half miles on Lake Erie, as well as on the Niagara River, and its location at the foot of the chain of great lakes, the reason why it plays such an active part in the commercial interests of the country is apparent.

The climate on account of the influence of the lake winds, is naturally salubrious in summer. On the whole the streets are broad, well paved and well lighted, and the city enjoys a good sewerage system. Large and stately shade trees give Buffalo a pretty appearance, and especially delightful spots are the numerous parks and squares that the city is noted for. The public squares are named Franklin, Niagara, Prospect, Johnsons, Lafayette, and the Terrace. They were designed and laid out by Frederic Law Olmstead, who acquired fame partly by the architectural skill he displayed in Central Park, New York City.

The number of public buildings and charitable institutions, and the beauty and cost of their erection, is a source of pride with the Buffalonians. As to private residences, the city can boast as many of great cost and beauty as any of its size in the United States.

Passengers for Niagara Falls and points west change cars here. Connections are made with all other roads with little or no inconvenience.

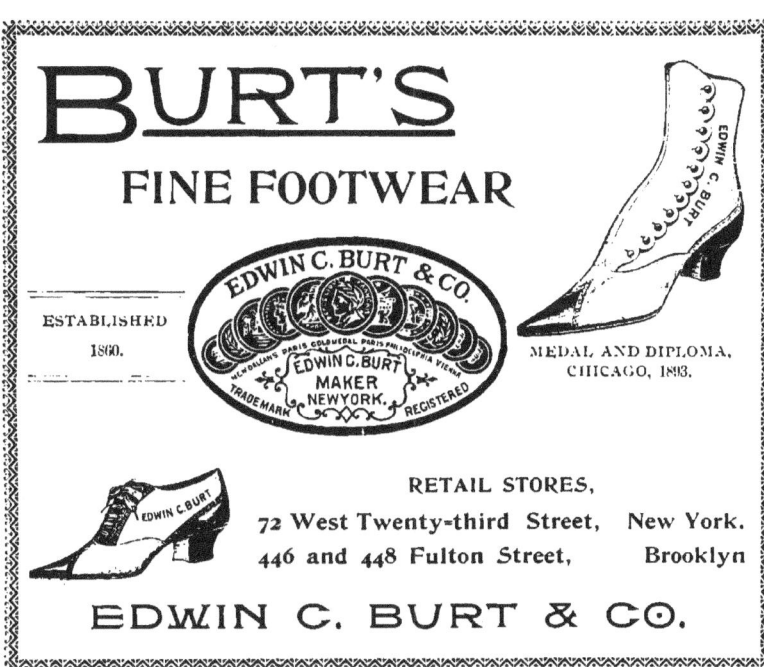

The Kittatinny, ✧ The Favorite Spring, Summer and Autumn Resort.

DELAWARE WATER GAP, MONROE CO., PENNA.

The "Kittatinny," open from May 1st to November, hardly needs introduction to people familiar with the beautiful Delaware Valley.

It is the pioneer of the resort hotels of the State, and enjoys the present distinction of being one of the best known and most fortunate in beauty of location. From a quaint mountain inn of half a century ago, the Kittatinny has grown continuously and so added to its appointment with its ever-increasing popularity that to-day it is the largest and one of the best hotels on the Delaware, receiving 350 guests and possessing a fame as wide as that of the storied Water Gap itself.

The house stands on a smooth plateau two hundred feet above the river, with the perfect picture of the river and the towering mountains that form the "Gap" on the one hand, and a wealth of natural beauty the background on the other.

One hundred and fifty acres of private grounds form a park, with the lake and mountain streams, rustic paths leading to every point of interest, and rustic structural to add to its effect. Within the hotel the appointments are complete, and suggestive in many details of the delightful outing life of which this is the centre.

The parlors, reception and reading rooms, office, corridors and bed-rooms are large, airy and tastefully furnished. A number of the bed-rooms are en suite with bath and private balconies.

An unlimited supply of purest water from mountain springs is furnished in each, both hot and cold.

The main dining-room, occupying the ground floor of the annex, built a year ago, seats three hundred. The cuisine is in charge of an experienced chef.

Other appointments include hydraulic elevator, gas, electric bells, billiard room, a well equipped livery, and an excellent orchestra.

The hotel is heated throughout by steam for the comfort of those desiring to come out in the early spring, or remaining through the fall.

Circulars and information as to how best to get here at our New York Office, care The Recreation Department, *The Outlook*, 13 Astor Place, New York City.

W. A. BRODHEAD & SONS,
Proprietors.

KING OF BICYCLES.

Light, graceful, strong, speedy, beautifully finished, exquisitively designed.

Four Models, $85 and $100.

ELEGANT 40 PAGE CATALOGUES FOR POSTAGE.

MONARCH CYCLE MFG. CO.,
LAKE AND HALSTED STREETS, CHICAGO.

Eastern Distributing and Sales Agents,
THE C. F. GUYON CO., Ltd., 79 Reade Street, New York.

Branches: San Francisco, Portland, Salt Lake City, Denver, Memphis, Detroit.

Near-by Trout and Other Waters.

Along the route of the

DELAWARE, LACKAWANNA & WESTERN RAILROAD

there are many very fine trout streams and black bass waters which are

OPEN TO THE PUBLIC,

and can be reached in a few hours from New York City. We name a few of them:

Alexander—Pickerel and black bass in waters near station.

Andover—The Pequest and tributaries, about one mile from station, afford fair trout fishing.

Apalachin—Trout are plentiful in lake Wyalusing, Cormalt Lake, and Lake of Meadows, all near station.

Atlanta—A few trout in adjacent creeks.

Augusta—Paulins Kill, one-eighth mile from station.

Baldwinsville—Seneca River; pike, pickerel and some small muscalonge.

Bath—In Keuka Lake, excellent fishing; salmon trout, black bass, etc.

Beach Haven—Susquehanna River near by is well known for its black bass and wall-eyed pike fishing.

Berwick—Excellent black bass fishing in Susquehanna River near station.

Bloomsburg—Trout in creek near by, and black bass and other fish in Susquehanna River ½ mile from station.

Branchville—Paulins Kill, one-half mile from station.

Bridgewater—Same fishing as in Atlanta, which see.

Bridgeville—Pequest, one-half mile, and Beaver Brook, one mile from station; both contain trout in fair numbers.

Budd's Lake—Black bass, &c.

Caroline—Six-Mile Brook, two miles from station; quite plentiful, and getting better each year; Boyer Creek, six miles from station; Willow Creek, four miles from station.

Catawissa—Good black bass fishing.

Chatham—Canoe Brook, one mile east of station; Spring Brook, three miles east of station; Sandy Brook, three miles west of station: trout are plentiful in all the above brooks; also in a number of nearby small streams; two good hotels.

Chenango Forks—Chenango River at station; black bass, perch and pickerel.

Chester—Two brooks contain trout, one two miles from station, the other two and one-half miles; also South Branch, one and one-half miles from station.

Corning—Black bass and perch in Chemung River one-quarter mile from station.

Cresco Station, Canadensis P. O., Pa.—Trout are very abundant in all the streams in this vicinity. Anglers who make this place their starting point will not have to go far to secure excellent trout fishing. We locate the following streams: Cranberry, one-quarter mile from station; Devil's Hole, two miles west of station; Broadhead Creek, east; Mill Creek, one mile north; Rattle Snake Creek, about one mile north; Stony Run, three miles east; Buck Hill, three miles north; Middle Branch, three miles north; Goose Pond Run, three miles northeast, and Spruce Cabin Run.

Cortland—Trout Brook, northeast of station; Hoxeyville Brook, southeast of station.

Danville—See Berwick.

Delaware Water Gap, Pa—Delaware River, near station, large but not very plentiful; Marshall Creek, one half mile from station, plenty; Brodhead's Creek, one-quarter mile from station, plenty; Caldeno Creek, half mile from station, plenty; Cherry Creek, one-quarter mile from station, abundant but small; Jersey Run, two miles from station, plentiful; first-class hotels. Good Black Bass fishing in the Delaware near the Hulies.

Dover—Numerous lakes and ponds, within five to nine miles, that gives good black bass, perch, and pickerel fishing.

Elmhurst—Excellent trout fishing in brooks near by.

Espy—Black bass in adjacent river, and trout in creeks.

Foster—The lakes close by give good black bass, pickerel and perch fishing, and trout are caught in brooks near station.

Franklin—Branch of Walkill River, near station; black bass, pickerel. etc.

Fulton—Rock and black bass in waters near by.

Gouldsboro—Same fishing as at Forks.

Henryville—At this station are the celebrated trout waters of the East and West branches of Brodhead's Creek.

Hick's Ferry—Black bass and wall-eyed pike in river near by.

Homer—Lakes containing black bass, and numerous trout streams within a radius of ten miles.

Hopatcong—Lake Hopatcong; black bass, rock bass, pike and pickerel are numerous.

Hunlocks—Same fishing as at Hick's Ferry.

Ithaca—In Cayuga Lake, one mile distant, black bass, rock bass, pike and pickerel are numerous.

Lyndhurst—Black and striped bass in the Passaic River about one-quarter mile from station.

Marathon—Black bass and pickerel near station.

Montrose—There are about thirty lakes in this vicinity that contain trout, black bass, pickerel and perch.

Morristown—Black bass, &c., in Lakes Pocahontas and Speedwell.

Moscow—Trout in brooks close to station.

Mount Pocono—Plenty of trout in adjacent streams.

Nanticoke—Good fishing for black bass, pickerel and wall-eyed pike.

North Brookfield—Trout are caught in Moscow Creek five miles from station.

Oxford—Black bass, pickerel and perch are plenty.

Pittston—Excellent black bass fishing.

Plymouth—See Pittston.

Pocono Summit—Good fishing for trout; two streams.

Portland—Black bass in Delaware River near station.

Preble—Numerous lakes close to station contain black bass and pickerel in numbers.

Richfield Springs—Pickerel, black bass and perch are caught freely in Canadarago Lake, about one mile from station.

Shickshinny—Black bass and wall-eyed pike are plenty.

Spragueville—Brodhead's Creek near station is famous for its trout fishing.

Stanhope—Budd's Lake, one to three miles; black bass, pickerel, etc.

Stroudsburg—Many good trout streams in this section.

Forest Park—"Bushkill," fifteen miles from Stroudsburg; excellent fishing; trout, black bass, perch, pickerel, etc.

Tobyhanna—In creek of this name trout are numerous.

Tully—Tully and Big Lakes, one and a half miles. Stocked with bass, perch or pickerel.

Whitney's Point—Good black bass fishing; also for pickerel, perch and sun-perch.

Willards—Same fishing as at Whitney's Point.

Willow Grove—Black bass in Susquehanna River, one-quarter mile distant.

GAME LAWS COMPILED BY
C. N. IRONSIDE,
OF LEEDS, PATRICK & IRONSIDE,
COUNSELORS AT LAW,
40 WALL ST., NEW YORK.

GAME LAWS

OF

New York, New Jersey and Pennsylvania.

♦

NEW YORK.

Act of May 5th, 1892, as amended May, 1895.

Deer.— Wild deer shall not be caught, shot at, hunted or killed except from the 16th day of August to the 31st day of October, both inclusive. No person shall kill or take alive more than two deer in any season. In the counties of Ulster, Greene, Sullivan and Delaware no wild deer shall be killed at any time within five years from the passage of this act. Deer shall not be hunted with dogs except from the 10th day of September to the 10th day of October, both inclusive. Deer shall not be hunted with dogs in the counties of St. Lawrence, Delaware, Greene, Ulster or Sullivan at any time. Dogs while chasing deer in violation of the law may be killed by any person, and dogs of the breed used for hunting deer shall not be permitted to run at large in forests inhabited by deer except between the days mentioned. Deer or venison killed in this State shall not be transported to any point within the State from or through any of the counties thereof, except that one carcass or a part thereof may be transported from the county where killed when accompanied by the owner. And no person shall so transport or accompany more than two deer in one year, but this does not apply to the head and feet or skin of deer severed from the body. No fawns shall be caught or killed at any time. No traps or any device whatever to catch or entice deer, including salt-licks, shall be used, nor shall deer be hunted, killed or captured by crusting nor while they are yarded. The above prohibitions apply also to moose, caribou and antelope. The provision as to close season does not apply to Long Island.

Black and Gray Squirrels, Hares and Rabbits.—Black and gray squirrels, hares and rabbits shall not be hunted, shot at, killed or possessed except during the months of September, October and November, but in the counties of St. Lawrence, Franklin, Essex, Clinton, Lewis, Warren, Hamilton, Herkimer, Saratoga, Washington, Onondaga, Oswego, Dutchess, Steuben, Richmond and Delaware, rabbits may be hunted, shot at, killed and possessed except from the 1st day of March to the 30th day of September, both inclusive. The use of ferrets in hunting rabbits is prohibited. The county of Wayne is exempt from the provisions of this section so far as it relates to the killing of hares and rabbits. This section does not apply to Long Island.

Wild Fowl.—Web-footed wild fowl, except geese and brant, shall not be pursued, shot at, hunted, killed, possessed or sold between the last day of April and the 1st day of September, and shall not be pursued, shot at, hunted or killed, except during the hours in each day commencing one hour before sunrise and terminating one hour after sunset. On the Hudson River below the dam at Troy, boats propelled by hand may be used for shooting web-footed fowl. Such fowl shall not be pursued, shot at, hunted, killed or caught in any way, save with the gun resting at arm's length, and fired from the shoulder without any other rest, nor from any boat other than a boat propelled by hand or floating device; nor from the use of any boughouse at a greater distance than fifty feet from the shore or from a natural growth of grass or flags. This section does not apply to Long Island and Long Island Sound.

Quail.—Quail shall not be pursued, shot at, hunted or killed except during the months of November and December; they shall not be sold or possessed except during the months of November, December and January, but possession in January is forbidden unless it be proved by the possessor that said birds were killed within the lawful periods for killing the same or outside of the State, and they shall not be killed or possessed in the counties of Genesee, Wyoming, Orleans, Livingston, Monroe, Cayuga, Seneca, Wayne, Tompkins, Tioga, Onondaga, Ontario, Steuben, Cortland and Otsego, prior to the 1st day of November, 1898. Robbin's Island and Gardiner's Island are exempt from the provisions of this section.

Woodcock and Grouse.—Woodcock, ruffed grouse, commonly known as partridge, or any member of the grouse family, shall not be pursued, shot at, hunted, or killed except from the 16th day of August to the 31st day of December, both inclusive. They shall not be sold or possessed except from the 16th day of August to the 31st day of January following; possession or sale thereof during the month of January is forbidden unless it be proved by the possessor or seller that said birds were killed within the lawful period for killing the same or outside of the State. This section does not apply to Long Island. These birds or quail killed within the State shall not be transported to any point within or without the State from or through any of the counties thereof, or possessed for that purpose, except that they may be transported from the county where killed when accompanied by the owner.

Plover, Snipe and other Birds.—Wilson's, commonly known as English snipe, plover, rail, mud-hen, gallinule, grebe, bittern, surf-bird, curlew, water chicken, bay snipe or shore bird shall not be shot at, hunted, killed or possessed during the months of May, June, July and August, except in Long Island.

Wild Birds other than Game.—These shall not be killed or caught at any time or possessed after the same are dead. This provision does not affect any birds the killing of which is prohibited between certain dates, nor does it protect the English sparrow, crow, hawk, crane, raven, crow blackbird, common blackbird and kingfisher.

Meadow Larks.—Meadow larks shall not be shot at, killed, or possessed after they are dead at any time, except in Long Island.

Nests.—The nests of wild birds shall not be robbed or willfully or needlessly destroyed, except when necessary to protect buildings or prevent their defacement. This section does not apply to the English sparrow, hawk, crane, crow, raven, blackbird, common blackbird and kingfisher.

Snaring.—English pheasants, ruffed grouse, commonly known as partridge, or any member of the grouse family, or quail, shall not be netted, trapped or snared, nor shall any person possess any of said birds so taken; nor shall any net, trap or snare of any kind be set for said birds. Such net, trap or snare may be summarily destroyed.

Mongolian Ring-Necked Pheasant.—No person shall kill, expose for sale or have in his or her possession after the same has been killed, any wild Mongolian ring-necked pheasant (*phasius tarquatus*) prior to the year 1897.

Authority to Collect Birds for Scientific Purposes.—Certificates may be granted by any incorporated society of natural history in the State, or by the regents of the University of the State of New York, to any properly accredited person of the age of eighteen years or upwards, permitting the holder thereof to collect birds, their nests or eggs, for strictly scientific purposes only.

Trout.—Trout shall not be fished for, caught, killed or possessed except from the 16th day of April to the 31st day of August, both inclusive, except in Long Island. They shall not be taken or possessed unless six inches in length, and if less than six inches in length and taken unintentionally shall be immediately replaced in the water from which taken without unnecessary injury.

Salmon Trout and Land-Locked Salmon.—Shall not be willfully molested or disturbed while upon their spawning beds during close season, nor shall such fish nor any spawn or milt from any such fish be carried away while upon the spawning beds.

Salmon Trout.—Sometimes known as lake trout, and land-locked salmon, shall not be caught or killed in inland waters of this State, except from the 1st day of May to the 30th day of September, both inclusive. Possession of such fish during close season is prohibited unless it be proved that such fish were not caught in this State during such season. The provisions of this section do not apply to Long Island. These fish caught in any inland waters of the State shall not be transported to any point within or without the State from or through any of the counties thereof, or possessed for that purpose except when accompanied by the owner.

Black Bass and Oswego Bass.—Black bass, Oswego bass, pickerel, pike or wall-eyed pike, shall not be fished for, caught or possessed, except from the 30th day of May to the 31st day of December, both inclusive, nor in Lake George except from the 1st of August to the 31st of December, both inclusive.

Pickerel, Pike and Wall-Eyed Pike—Shall not be fished for, caught, killed or possessed, except from the 1st day of May to the 31st day of January, both inclusive; except that pickerel, bull-heads, catfish, eels, perch and sunfish may be fished for through the ice with hooks and lines or tip-ups in Lake Keuka or Crooked Lake or in any of the waters of the State not inhabited by trout, lake trout, salmon trout, black or Oswego bass or land-locked salmon or muskallonge, and by set lines in the Susquehanna River, and in the waters of Port Bay in the County of Wayne. Suckers, bull-heads, eels and dogfish may be caught at any time by hooking and spearing in Oneida Lake or river, or in any of the waters of the State not inhabited by trout, lake trout, land-locked salmon, muskallonge, black bass or Oswego bass, but pike, pickerel and wall-eyed pike may be taken with hook and line or spear, and muskallonge with hook and line in any of the inland waters of this State not inhabited by trout or salmon of any kind, during December, January and February, except in the waters of Cortland County. Suckers, bull-heads and eels may be caught in Seneca Lake with seines after permission first obtained from the Commissioners of Fisheries, Game and Forests.

Bass.—Shall not be taken less than eight inches in length from any of the waters of this State, nor possessed; if such are caught they must be immediately replaced in the water whence taken, without injury.

Muskallonge shall not be fished for, caught or possessed, except from the 30th day of May to the last day of February, both inclusive.

Salmon shall not be fished for, caught, killed or possessed between the 15th day of August and the 1st day of March following. No salmon less than eighteen inches in length shall be intentionally taken alive from any of the waters of this State, nor possessed, and if taken shall be immediately returned to the waters from which it is taken without unnecessary injury.

Fishing within fifty rods of any fishway erected by the State, and any interference with the signboards there maintained, is forbidden.

Salt Water Striped Bass.—No salt water striped bass less than eight inches in length shall be intentionally taken from any of the waters of this State, nor possessed. If unintentionally taken shall be immediately replaced in the water from which it is taken without any unnecessary injury.

Pollution of Waters.—No dyestuff, coal tar, refuse from gas houses, sawdust, shavings, tanbark, lime, or other deleterious, or poisonous, substances shall be allowed to run into any of the waters of this State, either private or public, in quantities destructive to the life of fish inhabiting the same. Nor shall fish be taken by shutting or drawing off any water for that purpose. The use of dynamite or any other explosives in any of the waters of this State is prohibited except for mining and mechanical purposes.

Stocking Waters from Streams.—No trout of any kind, salmon trout, or land-locked salmon, shall be taken from any of the waters of this State for the purpose of stocking a private pond or stream.

Fishing Through the Ice in any waters inhabited by trout, salmon trout, or land-locked salmon, during the closed season for any such fish, is prohibited.

Waters of the Adirondacks.—No fish, fish fry, spawn or milt, except speckled trout, brook, brown, salmon and rainbow, trout, Adirondack frost fish, or land-locked salmon, shall be placed in waters of the Adirondack regions except under the immediate supervision of the Commissioners of Fisheries.

Unlawful Devices—Fishing by any device other than angling in the waters of the St. Lawrence or Niagara Rivers nor in Lake Champlain, except during the months of March, April and May, and in the

SUMMER EXCURSION ROUTES AND RATES.

waters of Niagara County, except during the months of November, December, January, February and March, no fish may be taken except black bass and muskallonge, after permission being first obtained from the Commissioners of Fisheries, Game and Forests. The use of any device, except angling, in the waters of Lake Erie within half a mile of the shore, or of any of the islands therein, nor in Cattaraugus Creek, or within five miles of the mouth thereof, or of any of the islands therein, nor within three miles of the mouth of the Niagara River, the waters of Lake Ontario, in the County of Jefferson, included between Blue Rock Point and the towns of Lyme and Cape Vincent, including Chaumont Bay, Griffin Bay and Three Mile Bay, in the County of Oswego, between the northerly line of the town of Mexico and Jefferson County line, are exempt from the provision of this act.

Salmon taken in nets from the Hudson River shall be immediately put back. Salmon, black bass, salmon trout and pike perch caught in nets in fishing for other fish in the Hudson River shall be thrown back into the water without unnecessary injury.

No Device except angling shall be used for the capture of any fish except menhaden, in the waters of Raritan Bay or waters adjacent thereto in Richmond County, except that shad may be taken in shad nets between the 15th day of March and the 15th day of June, both inclusive.

Nets, set-nets, pounds or fykes, except those used for catching lobsters or crabs, shall not be used in the Harlem River, or the East River, or in the adjacent water or confluent brooks.

NEW JERSEY.

BIRDS AND ANIMALS.	Open Season.		Open Season.
Ruffed Grouse	Oct. 31 to Dec. 16	Rabbit and Hare	Nov. 10 to Dec. 16
Quail	Nov. 10 to Dec. 16	Deer	Nov. 25 to Dec. 15
Woodcock	July and Sept. 30 to Dec. 16	FISH.	
Upland Plover	July 31 to Dec. 16	Salmon Trout	March 1 to Oct. 1
English Snipe	March, April and Aug. 26 to Dec. 16	Brook Trout	April 1 to July 15
Grouse and Pheasant	Oct. 31 to Dec. 16	Black and Oswego Bass	May 30 to Dec. 1
Wild Turkey	Oct. 31 to Dec. 16	Pickerel and Pike	April 1 to March 31
Web-Footed Wild Fowl	Aug. 31 to May 1		

PENNSYLVANIA.

BIRDS AND ANIMALS.	Open Season.	FISH.	Open Season.
Turkeys	Oct. 15 to Jan. 1	Wall-Eyed Pike	June 1 to Feb. 1
Ducks	Sept. 1 to May 1	Speckled Trout	April 15 to July 15
Plover	July 15 to Jan. 1	Salmon	May 30 to Jan. 1
Woodcock	July 4 to Jan. 1	Lake Trout	Jan 1 to Sept. 30
Quail	Nov. 1 to Dec. 15	Pickerel	June 1 to Jan. 31
Ruffed Grouse or Pheasant	Oct. 1 to Jan. 1	Black and Rock Bass	May 30 to Jan. 1
Rail and Reed Bird	Sept. 1 to Dec. 1	Hunting and Fishing on Sunday unlawful.	
Snipe and Wild Pigeons	Any time.		
Elk and Deer	Oct. 1 to Dec. 15		
Squirrels	Sept. 1 to Jan. 1		
Hares and Rabbits	Nov. 1 to Jan. 1		

In most of the States there is a penalty of from $5 to $50 for killing song-birds.

Stylish Cutting   **15th SEASON**   *Fine Workmanship*

MILLER & CO.
TAILORS
21 & 23 CENTRE STREET
Bet. Chambers & Reade Sts.   NEW YORK

One block North of City Hall Station

Reasonable Prices   *Fashionable Novelties*

The Jackson Sanatorium

DANSVILLE, NEW YORK

ESTABLISHED 1858.

Clear, dry Atmosphere, free from fogs and Malaria.

Pure Spring Water from rocky heights.

Perfect Drainage and Sewerage.

Main Building Absolutely Fire-proof.

A delightful home for those seeking health, rest or recreation. Under the personal care of regularly educated and experienced physicians. Hillside location in Woodland Park, overlooking extended views of the famous Genesee Valley region, unsurpassed for healthfulness and beauty.

Elegant modern fire-proof main building and twelve cottages, complete in all appliances for health and comfort. Extensive apartments for treatment arranged for individual privacy. Skilled attendants. All forms of fresh and salt water baths: Electricity, Massage, Swedish Movements, etc. Vacuum treatment. Delsarte system of Physical Culture. Frequent lectures and lessons on Health Topics. Especial provision for quiet and rest; also for recreation, amusement and regular outdoor Life. Delightful walks and drives.

Culinary Department under supervision of Mrs. Emma P. Ewing, Superintendent of Chautauqua Cooking School.

Steam heat, open fires, electric bells, safety elevator, telegraph, telephone, chapel, library, daily papers, and every provision for comfort, health and good cheer.

For illustrated pamphlet, testimonials, and other information, address

J. ARTHUR JACKSON, ...
. . . . Secretary . . .   P. O. BOX, 1874.

LAKE KEUKA PARK

ONE of the most restful and enjoyable resorts on Lake Keuka is Keuka Park. . . . . .
It occupies a beautiful slope on the west shore of the Lake, four miles from Penn Yan where steamers connect with the N. Y. C. and Fall Brook Railways and the N. C. Railway, and eighteen miles from Hammondsport where they connect with D., L. & W. and N. Y., L. E. & W. R. R. *via* Bath and Hammondsport Railway. .
The park contains 160 acres, with 30 acres of grove and 170 rods of Lake frontage . .

KEUKA COLLEGE

in this park opens its large new and elegant building for guests from June 20th to September 1st, at a charge of only $1.00 a day. The rooms are large, light and cheery, and the table service excellent. Tents and cottages in ample supply may be rented at moderate rates. Fresh milk, fruit and vegetables are abundant. The Summer assembly in the splendid natural amphitheatre offer instruction, diversion, amusement and society of a high order. . . . .

A well conducted sanatorium offer superior medical service, and Turkish, Russian, electric, medicated, perfumed and salt water baths. . . . .

The college reading room is well supplied with papers and free to guests. The name of the Post Office is Keuka College, and mail is received daily. . . . .

All the Trunk Lines sell tickets to Keuka Park at reduced rates. . . .

Mount Pocono
Pennsylvania

THIS Summer resort is situated on one of the spurs of the Pocono Mountains, in Monroe County, Pennsylvania, one and one-fourth miles from Mount Pocono Station.

The House commands a fine view of mountain, forest and valley, the picture framed by the Blue Ridge twenty miles distant, with Pocono Knob and Delaware Water Gap prominent features in the landscape.

The extensive grounds, covering several hundred acres, are well wooded, yellow pine predominating. The broad lawns afford ample facilities for out-door sports.

The accommodations are limited to one hundred guests. The house is heated with steam, and has ample parlors, sitting rooms, billiard room, dancing room, and children's play room. There are hot and cold water baths, and the sanitary arrangements are of the most approved system.

Wiscasset Spring Water is the only water used in the house. There are three miles of trout stream of which The Wiscasset's guests have exclusive use.

The elevation, delightful scenery, healthful and exhilarating climate, freedom from mosquitoes, and easy access, render The Wiscasset particularly desirable for a Summer sojourn. Applicants will please mention by whom, if any one, the house has been recommended. References will be exchanged with strangers.

ELEVATION, ONE THOUSAND
SEVEN HUNDRED FEET

I. D. IVISON
MANAGER

ROUTES AND RATES.

ALEXANDRIA BAY, N. Y.
THE THOUSAND ISLANDS.

JUST where the blue waters of Lake Ontario find their outlet between Cape Vincent, N. Y., and Kingston, Can., the Thousand Islands of the St. Lawrence have their beginning, extending some forty miles down the river in picturesque groups, and forming in their entirety one of the loveliest and most varied fishing regions in the world.

It is now hardly more than a dozen years since the Thousand Islands began to attract widespread attention, yet the visitor will find along the route of the steamer, which bears him down the crystal current, numbers of large hotels, and hundreds of costly and palatial summer homes, which increase in numbers annually.

The tourist portion of the Thousand Islands begins, practically speaking, at Clayton, the terminus of the Rome, Watertown & Ogdensburg Railroad. From this point steamers ply to Alexandria Bay, touching at intermediate points. The first landing is made at Round Island. This is a prominent cottage community. It is non-sectarian, and numbers among its permanent summer residents many prominent people from the large cities.

Thousand Island Park, a Methodist community, is two miles below, and also has its hotel and numerous cottages, as well as a large "tabernacle."

Central Park is prettily located midway down the American channel.

About ten miles below Clayton, Alexandria Bay is located. In the immediate vicinity are many of the most costly and beautiful summer villas. The "Bay" is the focus of a large summer travel, steamers coming and going constantly.

Near Alexandria Bay, and like that village, also upon the mainland, is Edgewood Park, chiefly occupied by Cleveland families; and one mile distant is Westminster Park, which has a good hotel and Presbyterian tendencies.

The fishing at the Thousand Islands will always be its chief charm with the general visitor, and, thanks to the protection of recently enacted State laws and the activity of the Angler's Association, the fishing is always improving. Boatmen, with safe and natty St. Lawrence skiffs, the most beautiful of all water craft, may be engaged at any of the hotels by the day or week.

Daily excursions are made among the islands from all the hotels, upon swift and roomy steamboats.

EXCURSION NO. 9.—ALEXANDRIA BAY AND RETURN.

Delaware, Lack. & Western R. R..to Utica.
Rome, Watertown & Ogdbg. R. R..to Clayton.
Thousand Island Steamboat Co...to Alexandria Bay.
Returning *via* same route.

THROUGH RATES.

New York	$16 00	Berwick	$14 80
Paterson	16 00	Bloomsburg	15 35
Newark	16 00	Danville	15 75
Morristown	16 00	Binghamton	10 55
Dover	16 00	Greene	9 80
Hackettstown	16 00	Oxford	9 25
Washington	16 00	Norwich	8 95
Water Gap	15 35	Sherburne	8 50
Stroudsburg	15 15	Waterville	7 65
Scranton	13 05	Richfield Springs	8 25
Pittston	13 45	Vestal	10 90
Kingston	13 75	Owego	11 40
Wilkesbarre	13 75	Waverly	12 15
Plymouth	13 90	Elmira	12 85
Nanticoke	14 00	Corning	13 35
Shickshinny	14 35	Bath	14 35

EXCURSION NO. 7.—ALEXANDRIA BAY AND RETURN.

Delaware, Lack. & Western R. R..to Syracuse.
Rome, Watertown & Ogdbg. R. R. to Clayton.
Thousand Island Steamboat Co...to Alexandria Bay.
Returning *via* same route.

THROUGH RATES.

New York	$16 00	Wilkesbarre	$13 10
Paterson	16 00	Plymouth	13 25
Newark	16 00	Nanticoke	13 35
Morristown	16 00	Shickshinny	13 75
Dover	16 00	Berwick	14 15
Hackettstown	15 95	Bloomsburg	14 70
Washington	15 55	Danville	15 15
Water Gap	14 75	Binghamton	9 95
Stroudsburg	14 55	Cortland	8 25
Scranton	12 45	Vestal	10 30
Pittston	12 80	Owego	10 75
Kingston	13 10	Waverly	11 25
Elmira	$11 25		

EXCURSION NO. 153.—ALEXANDRIA BAY AND RETURN.

Delaware, Lack. & Western R. R..to Oswego.
Rome, Watertown & Ogdbg. R. R..to Clayton.
Thousand Island Steamboat Co...to Alexandria Bay.
Returning *via* same route

THROUGH RATES.

New York	$16 00	Wilkesbarre	$14 05
Paterson	16 00	Plymouth	14 15
Newark	16 00	Nanticoke	14 25
Morristown	16 00	Shickshinny	14 65
Dover	16 00	Berwick	15 05
Hackettstown	16 00	Bloomsburg	15 60
Washington	16 00	Danville	16 05
Water Gap	15 65	Binghamton	10 85
Stroudsburg	15 45	Cortland	9 15
Scranton	13 35	Syracuse	7 65
Pittston	13 70	Owego	11 65
Kingston	14 05	Waverly	12 15
Elmira	$12 15		

EXCURSION NO. 154.—ALEXANDRIA BAY AND RETURN.

Delaware, Lack. & Western R. R...to Oswego.
Rome,Watertown & Ogdbg. R. R..to Clayton.
Thousand Island Steamboat Co...to Alexandria Bay.
Thousand Island Steamboat Co...to Clayton.
Rome,Watertown & Ogdbg. R. R..to Utica.
Delaware, Lack. & Western R. R..to starting point.

EXCURSION NO. 155.—REVERSE OF THE PRECEDING.

THROUGH RATES.

New York	$19 75	Plymouth	$14 75
Paterson	19 15	Nanticoke	14 90
Newark	19 55	Shickshinny	15 25
Morristown	18 70	Berwick	15 70
Dover	18 20	Bloomsburg	16 20
Hackettstown	17 45	Danville	16 65
Washington	17 10	Binghamton	11 25
Water Gap	16 25	Greene	11 05
Stroudsburg	16 05	Oxford	11 05
Scranton	13 95	Norwich	11 05
Pittston	14 35	Cortland	11 05
Kingston	14 65	Owego	12 30
Wilkesbarre	14 65	Waverly	13 05
Elmira	$13 75		

EXCURSION S T 16.—UTICA TO ALEXANDRIA BAY AND RETURN.

Rome,Watertown & Ogdbg. R. R..to Clayton.
Thousand Island Steamboat Co...to Alexandria Bay.
Returning *via* same route.
Sold only in connection with Summer Excursion Ticket passing through Utica.
Rate..............$6 75

ASHEVILLE, N. C.

In the centre of a region poetically designated as "The Land of the Sky," is Asheville, N. C.

In Western North Carolina, between the Blue Ridge on the east and the Alleghanies on the west, lies this beautiful valley. It is a land of bright skies, incomparable climate, and picturesque scenery, whose praises have been sung by poets and whose beauties of stream, valley and mountain height have furnished subject and inspiration to the sketcher's hand. The city is situated in the heart of the mountains, 2,300 feet above the level of the tide. Romantic scenery surrounds the town on every side, and the approach to it from either direction leads through a panorama of enchanting views. On the one hand there rises the beautiful Blue Ridge; on the other, the picturesque Alleghanies; at their feet flow the clear waters of the French Broad.

There is scarcely a more beautiful valley than this, and certainly none more rich in all that would attract health-seeker, lounger, invalid or dreamer. The climate is superb.

EXCURSION NO. 314 Y.—ASHEVILLE, N. C. AND RETURN.

Limited to three (3) months from date of sale.

Good for use south-bound only within fifteen (15) days from date of issue as stamped on back of ticket; and must be presented to the ticket agency of the initial line at the destination point for identification and validation before they can be used for the return trip, and are then good returning only within fifteen (15) days from such validation as stamped on the back of ticket; in all cases, however, tickets must be used within the extreme limit.

Del., Lack. & Western R. R.....to Manunka Chunk.
Pennsylvania Railroad..........to Washington.
Richmond & Danville Railroad..to Asheville.
Returning *via* same route.

THROUGH RATES.

Stroudsburg	$31 05	Syracuse	$37 65
Scranton	31 05	Fulton	38 65
Pittston	31 05	Oswego	39 05
Kingston	31 05	Owego	34 85
Wilkesbarre	31 05	Ithaca	36 25
Montrose	33 35	Waverly	34 85
Binghamton	34 85	Elmira	34 85
Greene	36 05	Corning	35 60
Oxford	36 60	Bath	35 60
Norwich	37 40	Atlanta	35 60
Sherburne	38 05	Wayland	35 60
Waterville	39 30	Dansville	35 60
Richfield Springs	41 10	Mt. Morris	35 60
Utica	40 55	Buffalo	35 60
Cortland	36 60		

EXCURSION NO. 333 Y.—ASHEVILLE, N. C. AND RETURN.

Limited to three (3) months from date of sale.

Delaware, Lack. & Western R. R.....to New York.
Pennsylvania Railroad...........to Washington.
Richmond & Danville Railroad.......to Asheville.
Returning *via* same route.

THROUGH RATES.

Summit	$30 80	Richfield Springs	$40 75
Morristown	31 25	Utica	39 25
Dover	31 75	Cortland	40 00
Hackettstown	32 45	Syracuse	40 00
Washington	32 85	Fulton	40 00
Stroudsburg	33 85	Oswego	40 00
Scranton	36 00	Owego	38 85
Pittston	36 55	Ithaca	40 50
Kingston	36 80	Waverly	39 60
Wilkesbarre	36 85	Elmira	40 25
Montrose	38 20	Corning	40 90
Binghamton	38 00	Bath	41 75
Greene	38 80	Atlanta	42 75
Oxford	39 00	Wayland	42 95
Norwich	39 00	Dansville	43 70
Sherburne	39 25	Mt. Morris	43 70
Waterville	39 25	Buffalo	46 00

ATLANTIC CITY, N. J.

Atlantic City claims for itself to be the most popular resort in this country—an all-year-round health-restoring and pleasure-giving place, unsurpassed in the plenitude of its accommodations.

Although immediately on the beach (many houses being but a few feet from the surf), it is a city of ten thousand inhabitants, which, at the height of the summer season, is increased to a hundred thousand.

In summer, bathing, fishing, driving, boating, and like sea-shore divertisements are its offerings to the well who go there for a rest and change from the monotony of every-day affairs.

For the invalid there is ozone-freighted air breezes, tempered by journeys over thousands of miles of ocean, cool, comfortable nights for repose, and all the facilities enjoyed in cities of the larger size.

Fine avenues, beautiful cottages, magnificently appointed hotels, street cars, electric lights, a perfect sewerage, and first-class drinking water, brought from the mainland.

Prominent as it is, as a summer resort, it is hardly less so as a winter sanitarium—many of its hotels being filled to their utmost.

SUMMER EXCURSION ROUTES AND RATES. 119

It lays claim to being only sixty miles from the gulf stream, the influence of which is directly attested by its temperature, being several degrees higher in winter than cities sixty miles inland.

EXCURSION NO. 65 Y.—ATLANTIC CITY AND RETURN.

Limited to six (6) months from date of sale.
Del., Lack. & Western R. R.....to Manunka Chunk.
Pennsylvania Railroad..........to Atlantic City.
Returning via same route.
(Good for passage via either Philadelphia (Broad St. Station) or Amboy Division to Camden.)

THROUGH RATES.

Stroudsburg	$ 6 10	Syracuse	$14 25
Scranton	8 50	Fulton	15 25
Pittston	8 50	Oswego	15 65
Kingston	8 50	Owego	11 50
Wilkesbarre	8 50	Ithaca	12 90
Montrose	10 80	Waverly	11 50
Binghamton	11 50	Elmira	11 50
Greene	12 30	Corning	12 45
Oxford	12 80	Bath	13 70
Norwich	13 15	Atlanta	14 80
Sherburne	13 60	Wayland	15 00
Waterville	14 25	Dansville	15 30
Richfield Springs	15 60	Mt. Morris	16 20
Utica	14 25	Buffalo	18 10
Cortland	14 10		

EXCURSION NO. 66 Y.—ATLANTIC CITY AND RETURN.

Limited to six (6) months from date of sale.
Delaware, Lack. & Western R. R....to New York.
Pennsylvania Railroad..........to Atlantic City.
Returning via same route.
(Good for passage via either Philadelphia (Broad St. Station) or Amboy Division to Camden.)

EXCURSION NO. 152 Y.—ATLANTIC CITY AND RETURN.

Limited to six (6) months from date of sale.
Delaware, Lack. & Western R. R...to New York.
Central Railroad of New Jersey.....to Bound Brook.
Philadelphia & Reading Railroad...to Atlantic City.
Returning via same route.

EXCURSION NO. 151 Y.—ATLANTIC CITY AND RETURN.

Limited to six (6) months from date of sale.
Delaware, Lack. & West. R. R...to New York.
C. R. R. of N. J. via Perth Amboy.to Winslow Junc'n.
Philadelphia & Reading R. R.....to Atlantic City.
Returning via same route.

THROUGH RATES FOR EITHER EXCURSION.

Summit	$ 5 80	Richfield Springs	$15 75
Morristown	6 25	Utica	14 25
Dover	6 75	Cortland	15 00
Hackettstown	7 45	Syracuse	15 00
Washington	7 85	Fulton	15 00
Stroudsburg	8 85	Oswego	15 00
Scranton	11 00	Owego	13 85
Pittston	11 40	Ithaca	15 50
Kingston	11 80	Waverly	14 60
Wilkesbarre	11 85	Elmira	15 25
Montrose	13 20	Corning	15 90
Binghamton	13 00	Bath	16 75
Greene	13 80	Atlanta	17 90
Oxford	14 00	Wayland	18 20
Norwich	14 00	Dansville	18 70
Sherburne	14 25	Mount Morris	18 70
Waterville	14 25	Buffalo	21 00

EXCURSION NO. 67 Y.—ATLANTIC CITY AND RETURN.

Limited to six (6) months from date of sale.
Del., Lack. & Western R. R.....to Manunka Chunk.
Pennsylvania Railroad ....to Atlantic City.
Pennsylvania Railroad ....to New York.
Del., Lack. & Western R. R.....to starting point.

EXCURSION NO. 68.—REVERSE OF THE PRECEDING.

(Good for passage via either Philadelphia (Broad St. Station) or Amboy Division to Camden.)

THROUGH RATES.

Stroudsburg	$ 8 80	Syracuse	$15 00
Scranton	10 00	Fulton	16 00
Pittston	10 45	Oswego	16 40
Kingston	10 80	Owego	13 75
Wilkesbarre	10 80	Ithaca	15 15
Montrose	12 30	Waverly	14 90
Binghamton	12 50	Elmira	15 90
Greene	13 30	Corning	16 85
Oxford	13 80	Bath	18 10
Norwich	14 15	Atlanta	19 25
Sherburne	14 30	Wayland	19 60
Waterville	14 30	Dansville	20 00
Richfield Springs	15 65	Mount Morris	21 75
Utica	14 30	Buffalo	21 75
Cortland	15 00		

BAR HARBOR, ME. (MT. DESERT.)

This island (named by Champlain in 1604, L'Isle des Monts Desert) is about one hundred miles (water route) east of Portland, Maine. Bar Harbor is the principal village, containing numerous residences and hotels. The island, which is about fourteen miles by eight, contains a wonderful variety of nature's beauties in the same line. Mountains, the highest on the Atlantic coast, beautiful valleys, lakes of great depth and peculiar surroundings, roaring streams, and great brooks. It is very popular from the fact that the varied character of its charms attracts alike the mountaineer, the hunter, the yachtsman, artist, naturalist, and the poet.

*EXCURSION S T 7.—BOSTON TO BAR HARBOR AND RETURN.

Boston & Maine Railroad............to Portland.
Maine Central Railroad ....to Bath.
Knox & Lincoln Railroad............to Rockland.
Boston & Bangor Steamship Co......to Bar Harbor.
Returning via same route.
Rate..................... $10 00

*EXCURSION S T 8.—BOSTON TO BAR HARBOR AND RETURN.

Boston & Maine Railroad.....to Portland.
Maine Central Railroad.............to Bath.
Knox & Lincoln Railroad............to Rockland.
Portland, Bangor, Mt. Desert and
  Machias Steamboat Co...........to Bar Harbor.
Returning via same route.
Rate..........................$10 00

*EXCURSION S T 11.—BOSTON TO BAR HARBOR AND RETURN.

Boston & Maine Railroad. ....to Portland.
Maine Central Railroad............to Bar Harbor.
Returning via same route.
Limited to continuous passage between Portland and Bar Harbor.
Rate $11 50

*EXCURSION S T 10.—BOSTON TO BAR HARBOR AND RETURN.

Boston & Bangor Steamship Co.'s to Bar Harbor
  Steamer........................ and return.
Rate......................... $7 50
* Sold only in connection with Summer Excursion Ticket to, or passing through Boston.

†EXCURSION S T 28.—PORTLAND TO BAR HARBOR AND RETURN.
Maine Central Railroad............. {to Bar Harbor and return.
Limited to continuous passage in both directions.
Rate........................ $8 50

†EXCURSION S T 29.—PORTLAND TO BAR HARBOR AND RETURN.
Maine Central Railroad.............. to Bath.
Knox & Lincoln Railroad........... to Rockland.
Boston & Bangor Steamship Co.......to Bar Harbor.
Returning *via* same route.
Rate.... .... $7 00

†EXCURSION S T 30.—PORTLAND TO BAR HARBOR AND RETURN.
Maine Central Railroad................to Bath.
Knox & Lincoln Railroad.......... to Rockland.
Portland, Bangor, Mt. Desert and Machias Steamboat Co............to Bar Harbor.
Returning *via* same route.
Rate........................ $7 00
† Sold only in connection with Summer Excursion Ticket to, or passing through Portland.

BARNEGAT CITY, N. J.

Barnegat is one of the oldest and most celebrated settlements on the Jersey coast, and many are the traditions that cluster about its shores, so full of peril to sailors. The very name means "dangerous breakers," and many an old sailor would testify to the fitness of the appellation.

The town, located near the shores of Barnegat Bay, is the metropolis of the fishing-grounds of New Jersey. The bay and inlet are the favorite haunts of bluefish as well as the home of every other species native to the waters of that section.

In addition to its fishing resources, oysters are plentiful, and wild fowl are found in great abundance.

Yachts, tackle, and sportsmen's supplies may be obtained from the seafaring people, of which the population is largely composed.

EXCURSION NO. 275.—BARNEGAT CITY AND RETURN.
Del., Lack. & Western R. R.....to Manunka Chunk.
Pennsylvania R. R. *via* Trenton.to Whiting's.
Tuckerton Railroad............to Manahawken.
Pennsylvania Railroad...........to Barnegat City.
Returning *via* same route.

THROUGH RATES.

Water Gap ....$ 6 00	Oxford.... ....$11 80
Stroudsburg....... 6 30	Norwich............ 12 10
Scranton 8 65	Sherburne.......... 12 55
Pittston.. .... 8 65	Waterville.......... 13 45
Kingston........... 8 50	Richfield Springs... 14 60
Wilkesbarre....... 8 65	Utica 14 25
Binghamton....... 10 45	Cortland............ 12 20
Greene............ 11 25	Syracuse........... 13 65
Oswego............ 15 05	Bath................ 14 25
Owego............. 11 30	Atlanta............. 15 25
Ithaca 12 65	Wayland 15 55
Waverly.......... 12 05	Dansville.......... 15 55
Elmira............ 12 75	Mount Morris...... 16 10
Corning 13 00	Buffalo............ . 18 10

EXCURSION NO. 276.—BARNEGAT CITY AND RETURN.
Del., Lack. & Western R. R. ....to New York.
Pennsylvania R. R. *via* Trenton....to Whiting s.
Tuckerton Railroad................to Manahawken.
Pennsylvania Railroad..............to Barnegat City.
Returning *via* same route.

THROUGH RATES.

Morristown ....$ 5 75	Utica $13 75
Dover............. 6 25	Richfield Springs.. 15 25
Hackettstown...... 6 95	Cortland............ 14 50
Washington....... 7 35	Syracuse........... 14 50
Water Gap.. ...... 8 20	Oswego............ 14 50
Stroudsburg........ 8 35	Owego............. 13 40
Scranton........... 10 50	Ithaca 15 00
Pittston........... 10 90	Waverly........... 14 10
Kingston.......... 11 65	Elmira............ 14 75
Wilkesbarre........ 11 70	Corning............ 15 40
Binghamton....... 12 50	Bath................ 16 25
Greene............ 13 30	Atlanta............. 17 40
Oxford 13 50	Wayland.......... 17 70
Norwich........... 13 50	Dansville.......... 18 20
Sherburne......... 13 75	Mount Morris...... 18 20
Waterville......... 13 75	Buffalo 20 50

BEACH HAVEN, N. J.

EXCURSION NO. 277.—BEACH HAVEN AND RETURN.
Del., Lack. & Western R. R.....to Manunka Chunk.
Pennsylvania R. R. *via* Trenton .to Whiting's.
Tuckerton Railroad..............to Manahawken.
Pennsylvania Railroad..........to Beach Haven.
Returning *via* same route.

THROUGH RATES.

Water Gap.........$ 6 00	Cortland.. ....$12 20
Stroudsburg........ 6 30	Syracuse........... 13 65
Scranton 8 65	Oswego............. 15 05
Pittston............ 8 65	Owego............. 11 30
Kingston........... 8 65	Ithaca 12 65
Wilkesbarre....... 8 65	Waverly........... 12 05
Binghamton....... 10 45	Elmira 12 75
Greene............ 11 25	Corning 13 40
Oxford 11 80	Bath................ 14 25
Norwich........... 12 10	Atlanta............. 15 05
Sherburne......... 12 55	Wayland 15 25
Waterville......... 13 45	Dansville.......... 15 55
Richfield Springs... 14 60	Mount Morris...... 16 10
Utica.............. 14 25	Buffalo 18 10

EXCURSION NO. 278.—BEACH HAVEN AND RETURN.
Delaware, Lack. & Western R. R...to New York.
Pennsylvania R. R. *via* Trenton...to Whiting's.
Tuckerton Railroad................to Manahawken.
Pennsylvania Railroad.............to Beach Haven.
Returning *via* same route.

THROUGH RATES.

Morristown........ $ 5 75	Richfield Springs..$15 25
Dover 6 25	Utica 13 75
Hackettstown..... 6 95	Cortland............ 14 50
Washington....... 7 35	Syracuse........... 14 50
Water Gap....... 8 20	Oswego............ 14 50
Stroudsburg........ 8 35	Owego............. 13 40
Scranton 10 50	Ithaca 15 00
Pittston........... 10 90	Waverly........... 14 10
Kingston 11 65	Elmira............. 14 75
Wilkesbarre....... 11 70	Corning............ 15 40
Binghamton....... 12 50	Bath................ 16 25
Greene............ 13 30	Atlanta............. 17 40
Oxford............ 13 50	Wayland.......... 17 70
Norwich. 13 50	Dansville.......... 18 20
Sherburne......... 13 75	Mount Morris...... 18 20
Waterville......... 13 75	Buffalo............ 20 50

BETHLEHEM, N. H.
(WHITE MOUNTAINS.)

This village is said to be the highest of any east of the Rocky Mountains—*i. e.*, 1,500 feet above the level of the ocean. It is quite famous as a resort for persons afflicted with hay-fever, who find here a relief. The Hay-FeverClub assembles at Bethlehem annually. Pure air, convenience to the many attractive

SUMMER EXCURSION ROUTES AND RATES.

resorts in the Presidential range in the White Mountains and the facilities offered by a good sized village, are only a few of the claims of this pretty region.

EXC. S T 37.—BOSTON TO BETHLEHEM AND RETURN.

Bos. & Maine R. R. (Lowell Sys.).to Nashua.
Concord & Montreal R. R.........to Concord.
Concord & Montreal R. R. ......to Bethlehem Junc.
Profile & Franconia Notch R. R..to Bethlehem.
Returning *via* same route.
Sold only in connection with Summer Excursion Ticket to, or passing through Boston.
Rate................$10 75

EXC. S T 46.—BOSTON TO BETHLEHEM AND RETURN.

Boston & Maine Railroad,........to North Conway.
Me. C. R. R. (White Moun. Line).to Crawford House.
Me. C. R. R. (White Moun. Line).to Fabyan's.
Concord & Montreal Railroad....to Bethlehem Junc.
Profile & Franconia Notch R.R...to Bethlehem.
Returning *via* same route.
Sold only in connection with Summer Excursion Ticket to, or passing through Boston.
Rate...............$10 75

EXC. S T 38.—BETHLEHEM JUNCTION TO BETHLEHEM AND RETURN.

Profile & Fran. Notch R. R.to Bethlehem and return.
Sold only in connection with Summer Excursion Ticket passing through Bethlehem Junction.
Rate...............$1 00

BLOCK ISLAND, R. I.

To be at once far out at sea and yet on terra firma—is what Block Island offers to the dwellers of the city and country. A change of air is certainly to be obtained here if anywhere, for it is a sea island—south from Point Judith about ten miles. It is reached by steamer from New London.

EXCURSION NO. 35.—BLOCK ISLAND AND RETURN.

Delaware, Lack. & Western R. R....to New York.
Norwich Line Steamers.............to New London.
Steamer Block Island..............to Block Island.
Returning *via* same route.

THROUGH RATES.

Morristown ....$ 5 55	Waterville.........$14 30
Dover.............. 6 05	Cortland........... 14 30
Hackettstown..... 6 75	Syracuse.......... 14 30
Washington....... 7 15	Oswego........... 14 30
Water Gap........ 8 00	Owego............ 13 15
Stroudsburg...... 8 15	Ithaca............. 14 80
Scranton......... 10 30	Waverly 13 90
Pittston.......... 10 70	Elmira............ 14 55
Kingston......... 11 10	Corning........... 15 20
Wilkesbarre...... 11 15	Bath.............. 16 05
Binghamton...... 12 30	Atlanta............ 17 20
Greene........... 13 10	Wayland........... 17 50
Oxford........... 13 30	Dansville.......... 17 75
Norwich.......... 13 30	Mount Morris...... 17 75
Sherburne........ 14 00	Buffalo............ 20 30

EXCURSION NO. 176.—BLOCK ISLAND AND RETURN.

Delaware, Lack. & Western R. R.....to New York.
Fall River Line Steamers..............to Newport.
Steamer .... to Block Island.
Returning *via* same route.

THROUGH RATES.

Morristown.........$ 8 00	Waterville..........$16 75
Dover.......... .. 8 50	Cortland 16 75
Hackettstown...... 9 20	Syracuse 16 75
Washington...... . 9 60	Oswego 16 75
Water Gap 10 45	Owego...... .... 15 60
Stroudsburg........ 10 60	Ithaca............. 17 25
Scranton 12 75	Waverly........... 16 35
Pittston............ 13 15	Elmira............. 17 00
Kingston........... 13 90	Corning........... 17 65
Wilkesbarre....... 13 95	Bath............... 18 50
Binghamton........ 14 75	Atlanta............ 19 65
Greene............. 15 55	Wayland 19 95
Oxford............. 15 75	Dansville.......... 20 45
Norwich........... 15 75	Mount Morris...... 20 45
Sherburne 16 45	Buffalo............ 22 75

BOSTON, MASS.

These Excursion Tickets to Boston have been prepared for use in connection with extension tickets of D., L. & W. R. R. issue, from Boston and returning to Boston, thus making complete round-trip tickets from point of sale. *These forms are not for sale except in connection with the extension tickets.*

EXCURSION NO. 125.—BOSTON AND RETURN.

Delaware, Lack. & Western R. R.......to New York.
Fall River Line Steamers................to Fall River.
Old Colony Railroad.................... to Boston.
Returning *via* same route.

THROUGH RATES.

Morristown... ...$ 9 25	Waterville,........$18 00
Dover............. 9 75	Cortland 18 00
Hackettstown..... 10 45	Syracuse 18 00
Washington....... 10 85	Oswego............ 18 00
Water Gap 11 70	Owego .,.......... 16 85
Stroudsburg 11 85	Ithaca............. 18 50
Scranton........... 14 00	Waverly............ 17 60
Pittston........... 14 40	Elmira............. 18 25
Kingston.......... 15 15	Corning 18 90
Wilkesbarre....... 15 20	Bath.............. 19 75
Binghamton....... 16 00	Atlanta.... .... 20 90
Greene............ 16 80	Wayland 21 20
Oxford............ 17 00	Dansville.......... 21 70
Norwich 17 00	Mount Morris...... 21 70
Sherburne 17 70	Buffalo............ 24 00

EXCURSION NO. 126.—BOSTON AND RETURN.

Delaware, Lack. & Western R. R...to New York.
Fall River Line Steamers.... ......to Fall River,
Old Colony Railroad.................to Boston.
Fitchburg Railroad..................to Saratoga.
Delaware & Hudson Canal Co. (*via* Howe's Cave).................to Binghamton.
Delaware, Lack. & Western R. R...to starting point.

EXCURSION NO. 127.—REVERSE OF THE PRECEDING.

THROUGH RATES.

Scranton...........$17 00	Ithaca ,.........$19 25
Pittston. 17 35	Waverly........... 18 60
Kingston.......... 17 65	Elmira 19 30
Wilkesbarre 17 70	Corning........... 19 85
Binghamton...... 16 95	Bath............. 20 60
Greene..... ... 17 75	Atlanta............ 21 35
Oxford............ 18 30	Wayland 21 70
Norwich.......... 18 55	Dansville.......... 22 05
Cortland.......... 18 70	Mount Morris...... 22 60
Owego 17 85	Buffalo 24 90

EXCURSION NO. 129.—BOSTON AND RETURN.

Delaware, Lack. & Western R. R...to New York.
Fall River Line Steamers......... ..to Fall River.
Old Colony Railroad................to Boston.
Fitchburg Railroad..................to Troy.
Delaware & Hudson Canal Co. (*via* Howe's Cave).................to Binghamton.
Delaware, Lack. & Western R. R...to starting point.

EXCURSION No. 130.—REVERSE OF THE PRECEDING.

THROUGH RATES.

Scranton	$15 50	Ithaca	$17 80
Pittston	15 85	Waverly	17 50
Kingston	16 15	Elmira,	17 85
Wilkesbarre	16 15	Corning	18 40
Binghamton	15 50	Bath	19 15
Greene	16 30	Atlanta	19 90
Oxford	16 85	Wayland	20 25
Norwich	17 20	Dansville	20 60
Cortland	17 25	Mount Morris	21 15
Owego	16 40	Buffalo	22 50

EXCURSION No. 128.—BOSTON AND RETURN.

Delaware, Lack. & Western R. R.....to Binghamton.
Delaware & Hudson Canal Co. (via Howe's Cave).....................to Troy.
Fitchburg Railroad...................to Boston.
Returning via same route.

THROUGH RATES.

Scranton	$16 20	Elmira	$16 05
Greene	14 50	Corning	16 60
Oxford	15 05	Bath	17 35
Norwich	15 40	Atlanta	18 10
Cortland	15 45	Wayland	18 45
Owego	14 60	Dansville	18 80
Ithaca	16 00	Mount Morris	19 35
Waverly	15 35	Buffalo	19 50

EXCURSION No. 131.—BOSTON AND RETURN.

Delaware, Lack. & Western R. R....to Binghamton.
Del. & Hud. C. C. .via Howe's Cave,..to Saratoga.
Fitchburg Railroad..................to Boston.
Fitchburg Railroad.. ....to Troy.
Delaware & Hudson Canal Co......to Binghamton.
Delaware, Lack. & Western R. R...to starting point.

EXCURSION No. 132.—REVERSE OF THE PRECEDING.

THROUGH RATES.

Scranton	$18 65	Elmira	$18 50
Greene	16 95	Corning	19 05
Oxford	17 50	Bath	19 80
Norwich	17 85	Atlanta	20 55
Cortland	17 90	Wayland	20 90
Owego	17 05	Dansville	21 25
Ithaca	17 15	Mount Morris	21 80
Waverly	17 80	Buffalo	22 20

CALDWELL, N. Y. (Lake George.)

EXC. S T 18.—SARATOGA TO CALDWELL AND RETURN.

Delaware & Hud. Canal Co ..to Caldwell and return.
Sold only in connection with Summer Excursion Ticket to, or passing through Saratoga.
Rate................$2 90

CAPE MAY, N. J.

The distinctive characteristics of Cape May are its delightful temperature, magnificent beach and surf, grand ocean view, and the charm of its refined society. The beach is probably the finest for surf bathing in the world.

EXCURSION No. 60 Y.—CAPE MAY AND RETURN.

Limited to six (6) months from date of sale.
Del., Lack. & Western R. R.....to Manunka Chunk.
Pennsylvania Railroad......... to Philadelphia.
West Jersey Railroad.........to Cape May.
Returning via same route.
(Good for passage via either Philadelphia (Broad Street Station) or Amboy Division via Camden.)

THROUGH RATES.

Stroudsburg	$6 60	Syracuse	$14 65
Scranton	9 00	Fulton	15 65
Pittston	9 00	Oswego	16 05
Kingston	9 00	Owego	12 00
Wilkesbarre	9 00	Ithaca	13 40
Montrose	11 30	Waverly	12 00
Binghamton	11 50	Elmira	12 00
Greene	12 30	Corning	12 95
Oxford	12 80	Bath	14 20
Norwich	13 15	Atlanta	15 30
Sherburne	13 60	Wayland	15 70
Waterville	14 45	Dansville	16 10
Richfield Springs	15 60	Mount Morris	16 80
Utica	14 75	Buffalo	18 60
Cortland	13 20		

EXCURSION No. 61 Y.—CAPE MAY AND RETURN.

Limited to six (6) months from date of sale.
Delaware, Lack. & Western R. R....to New York.
Pennsylvania Railroad..............to Philadelphia.
West Jersey Railroad..............to Cape May.
Returning via same route.
(Good for passage via either Philadelphia (Broad Street Station) or Amboy Division via Camden.)

THROUGH RATES.

Summit	$6 30	Richfield Springs	$16 25
Morristown	6 75	Utica	14 75
Dover	7 25	Cortland	15 50
Hackettstown	7 95	Syracuse	15 50
Washington	8 35	Fulton	15 50
Stroudsburg	8 35	Oswego	15 50
Scranton	11 50	Owego	14 35
Pittston	11 90	Ithaca	15 75
Kingston	12 30	Waverly	15 10
Wilkesbarre	12 35	Elmira	15 75
Montrose	13 70	Corning	16 40
Binghamton	13 50	Bath	17 25
Greene	14 30	Atlanta	18 40
Oxford	14 50	Wayland	18 70
Norwich	14 50	Dansville	19 20
Sherburne	14 75	Mount Morris	19 50
Waterville	14 75	Buffalo	21 50

EXCURSION No. 62 Y.—CAPE MAY AND RETURN.

Limited to six (6) months from date of sale.
Del., Lack. & Western R. R.....to Manunka Chunk.
Pennsylvania Railroad ....to Philadelphia.
West Jersey Railroad.............to Cape May.
West Jersey Railroad... ....to Philadelphia.
Pennsylvania Railroad ....to New York.
Del., Lack. & Western R. R.....to starting point.

EXCURSION No. 63 Y.—REVERSE OF THE PRECEDING.

Limited to six (6) months from date of sale.
(Good for passage via either Philadelphia (Broad Street Station) or Amboy Division via Camden.)

THROUGH RATES.

Stroudsburg	$9 30	Syracuse	$16 00
Scranton	10 50	Fulton	16 50
Pittston	10 95	Oswego	16 90
Kingston	11 30	Owego	14 25
Wilkesbarre	11 30	Ithaca	15 65
Montrose	12 80	Waverly	15 40
Binghamton	13 00	Elmira	16 40
Greene	13 80	Corning	17 35
Oxford	14 20	Bath	18 60
Norwich	14 65	Atlanta	19 75
Sherburne	14 80	Wayland	20 10
Waterville	14 80	Dansville	20 50
Richfield Springs	16 15	Mount Morris	22 25
Utica	14 80	Buffalo	22 25
Cortland	15 50		

CAPE VINCENT, N. Y.

EXCURSION No. 177.—CAPE VINCENT AND RETURN.

Delaware, Lack. & Western R. R. ..to Utica.
Rome, Watert'n & Ogdenb'g R. R....to Cape Vincent.
Returning via same route.

SUMMER EXCURSION ROUTES AND RATES. 123

THROUGH RATES.

New York	$15 25	Berwick	$14 05
Paterson	15 25	Bloomsburg	14 60
Newark	15 25	Danville	15 00
Morristown	15 25	Binghamton	9 80
Dover	15 25	Greene	9 05
Hackettstown	15 25	Oxford	8 50
Washington	15 25	Norwich	8 20
Water Gap	14 60	Sherburne	7 75
Stroudsburg	14 40	Waterville	6 90
Scranton	12 30	Richfield Springs	7 50
Pittston	12 70	Vestal	10 15
Kingston	13 00	Owego	10 65
Wilkesbarre	13 00	Waverly	11 40
Plymouth	13 15	Elmira	12 10
Nanticoke	13 25	Corning	12 60
Shickshinny	13 60	Bath	13 60

EXCURSION NO. 178.—CAPE VINCENT AND
RETURN.
Delaware, Lack. & Western R. R....to Syracuse.
Rome, Watert'n & Ogdensb'g R. R..to Cape Vincent.
Returning *via* same route.

THROUGH RATES.

New York	$15 25	Plymouth	$12 00
Paterson	15 25	Nanticoke	12 10
Newark	15 25	Shickshinny	12 50
Morristown	15 25	Berwick	12 90
Dover	15 25	Bloomsburg	13 45
Hackettstown	14 70	Danville	13 90
Washington	14 30	Binghamton	8 70
Water Gap	13 50	Cortland	7 00
Stroudsburg	13 30	Vestal	9 05
Scranton	11 20	Owego	9 50
Pittston	11 55	Waverly	10 00
Kingston	11 85	Elmira	10 00
Wilkesbarre	11 85		

EXCURSION NO. 179.—CAPE VINCENT AND
RETURN.
Delaware, Lack. & Western R. R....to Oswego.
Rome, Watert'n & Ogdensb'g R. R..to Cape Vincent.
Returning *via* same route.

THROUGH RATES.

New York	$15 25	Wilkesbarre	$12 80
Paterson	15 25	Plymouth	12 90
Newark	15 25	Nanticoke	13 80
Morristown	15 25	Shickshinny	13 40
Dover	15 25	Berwick	13 80
Hackettstown	15 25	Bloomsburg	14 35
Washington	15 25	Danville	14 80
Water Gap	14 40	Binghamton	9 60
Stroudsburg	14 20	Cortland	7 90
Scranton	12 10	Syracuse	6 40
Pittston	12 45	Vestal	9 95
Kingston	12 80		

CHATHAM, MASS.
EXCURSION NO. 280.—CHATHAM AND
RETURN.
Delaware, Lack. & Western R. R.......to New York.
Fall River Line Steamers..........to Fall River.
Old Colony Railroad................to Chatham.
Returning *via* same route.

THROUGH RATES.

Morristown	$10 25	Pittston	$15 40
Dover	10 75	Kingston	16 15
Hackettstown	11 45	Wilkesbarre	16 20
Washington	11 85	Binghamton	17 00
Water Gap	12 70	Greene	17 80
Stroudsburg	12 85	Oxford	18 00
Scranton	15 00	Norwich	18 00
Sherburne	18 70	Elmira	19 25
Waterville	19 00	Corning	19 90
Cortland	19 00	Bath	20 75
Syracuse	19 00	Atlanta	21 90
Oswego	19 00	Wayland	22 25
Owego	17 85	Dansville	22 70
Ithaca	19 50	Mount Morris	22 70
Waverly	18 60	Buffalo	25 00

CHAUTAUQUA LAKE, N. Y.

This magnificent sheet of water is situated on a table land 1,400 feet above the sea level, and enjoys the distinction of being the highest navigable inland sea on the continent. Situated in Western New York, in the county of Chautauqua, it is eighteen miles long and ranges from one to five miles in width.

In many respects this lake is the most magnificent in this country. Aside from its altitude, the scenery along its shores is of such a beautiful character that artists find fresh snatches to paint each recurring season. The water is deep and transparent, and as pure as crystal. No wonder, then, that it should abound in fine game fish, and yearly attract anglers to its shores. The air is always cool and invigorating, and here malaria is absolutely unknown. The boating and bathing are superb, and the drives along the shores of the lake and back in the hills are unsurpassed, and scarcely to be equalled anywhere. These features have combined to draw admiring thousands of intellectual holiday-seekers here every summer, and to establish several large well-appointed hotels.

The class of people that patronize Chautauqua are lovers of the beautiful in nature, who appreciate all that the Creator has bestowed upon it, and know how to get pleasure out of every daylight moment, and invigorating and restful sleep out of the calm, cool nights

A fleet of steamers ply on the lake daily, and carry excursionists all around it. The scene on the water in the daytime, and for that matter after moondawn, is one of animation. Steam yachts, launches, row boats and shells are darting in all directions, and the "lone fisherman" sits in quiet contemplation, awaiting the "tug" of a bass or pickerel. In the fall the duck shooting about the coves and nooks is excellent, and gunners flock there with the same regularity as the wild fowl.

The *Chautauqua Assembly*, organized in 1874, holds its meetings every July and August. The purpose of the enterprise is to combine the recreations of a summer resort with intellectual culture and improvement. The Assembly is a great educational institution that attracts teachers of all grades here, both for information and to commune about their fraternal interests, and this has proved itself one of the most prominent features of attraction. The Assembly grounds are at Point Chautauqua. To lovers of gaiety, Lakewood, a few miles distant, offers every opportunity. And among many of the most beautiful drives in this neighborhood, is from Jamestown to Mayville; and, as for aquatic attractions, a sail on the lake is a beautiful sight that awaits the person who will spend the time in steaming from Jamestown through the narrows.

EXCURSION NO. 4.—CHAUTAUQUA AND
RETURN.

Delaware, Lack. & Western R. R.....to Buffalo.
Western New York & Penn. R. R.....to Mayville.
Chautauqua Lake Steamboat Co......to Chautauqua.
Returning via same route.

EXCURSION NO. 345.—CHAUTAUQUA AND
RETURN.

Delaware, Lack. & Western R. R ....to Buffalo.
Western New York & Penn, R, R.....to Mayville.
Chautauqua Lake Railway............to Chautauqua.
Returning via same route.

THROUGH RATES FOR EITHER EXCURSION.

New York.........	$17 00	Greene.............	$11 20
Paterson..........	17 00	Oxford.............	12 00
Newark...........	17 00	Norwich............	12 50
Morristown.......	17 00	Sherburne..........	13 00
Dover.............	17 00	Owego.............	9 10
Hackettstown.....	16 90	Ithaca.	9 50
Washington.......	16 50	Waverly............	8 35
Water Gap........	15 70	Elmira............	7 50
Stroudsburg.......	15 50	Corning............	6 95
Scranton..........	12 00	Bath...............	6 95
Pittston...........	12 10	Atlanta............	5 95
Kingston..........	12 45	Wayland...........	5 75
Wilkesbarre.......	12 45	Dansville..........	5 75
Binghamton.......	10 00	Mount Morris......	5 30

CLAYTON, N. Y.

EXCURSION NO. 13.—CLAYTON AND
RETURN.

Delaware, Lack. & Western R. R..........to Utica.
Rome, Watertown & Ogdensburg R. R....to Clayton.
Returning via same route.

THROUGH RATES.

New York.........	$15 25	Berwick...........	$14 05
Paterson..........	15 25	Bloomsburg........	14 60
Newark...........	15 25	Danville...........	15 00
Morristown.......	15 25	Binghamton........	9 80
Dover.............	15 25	Greene.............	9 05
Hackettstown.....	15 25	Oxford.............	8 50
Washington.......	15 25	Norwich............	8 20
Water Gap........	14 60	Sherburne..........	7 75
Stroudsburg.......	14 40	Waterville..........	6 90
Scranton..........	12 30	Richfield Springs...	7 50
Pittston...........	12 70	Vestal..............	10 15
Kingston..........	13 00	Owego.............	10 65
Wilkesbarre.......	13 00	Waverly............	11 40
Plymouth.........	13 15	Elmira.............	12 10
Nanticoke.........	13 25	Corning............	12 60
Shickshinny.......	13 60	Bath	13 60

EXCURSION NO. 11.—CLAYTON AND
RETURN.

Delaware, Lack. & Western R. R........to Syracuse.
Rome, Watertown & Ogdensburg R. R. to Clayton.
Returning via same route.

THROUGH RATES.

New York.........	$15 25	Washington........	$14 80
Paterson..........	15 25	Water Gap........	14 00
Newark...........	15 25	Stroudsburg........	13 80
Morristown.......	15 25	Scranton...........	11 70
Dover.....	15 25	Pittston............	12 05
Hackettstown.....	15 20	Kingston...........	12 35
Wilkesbarre.......	12 35	Danville...........	14 40
Plymouth.........	12 50	Binghamton........	9 20
Nanticoke.........	12 60	Cortland...........	7 50
Shickshinny.......	13 00	Vestal..............	9 55
Berwick...........	13 40	Owego.............	10 00
Bloomsburg.......	13 95	Waverly............	10 50
Elmira......	$10 50		

EXCURSION NO. 180.—CLAYTON AND
RETURN.

Delaware, Lackawanna & Western R. R..to Oswego.
Rome, Watertown & Ogdensburg R. R ...to Clayton.
Returning via same route.

THROUGH RATES.

New York.........	$15 25	Kingston.....	...$13 30
Paterson..........	15 25	Wilkesbarre........	13 30
Newark...........	15 25	Plymouth..........	13 40
Morristown........	15 25	Nanticoke..........	13 50
Dover.............	15 25	Shickshinny........	13 90
Hackettstown.....	15 25	Berwick............	14 30
Washington.......	15 25	Bloomsburg........	14 85
Water Gap........	14 90	Danville...........	15 30
Stroudsburg.......	14 70	Binghamton........	10 10
Scranton....	12 60	Cortland...........	8 40
Pittston...........	12 95	Syracuse...........	6 90
Vestal..............	$10 45.		

COLORADO EXCURSIONS.

EXCURSION NO. 258.

Excursion Tickets may be sold to Colorado Springs, Denver or Pueblo.

1. These tickets contain an Exchange Ticket Order, in exchange for which Excursion Tickets will be issued by lines starting from Chicago or St. Louis.

2. Agents should be careful in issuing tickets to secure signature of purchaser (with ink) to contract, to properly witness same, and to write the destination in stub, in contract, and in Exchange Order; also to fill up *all blanks* in the Exchange Order and stub.

3. Passengers desiring to return over lines other than those traveled going west must be informed at the time Exchange Order is purchased that such arrangements must be made with the ticket agent *at the eastern terminal point, and at the time the order is presented for exchange;* but it is agreed by the Eastern Trunk Lines that when tickets are sold with going coupons via Chicago or St. Louis, the route returning *from those cities* to the original starting point shall be the same as on the going trip.

4. The ultimate limit of Excursion Tickets will be October 31st in year sold.

5. By agreement of the western lines all excursion Tickets issued by them on Exchange Orders will be limited to continuous passage in each direction, except that stop-over will be allowed between Cheyenne, Wyoming, and Pueblo, Colorado, by lines in interest, and upon return passengers will be required to have their tickets *vised* by the ticket agent at the last stop between said points.

6. No stop-over will be allowed at stations on this line nor at any point east of the Missouri River.

7. Form Excursion 258, issued for this business, may be filled out to read over any regular route to Chicago or St. Louis.

THROUGH RATES.

New York.........	$76 80	Waterville.........	$74 70
Paterson..........	76 80	Richfield Springs...	75 60
Newark...........	76 80	Cortland	74 35
Morristown.......	76 80	Homer.............	74 35
Dover.............	76 80	Fulton.............	72 20
Hackettstown.....	76 80	Oswego............	72 60
Washington.......	76 80	Owego.............	71 40
Stroudsburg.......	76 80	Ithaca..............	71 40
Scranton..........	75 85	Waverly............	71 40
Pittston...........	75 85	Elmira.............	70 35
Kingston..........	76 30	Corning............	69 40
Wilkesbarre.......	76 30	Bath...............	68 15
Binghamton.......	72 60	Atlanta............	67 40
Greene............	73 80	Wayland...........	67 20
Oxford............	74 60	Dansville..........	66 90
Norwich...........	74 60	Mount Morris......	66 30
Sherburne.........	74 60		

CONEY ISLAND, N. Y.

EXCURSION NO. 174.—CONEY ISLAND AND
RETURN.

Delaware, Lack. & Western R. R....to New York.
Iron Steamboat Co..................to Coney Island.
Returning via same route.

THROUGH RATES.

Binghamton........	$8 40	Bath	$12 15
Owego.............	9 25	Atlanta............	13 30
Ithaca.............	10 90	Wayland...........	13 60
Waverly...........	10 00	Dansville..........	14 10
Elmira............	10 65	Mount Morris.....	14 10
Corning...........	11 30	Buffalo............	16 40

COOPERSTOWN, N. Y.

EXCURSION NO 14.—COOPERSTOWN AND RETURN.

Delaware, Lack & Western R R..to Richfield Sp'gs.
Otsego L. Steamboat Co. and stage to Cooperstown.
Returning via same route.

THROUGH RATES.

New York	$11 45	Oxford	$ 4 85
Paterson	11 45	Norwich	4 55
Newark	11 45	Sherburne	4 05
Morristown	11 45	Waterville	3 20
Dover	11 45	Bridgewater	2 70
Hackettstown	11 45	West Winfield	2 60
Washington	11 45	Clayville	3 00
Water Gap	10 95	Sauquoit	3 05
Stroudsburg	10 80	Utica	3 50
Scranton	8 65	Owego	7 00
Pittston	9 00	Ithaca	8 35
Kingston	9 35	Waverly	7 75
Wilkesbarre	9 35	Elmira	8 45
Plymouth	9 45	Corning	9 10
Nanticoke	9 60	Bath	9 90
Shickshinny	10 00	Atlanta	10 70
Berwick	10 40	Wayland	10 95
Bloomsburg	10 90	Dansville	11 20
Danville	11 40	Mount Morris	11 80
Binghamton	6 20	Buffalo	12 00
Greene	5 40		

EXCURSION NO. 395.—COOPERSTOWN AND RETURN.

Del., Lack. & Western R. R..to Binghamton.
Delaware & Hud. Canal Co..to C. & C. V, R. R. Junc.
Cooperst'n & Char.Val'y R.R. to Cooperstown.
Returning via same route.

THROUGH RATES.

New York	$12 00	Berwick	$ 8 25
Paterson	11 70	Bloomsburg	8 75
Newark	12 00	Danville	9 20
Morristown	11 20	Cortland	5 70
Dover	10 75	Owego	4 85
Hackettstown	10 00	Ithaca	6 25
Washington	9 60	Waverly	5 55
Water Gap	8 75	Elmira	6 30
Stroudsburg	8 70	Corning	6 90
Scranton	6 50	Bath	7 65
Pittston	6 85	Atlanta	8 40
Kingston	7 20	Wayland	8 75
Wilkesbarre	7 20	Dansville	9 10
Plymouth	7 30	Mount Morris	9 65
Nanticoke	7 45	Buffalo	11 50
Shickshinny	7 80		

EXCURSION NO. 2.—COOPERSTOWN AND RETURN.

Del., Lack. & Western R. R..to Binghamton.
Delaware & Hud. Canal Co..to C. & C. V. R. R. Junc.
Cooperst'n & Char. Val'y R.R.to Cooperstown.
Otsego L.Stea'b't Co. & Stage.to Richfield Springs.
Del., Lack. & Western R. R...to starting point.

EXCURSION NO. 3.—REVERSE OF THE PRECEDING.

THROUGH RATES.

New York	$11 65	Berwick	$ 9 70
Paterson	11 65	Bloomsburg	10 20
Newark	11 65	Dansville	10 70
Morristown	11 65	Binghamton	5 50
Dover	11 65	Cortland	6 75
Hackettstown	11 50	Owego	6 30
Washington	11 10	Ithaca	7 70
Water Gap	10 25	Waverly	7 05
Stroudsburg	10 10	Elmira	7 75
Scranton	8 00	Corning	8 40
Pittston	8 35	Bath	9 25
Kingston	8 65	Atlanta	9 85
Wilkesbarre	8 65	Wayland	10 05
Plymouth	8 80	Dansville	10 55
Nanticoke	8 90	Mount Morris	11 10
Schickshinny	9 30	Buffalo	12 50

EXC. S. T. 32.—C. & C. V. JUNCTION TO COOPERSTOWN AND RETURN.

C. & C. Valley Railroad..to Cooperstown and return.
Sold only in connection with Summer Excursion Ticket to, or passing through Cooperstown & Charlotte Valley R. R. Junction.
Rate..................$1 30.

COTTAGE CITY (Martha's Vineyard), MASS.

Cottage City developed into a summer resort through the ministrations of the Methodists. Captivated by the beauty and healthfulness of the location, they built an enormous tabernacle for public worship and set up their tents around it. Presently the tents became cottages, and, as the population increased, a large summer town was built, which has attracted many visitors other than those who came to worship.

The shores of Martha's Vineyard, on which Cottage City is located, are exceedingly attractive, and their fascinations are greatly enhanced by the animation which always prevails upon the surrounding waters. All the marine travel between New York and Boston, and between Boston and the South passes through Holmes' Hole and Vineyard Sound, and these bits of ocean are always alive with shipping. Bluffs and cliffs overhang the shore in many places, and many beautiful islets are separated from the mother island by a narrow strip of water.

EXC. NO. 20.—COTTAGE CITY (MARTHA'S VINEYARD) AND RETURN.

Delaware, Lack. & Western R. R....to New York.
Fall River Line Steamers..............to Fall River.
Old Colony Railroad ....to New Bedford.
New Bedford, Vineyard, Nantucket } to Cottage City.
& Cape Cod S. B. Line............... }
Returning via same route.

THROUGH RATES.

Morristown	$ 8 50	Binghamton	$15 25
Dover	9 00	Greene	16 05
Hackettstown	9 70	Oxford	16 25
Washington	10 10	Norwich	16 25
Water Gap	10 95	Sherburne	16 95
Stroudsburg	11 10	Waterville	17 25
Scranton	13 25	Cortland	17 25
Pittston	13 65	Syracuse	17 25
Kingston	14 40	Oswego	17 25
Wilkesbarre	14 45	Owego	16 10
Ithaca	17 75	Atlanta	20 15
Waverly	16 85	Wayland	20 45
Elmira	17 50	Dansville	20 45
Corning	18 15	Mount Morris	20 95
Bath	19 00	Buffalo	23 25

CRAWFORD HOUSE, N. H. (WHITE MOUNTAINS.)

The Crawford House is situated on a plateau 2,000 feet above the sea, and commands a magnificent view of Mt. Washington (6,293 feet), and Mt. Monroe (5,349 feet). The bridle path up Mt. Washington passes over Mounts Pleasant, Monroe, Franklin and Clinton, and is said to afford finer views than any other route.

Within easy reach of the Crawford House are, the Notch, a huge chasm in the mountains, which rises 2,000 feet on either side; Silver Cascade and Sylvan Glade Cataract, between which it is hard to award the palm; and Mount Willard, commanding a view down the Notch.

EXC. S. T. 39.—FABYAN'S TO CRAWFORD HOUSE AND RETURN.

Me. C. R. R (White Moun. Line)..to Crawford House.
Sold only in connection with Summer Excursion Ticket to, or passing through Fabyan's.
Rate............50 cents.

EXC. S. T. 40.—BOSTON TO CRAWFORD HOUSE AND RETURN.

Boston and Maine Railroad ......to North Conway.
Me. C. R. R. (White Moun. Line)..to Crawford House.
Returning *via* same route.
Sold only in connection with summer Excursion Ticket to, or passing through Boston.
Rate............$9 75.

CRESCO, PA.

LOCAL EXCURSION.

(Good for continuous passage only.)

THROUGH RATES.

*New York	$4 45	Shickshinny	$3 25
Passaic	4 05	Berwick	3 75
Paterson	3 90	Bloomsburg	4 05
Boonton	3 35	Danville	4 40
*Newark	4 35	Great Bend	3 55
*Roseville Ave	4 35	Binghamton	4 10
Orange	4 15	Greene	4 90
Mountain	4 05	Oxford	5 40
South Orange	4 00	Norwich	5 75
Milburn	3 85	Sherburne	6 20
Short Hills	3 80	Waterville	7 05
Summit	3 80	Richfield Springs	8 20
Chatham	3 60	Utica	7 90
Madison	3 50	Cortland	5 80
Morristown	3 35	Syracuse	7 25
Dover	2 85	Oswego	8 65
Andover	2 55	Owego	4 95
Newton	2 85	Ithaca	6 30
Franklin	3 35	Waverly	5 65
Hackettstown	2 15	Elmira	6 40
Washington	1 75	Corning	7 00
Scranton	2 15	Bath	7 85
Pittston	2 55	Atlanta	8 65
Kingston	2 90	Wayland	8 90
Wilkesbarre	2 90	Dansville	9 20
Plymouth	3 05	Mount Morris	9 75
Nanticoke	3 20	Buffalo	12 20

*Tickets good until used.

DANSVILLE, N. Y.

LOCAL EXCURSION.

(Good for continuous passage only.)

THROUGH RATES.

*New York	$13 30	Morristown	$12 30
Passaic	12 90	Dover	11 80
Paterson	12 80	Andover	11 60
Boonton	12 20	Newton	11 80
*Newark	13 20	Franklin	12 30
Roseville Ave	13 20	Hackettstown	11 10
Orange	13 00	Washington	10 70
Mountain	13 00	Portland	10 05
South Orange	12 95	Water Gap	9 85
Milburn	12 80	Stroudsburg	9 70
Short Hills	12 80	Scranton	7 60
Summit	12 70	Pittston	8 00
Chatham	12 55	Kingston	8 45
Madison	12 05	Wilkesbarre	8 45

Plymouth	$8 55	Waterville	$8 05
Nanticoke	8 80	Richfield Springs	9 20
Shickshinny	9 05	Utica	8 90
Berwick	9 05	Owego	4 25
Bloomsburg	10 00	Ithaca	5 60
Danville	10 50	Waverly	3 55
Great Bend	5 65	Elmira	2 80
Binghamton	5 10	Corning	2 20
Greene	5 85	Bath	1 35
Oxford	6 40	Atlanta	60
Norwich	6 75	Buffalo	2 70
Sherburne	7 20		

*Good for stop-over.

DELAWARE WATER GAP, PA.

LOCAL EXCURSION.

(Good for continuous passage only.)

THROUGH RATES.

‡New York	$3 70	Shickshinny	$4 25
Passaic	3 25	Berwick	4 55
Paterson	3 10	Bloomsburg	4 85
Boonton	2 55	Danville	5 20
‡Newark	3 55	Great Bend	4 25
‡Roseville Ave	3 55	Binghamton	4 80
Orange	3 35	Greene	5 60
Mountain	3 25	Oxford	6 15
South Orange	3 20	Norwich	6 45
Milburn	3 05	Sherburne	6 90
Short Hills	3 00	Waterville	7 75
Summit	3 00	Richfield Springs	8 95
Chatham	2 80	Utica	8 60
Madison	2 70	Cortland	6 55
Morristown	2 55	Syracuse	8 00
Dover	2 05	Oswego	9 40
Andover	1 85	Owego	5 60
Newton	2 05	Ithaca	7 00
Franklin	2 55	Waverly	6 40
Hackettstown	1 35	Elmira	7 10
Washington	95	Corning	7 75
Scranton	2 95	Bath	8 55
Pittston	3 35	Atlanta	9 35
Kingston	3 70	Wayland	9 00
Wilkesbarre	3 70	Dansville	9 90
Plymouth	3 85	Mount Morris	10 40
Nanticoke	4 00	Buffalo	12 95

‡Tickets good until used.

DENMARK LAKE, N. J

EXCURSION NO. 291.—LAKE DENMARK AND RETURN.

Del. Lack. & Western R. R.....to Chester Junction.
Morris County Railroad........to Lake Denmark.
Returning *via* same route.

THROUGH RATES.

New York	$2 25	South Orange	$1 75
Paterson	1 55	Milburn	1 55
Boonton	90	Summit	1 40
Newark	2 00	Madison	1 20
Orange	1 80	Morristown	1 00

ELMHURST, PA.

LOCAL EXCURSION.

(Good for continuous passage only.)

THROUGH RATES.

‡New York	$5 60	Short Hills	$5 50
Passaic	5 75	Summit	5 50
Paterson	5 60	Chatham	5 30
Boonton	5 05	Madison	5 20
‡Newark	5 60	Morristown	5 05
‡Roseville	5 60	Dover	4 55
Orange	5 90	Andover	4 35
Mountain	5 75	Newton	4 55
South Orange	5 70	Franklin	5 05
Milburn	5 55	Hackettstown	3 85

SUMMER EXCURSION ROUTES AND RATES.

Washington	$3 45	Waterville	5 85
Scranton	50	Richfield Springs	7 05
Pittston	90	Utica	6 70
Kingston	1 25	Cortland	4 65
Wilkesbarre	1 25	Syracuse	6 05
Plymouth	1 40	Oswego	7 45
Nanticoke	1 55	Owego	3 75
Shickshinny	1 80	Ithaca	5 10
Berwick	2 10	Waverly	4 45
Bloomsburg	2 40	Elmira	5 20
Danville	2 75	Corning	5 85
Great Bend	2 35	Bath	6 65
Binghamton	2 90	Atlanta	7 45
Greene	3 70	Wayland	7 65
Oxford	4 25	Dansville	8 00
Norwich	4 55	Mount Morris	8 55
Sherburne	5 00	Buffalo	11 00

‡Tickets good until used.

FABYAN'S, N. H. (WHITE MOUNTAINS.)

Possessing, as it does, a most central location in the famous White Mountain region, Fabyan's presents to the summer tourist not only the attractions usual to mountain resorts, but the unceasing novelty which is invariably part of a thoroughfare of travel. It is the starting point for the ascent by rail of Mt. Washington. The hotel is as popular as any in the White Mountains, possesses all the modern conveniences, and from its porches and windows a very extended view of the entire White Mountain region is to be had.

EXCURSION S. T. 41.—BOSTON TO FABYAN'S AND RETURN.

Boston & Maine Railroad..........to North Conway.
Me. C. R. R. (White Moun. Line)..to Fabyan's.
Returning *via* same route.
Sold only in connection with Summer Excursion Ticket to, or passing through Boston.
Rate............$9 75.

FALMOUTH, MASS.

EXCURSION No. 281.—FALMOUTH AND RETURN.

Delaware, Lack. & Western R. R........to New York.
Fall River Line Steamers................to Fall River
Old Colony Railroad...................to Falmouth.
Returning *via* same route

THROUGH RATES.

Morristown	$ 8 75	Greene	$16 30
Dover	9 25	Oxford	16 50
Hackettstown	9 95	Norwich	16 50
Washington	10 35	Sherburne	17 20
Water Gap	11 20	Waterville	17 50
Stroudsburg	11 35	Cortland	17 50
Scranton	13 50	Syracuse	17 50
Pittston	13 90	Oswego	17 50
Kingston	14 65	Owego	16 35
Wilkesbarre	14 70	Ithaca	18 00
Binghamton	15 50	Waverly	17 10
Elmira	17 75	Wayland	20 75
Corning	18 40	Dansville	21 20
Bath	19 25	Mount Morris	21 20
Atlanta	20 40	Buffalo	23 50

FORT TICONDEROGA, N. Y. (LAKES GEORGE and CHAMPLAIN.)

*EXCURSION S. T. 19—SARATOGA TO LAKE CHAMPLAIN AND RETURN (*via* LAKE GEORGE.)

Delaware & Hudson Canal Co....to Ft. Ticonderoga.
Delaware & Hudson Canal Co....to Baldwin.
Lake George Steamer.............to Caldwell.
Delaware & Hudson Canal Co....to Saratoga.
Rate............$6 00.

EXCURSION S. T. 20.—SARATOGA TO LAKE CHAMPLAIN AND RETURN (*via* LAKE GEORGE.)

Delaware & Hudson Canal Co .. to Caldwell.
Lake George Steamer ....to Baldwin.
Delaware & Hudson Canal Co.....to Ft. Ticonderoga.
Delaware & Hudson Canal Co.....to Saratoga.
Rate............$6 00.

*Sold only in connection with Summer Excursion Ticket to, or passing through Saratoga.

GENEVA, N. Y. (SENECA LAKE).

The pretty town of Geneva, with a population of 9,000, is pleasantly situated on the shores of Seneca Lake. It is celebrated as well for its schools and churches, as for the fertility and beauty of the surrounding country. It was the principal seat of the Senecas, and there still remains in the vicinity an ancient fortification erected by the "mound builders," as well as an old Indian cemetery, which has not as yet been desecrated by the plow. The climate of this section is fine, and the means of living abundant. The mineral springs near by are highly esteemed for their health restoring properties.

Seneca Lake (thirty-six miles by two) is one of the largest and most beautiful in New York State.

EXCURSION No. 165.—GENEVA (SENECA LAKE) AND RETURN.

Delaware Lack. & Western R. R........to Elmira.
Pennsylvania R. R. (*via* Havana Glen)..to Watkins.
Seneca Lake Steamer............. .. to Geneva.
Returning *via* same route.

THROUGH RATES.

New York	$12 40	Danville	$ 9 45
Paterson	12 15	Binghamton	4 90
Newark	12 40	Greene	5 25
Morristown	11 65	Oxford	5 75
Dover	11 15	Norwich	6 10
Hackettstown	10 45	Sherburne	6 55
Washington	10 05	Waterville	7 40
Water Gap	9 25	Richfield Springs	8 60
Stroudsburg	9 05	Utica	8 25
Scranton	7 00	Owego	4 00
Pittston	7 00	Waverly	3 00
Kingston	7 00	Corning	3 00
Wilkesbarre	7 40	Bath	3 95
Plymouth	7 65	Atlanta	4 75
Nanticoke	6 75	Wayland	5 00
Shickshinny	6 85	Dansville	5 95
Berwick	8 50	Mount Morris	5 55
Bloomsburg	9 00	Buffalo	7 30

EXCURSION S. T. 21.—ELMIRA TO GENEVA (SENECA LAKE) AND RETURN.

Pennsylvania Railroad...................to Watkins.
Seneca Lake Steamer...................to Geneva.
Returning *via* same route.
Sold only in connection with Summer Excursion Ticket passing through Elmira.
Rate............$2 15

EXCURSION S. T. 33.—CORNING TO GENEVA AND RETURN.

Fall Brook Railway............to Geneva and return.
Sold only in connection with Summer Excursion Ticket passing through Corning.
Rate............$2 30

GETTYSBURG, PA.

This field of action of the battle that was the turning point of the late war becomes each year a greater attraction to the old soldier, the student and tourist in general. The most important locations of the forces when at rest and in action have been designated by monuments, tablets, or the like.

EXCURSION 335 Y.—GETTYSBURG, PA. AND RETURN.

Limited to six (6) months from date of sale.
Dela., Lack. & Western R. R...to Northumberland.
Pennsylvania Railroad.........to Hanover.
Western Maryland Railroad...to Gettysburg
Returning via same route.

THROUGH RATES.

Paterson...........$9 45	Bloomsburg........$ 5 15
Boonton............ 9 45	Danville............ 4 65
Morristown......... 9 45	Montrose........... 9 75
Dover............... 9 45	Binghamton........ 10 05
Hackettstown...... 9 45	Greene............. 10 85
Washington........ 9 45	Oxford............. 11 40
Stroudsburg........ 9 45	Norwich............ 11 75
Scranton........... 7 45	Sherburne.......... 12 15
Pittston............ 7 15	Waterville......... 13 00
Kingston........... 6 70	Richfield Springs.. 14 20
Wilkesbarre........ 6 70	Utica............... 13 85
Plymouth.......... 6 60	Cortland........... 11 75
Nanticoke.......... 6 45	Syracuse........... 13 25
Shickshinny....... 6 05	Fulton............. 14 25
Berwick........... 5 65	Oswego............ 14 25

EXCURSION 334 Y.—GETTYSBURG, PA. AND RETURN.

Limited to six (6) months from date of sale.
Delaware, Lack. & Western R. R......to Easton
Lehigh Valley Railroad................to Allentown.
Philadelphia & Reading Railroad......to Gettysburg
Returning via same route.

THROUGH RATES.

New York..........$9 65	Morristown........$9 65
Newark............ 9 65	Dover.............. 8 85
Paterson.......... 9 65	Hackettstown...... 7 95
Boonton........... 9 65	Washington........ 7 35

EXCURSION 348 Y.—GETTYSBURG, PA. AND RETURN.

Limited to six (6) months from date of sale.
Delaware, Lack. & Western R. R....to Elmira.
Pennsylvania Railroad................to Hanover.
Western Maryland Railroad.......to Gettysburg.
Returning via same route.

THROUGH RATES.

Binghamton.......$10 05	Atlanta...........$12 15
Owego............. 9 75	Wayland.......... 12 55
Ithaca............ 10 70	Dansville......... 12 95
Waverly........... 8 85	Mount Morris..... 13 65
Corning........... 9 80	Buffalo............ 15 45
Bath.............. 11 05	

GLEN HOUSE, N. H.
(WHITE MOUNTAINS.)

This mountain house is located fourteen miles from Glen Station on the Portland and Ogdensburg Division of Maine Central R. R. or it can be reached by regular carriage line from summit of Mount Washington.

From this hotel there is an uninterrupted view of the Presidential Peaks; Mount Washington, 6,300 feet; Mount Clay, 5,400 feet; Mount Jefferson, 5,700 feet; Mount Adams, 5,800 feet; and Mount Madison, 5,400 feet.

EXCURSION S. T. 42.—BOSTON TO GLEN HOUSE AND RETURN.

Boston & Maine Railroad..........to North Conway.
Me. C. R. R. (White Moun. Line'...to Glen Station.
Milliken's Stage Line................to Glen House.
Returning via same route.
Sold only in connection with Summer Excursion Tickets to, or passing through Boston.
Rate............$11 00

GLEN ISLAND, N. Y.

EXCURSION NO. 390.—GLEN ISLAND AND RETURN.

Delaware Lack. & Western R. R.....to New York.
Starin's Glen Island Line, from Pier } to Glen Island.
18 North River....................}
Returning via same route.

THROUGH RATES.

Grove Street.......$ 70	Short Hills........$1 20
East Orange....... 75	Summit............ 1 20
Brick Church...... 80	Chatham........... 1 40
Orange............ 80	Madison........... 1 50
Highland Avenue.. 90	Morristown........ 1 65
Mountain.......... 95	Morris Plains...... 1 75
South Orange..... 1 00	Rockaway.......... 2 00
Maplewood........ 1 05	Dover.............. 2 15
Milburn........... 1 15	

HA-HA BAY AND LAKE ST. JOHN, P. Q.

EXCURSION S. T. 25.—MONTREAL TO HA-HA BAY OR CHICOUTIMI AND RETURN.

Richelieu & Ontario Nav. Co.'s } Montreal to Quebec.
Strs. or Grand Trunk R'y....}
Richelieu & Ontario Nav. Co's } Quebec to Ha-Ha Bay
Steamers, Canada or Union. } or Chicoutimi and
 } return.
Returning via same route.
Sold only in connection with Summer Excursion Ticket to, or passing through Montreal.
Rate............$13 00

EXCURSION S. T. 22.—QUEBEC TO HA-HA BAY OR CHICOUTIMI AND RETURN.

Richelieu & Ontario Nav. Co.'s } to Ha-Ha Bay or Chi-
Steamers, Canada or Union. } coutimi and return.
Sold only in connection with Summer Excursion Ticket to, or passing through Quebec.
Rate........$8 00

EXCURSION S. T. 52.—QUEBEC TO ROBERVAL AND RETURN.

Quebec and Lake St. John } to Roberval and Re-
Railway.................} turn.
Sold only in connection with Summer Excursion Ticket to, or passing through Quebec.
Rate............$7 50

EXCURSION S. T. 53.—QUEBEC TO CHICOUTIMI AND RETURN.

Quebec & Lake St. John Railway......to Roberval
Quebec & Lake St. John Railway......to Chicoutimi.
Returning via same route.
Sold only in connection with Summer Excursion Ticket to, or passing through Quebec.
Rate............$9 00

EXCURSION S. T. 54.—QUEBEC TO CHICOUTIMI AND RETURN.

Quebec & Lake St. John Railway......to Roberval.
Quebec & Lake St. John Railway......to Chicoutimi.
Richelieu & Ontario Nav. Co.'s Strs., } to Quebec.
Canada or Union............... }
Sold only in connection with Summer Excursion Ticket to, or passing through Quebec.
Rate...............$10 00

HACKETTSTOWN, N. J.
STATION FOR SCHOOLEY'S MOUNTAIN.
LOCAL EXCURSION.
(Good for continuous passage only.)

THROUGH RATES.

*New York	$2 45	Madison	$1 35
Passaic	1 90	Morristown	1 20
Paterson	1 75	Dover	75
Boonton	1 20	Andover	55
*Newark	2 25	Newton	75
*Roseville Ave.	2 25	Franklin	1 25
Orange	2 00	Washington	40
Mountain	1 90	Phillipsburg	1 00
South Orange	1 90	Easton	1 10
Milburn	1 75	Portland	1 15
Short Hills	1 65	Water Gap	1 35
Summit	1 65	Stroudsburg	1 55
Chatham	1 45	Scranton	3 55

* Tickets Good until used.

HART LAKE, PA.
EXCURSION NO. 350 L.—HART LAKE AND RETURN.

(Good for continuous passage only.)
Delaware, Lack. & Western R. R......to Alford.
Lackawanna & Montrose Railroad.....to Hart Lake.
Returning via same route.

THROUGH RATES

Water Gap	$4 65	Wilkesbarre	$2 90
Stroudsburg	4 45	Plymouth	2 90
Spragueville	4 25	Nanticoke	3 05
Henryville	4 05	Shickshinny	3 45
Cresco	3 85	Clark's Summit	1 65
Mount Pocono	3 70	Gleuburn	1 50
Pocono Summit	3 45	Dalton	1 45
Tobyhanna	3 30	La Plume	1 25
Gouldsboro	3 00	Factoryville	1 25
Moscow	2 60	Nicholson	95
Elmhurst	2 50	Foster	70
Scranton	2 00	Kingsley	55
Pittston	2 40	New Milford	70
Wyoming	2 60	Great Bend	95
Kingston	2 80	Binghamton	1 55

HARWICH, MASS.
EXCURSION NO. 282.—HARWICH AND RETURN.

Delaware, Lack. & Western R. R......to New York.
Fall River Line Steamers................to Fall River.
Old Colony Railroad.....................to Harwich.
Returning via same route.

THROUGH RATES.

Morristown	$9 55	Waterville	$18 30
Dover	10 05	Cortland	18 30
Hackettstown	10 75	Syracuse	18 30
Washington	11 15	Oswego	18 30
Water Gap	12 00	Owego	17 15
Stroudsburg	12 15	Ithaca	18 80
Scranton	14 30	Waverly	17 90
Pittston	14 70	Elmira	18 55
Kingston	15 45	Corning	19 20
Wilkesbarre	15 50	Bath	20 05
Binghamton	16 30	Atlanta	21 20
Greene	17 10	Wayland	21 55
Oxford	17 30	Dansville	22 00
Norwich	17 30	Mount Morris	22 00
Sherburne	18 00	Buffalo	24 30

HENRYVILLE, PA.
LOCAL EXCURSION.
(Good for continuous passage only.)

THROUGH RATES.

*New York	$4 20	Shickshinny	$3 70
Passaic	3 80	Berwick	4 00
Paterson	3 65	Bloomsburg	4 30
Boonton	3 10	Danville	4 65
*Newark	4 10	Great Bend	3 80
*Roseville Ave.	4 10	Binghamton	4 35
Orange	3 90	Greene	5 10
Mountain	3 80	Oxford	5 65
South Orange	3 75	Norwich	6 00
Milburn	3 60	Sherburne	6 40
Short Hills	3 55	Waterville	7 25
Summit	3 55	Richfield Springs	8 45
Chatham	3 35	Utica	8 15
Madison	3 25	Cortland	6 05
Morristown	3 10	Syracuse	7 50
Dover	2 60	Oswego	8 90
Andover	2 40	Owego	6 15
Newton	2 60	Ithaca	6 50
Franklin	3 10	Waverly	5 90
Hackettstown	1 90	Elmira	6 60
Washington	1 50	Corning	7 20
Scranton	2 40	Bath	8 05
Pittston	2 80	Atlanta	8 85
Kingston	3 15	Wayland	9 10
Wilkesbarre	3 15	Dansville	9 40
Plymouth	3 30	Mount Morris	9 95
Nanticoke	3 45	Buffalo	12 45

* Ticket good until used.

HONESDALE, PA.
EXCURSION NO. 396.—HONESDALE, PA., AND RETURN.

Delaware, Lack. & Western R. R......to Scranton.
Delaware and Hudson Canal Co........to Honesdale.
Returning via same route.

THROUGH RATES.

New York	$8 20	Oxford	$5 75
Paterson	8 00	Norwich	6 10
Boonton	7 45	Sherburne	6 55
Newark	8 20	Waterville	7 40
Morristown	7 45	Richfield Springs	8 55
Dover	6 95	Utica	8 25
Hackettstown	6 70	Cortland	6 15
Washington	5 85	Syracuse	7 60
Water Gap	4 00	Oswego	9 00
Stroudsburg	4 70	Owego	5 30
Pittston	2 40	Ithaca	6 70
Kingston	2 75	Waverly	6 00
Wilkesbarre	2 80	Elmira	6 75
Plymouth	2 85	Corning	7 35
Nanticoke	3 00	Bath	8 20
Shickshinny	3 40	Atlanta	9 00
Berwick	3 85	Wayland	9 20
Bloomsburg	4 35	Dansville	9 53
Danville	4 85	Mount Morris	10 10
Binghamton	4 45	Buffalo	12 55
Greene	5 25		

HOPATCONG STATION, N. J.
LOCAL EXCURSION.
(Good for continuous passage only.)

THROUGH RATES.

*New York	$2 05	Dover	$0 35
Passaic	1 50	Andover	55
Paterson	1 35	Newton	75
Boonton	1 80	Franklin	1 25
*Newark	1 85	Hackettstown	50
*Roseville Ave.	1 85	Washington	85
Orange	1 65	Phillipsburg	1 40
Mountain	1 55	Easton	1 50
South Orange	1 50	Oxford Furnace	1 10
Milburn	1 35	Bridgeville	1 25
Short Hills	1 25	Delaware	1 40
Summit	1 25	Portland	1 55
Chatham	1 05	Water Gap	1 75
Madison	95	Stroudsburg	1 95
Morristown	80	Scranton	4 00
Denvill	75		

* Tickets good until used.

HOT SPRINGS, N. C.

EXCURSION 336 Y.—HOT SPRINGS, N. C., AND RETURN.

Limited to three (3) months from date of sale.

Good for use south-bound only within fifteen (15) days from date of issue as stamped on back of ticket, and must be presented at the ticket agency of the initial line at the destination point for identification and validation before they can be used for the return trip, and are then good returning only within fifteen (15) days from such validation as stamped on back of ticket; in all cases, however, tickets must be used within the extreme limit.

Del., Lack. & Western R. R .....to Manunka Chunk.
Pennsylvania Railroad. .. ..to Washington.
Richmond & Danville Railroad..to Hot Springs.
Returning via same route.

Stroudsburg	$31 05	Sherburne	$38 05
Scranton	31 05	Waterville	39 30
Pittston	31 05	Richfield Springs	41 10
Kingston	31 05	Utica	40 55
Wilkesbarre	31 05	Owego	37 85
Montrose	33 35	Ithaca	36 25
Binghamton	34 85	Waverly	34 85
Cortland	36 60	Elmira	34 85
Syracuse	37 65	Corning	35 60
Fulton	38 65	Bath	35 60
Oswego	39 05	Dansville	35 60
Greene	36 05	Mount Morris	35 60
Oxford	36 90	Buffalo	35 60
Norwich	37 40		

EXCURSION 337 Y.—HOT SPRINGS, N. C., AND RETURN.

Limited to three (3) months from date of sale.
Delaware, Lack. & Western R. R .....to New York.
Pennsylvania Railroad .. ..to Washington.
Richmond & Danville Road .... to Hot Springs.
Returning via same route.

THROUGH RATES.

Summit	$30 60	Richfield Springs	$40 75
Morristown	31 25	Utica	39 25
Dover	31 75	Cortland	40 00
Hackettstown	32 45	Syracuse	40 00
Washington	32 85	Fulton	40 00
Stroudsburg	33 85	Oswego	40 00
Scranton	36 00	Owego	38 85
Pittston	36 40	Ithaca	40 50
Kingston	36 80	Waverly	39 60
Wilkesbarre	36 85	Elmira	40 25
Montrose	38 20	Corning	40 90
Binghamton	38 00	Bath	41 75
Greene	39 00	Atlanta	42 75
Oxford	39 00	Wayland	42 95
Norwich	39 25	Dansville	43 70
Sherburne	39 25	Mount Morris	43 70
Waterville	39 25	Buffalo	46 00

HYANNIS, MASS.

EXCURSION NO. 283.—HYANNIS AND RETURN.

Delaware, Lack. & Western R. R......to New York.
Fall River Line Steamers................to Fall River.
Old Colony Railroad...... ....to Hyannis.
Returning via same route.

THROUGH RATES.

Morristown	$9 25	Waterville	$18 00
Dover	9 75	Cortland	18 00
Hackettstown	10 45	Syracuse	18 00
Washington	10 85	Oswego	18 00
Water Gap	11 70	Owego	16 85
Stroudsburg	11 85	Ithaca	18 50
Scranton	14 00	Waverly	17 60
Pittston	14 40	Elmira	18 25
Kingston	15 15	Corning	18 90
Wilkesbarre	15 20	Bath	19 75
Binghamton	16 00	Atlanta	20 90
Greene	16 80	Wayland	21 25
Oxford	17 00	Dansville	21 70
Norwich	17 00	Mount Morris	21 70
Sherburne	17 70	Buffalo	24 00

ITHACA, N. Y.

LOCAL EXCURSION.
(Good for continuous passage only.)

THROUGH RATES.

*New York	$10 50	Water Gap	$7 00
Passaic	9 95	Stroudsburg	6 80
Paterson	9 90	Scranton	5 00
Boonton	9 30	Pittston	5 00
*Newark	10 50	Kingston	5 40
Roseville Ave	10 50	Wilkesbarre	5 40
Orange	10 30	Plymouth	5 50
Mountain	10 20	Nanticoke	5 65
South Orange	10 05	Shickshinny	6 00
Milburn	9 95	Berwick	6 45
Short Hills	9 80	Bloomsburg	6 95
Summit	9 80	Danville	7 40
Chatham	9 70	Great Bend	2 80
Madison	9 60	Binghamton	2 20
Morristown	9 40	Greene	3 00
Dover	8 95	Oxford	3 55
Andover	8 70	Norwich	3 85
Newton	8 90	Sherburne	4 30
Franklin	9 40	Waterville	5 20
Hackettstown	8 20	Richfield Springs	6 35
Washington	7 80	Utica	6 00
Portland	7 20		

*Tickets good until used and for stop-over.

EXCURSION S. T. 2.—OWEGO TO ITHACA AND RETURN.

Delaware, Lack. & Western Railroad......to Ithaca.
Returning via same route.
Sold only in connection with Summer Excursion Ticket passing through Owego.
Rate..............$1 40

HAMMONDSPORT, N. Y.

LAKE KEUKA, STEUBEN COUNTY, N. Y.

The Delaware, Lackawanna & Western Railroad connects at Bath with the Bath & Hammondsport Railroad, and a ride through the far-famed Pleasant Valley brings the traveler to Hammondsport, N. Y., at the head of Lake Keuka.

Here nestled among the vine-clad hills of Yates and Steuben Counties, lies Lake Keuka, "The Queen of Lakes," the most beautiful of the smaller lakes in America. In a country whose picturesqueness is far famed, in the midst of scenery for which western New York is noted, this gem of inland waters has rapidly increased in fame and popularity. The quiet beauty of its waters, the novelty of its scenery, the salubrity of its atmosphere have gradually extended its name until to day Lake Keuka is recognized as one of the most famous resorts in New York State. It is the land of health and recreation. No swamp land or malaria is found, no mosquitos are bred in the dry healthy air, and hay fever is unknown.

Sailing, rowing, fishing and bathing are pastimes with which one wiles away the summer hours. From all parts of the country enthusiastic fishermen come to lure from the depths the fish which everywhere abound. The following endorsement from Seth Green, the late veteran fisherman and United States Fish Commissioner, speaks for itself:

"I think Lake Keuka unsurpassed by any waters in America as a fishing resort. The purity of the water, the large amount of fish food contained in the Lake, tend to put the fish in the finest condition for the table, and render them very strong and gamey when on the hook and line. During one of my sojourns in August, I took by hook and line 19 salmon trout weighing 113 pounds, and one day in October, 33 black bass, weighing 106 pounds."

The Lake is 22 miles long, divided about midway by a long bold promotory extending southward into its waters and terminating in "Bluff Point," one of the notable landmarks of this section, from whose lofty summits seven counties can be seen. Lake Keuka is 780 feet above sea level, (and over 270 feet above its larger neighbor "Seneca" Lake at the head of which is the famous Watkins Glen) and its shores and lofty hills remind the traveler of the banks of the River Rhine where the wooded hills are covered for miles with vineyards. The precipitous sides of the Lake for miles are covered with farm houses, woodland glens and vineyards, while its water's edge is dotted with hotels and cottages, affording a panorama of unceasing beauty and interest to the tourist when viewed from the deck of the passing steamer.

The hotels of Lake Keuka are "Grove Springs," "Ogoyago," "Keuka," "Gibson's," "Idlewild," and "The Ark," while at the head of the Lake is the "Fairchild House." All the hotels have spacious, cool rooms, broad verandas, and handsome surroundings of groves and grassy lawns, and connected with each, besides the dancing pavilions, bath houses, etc., are many cottages which are rented to families and parties.

Keuka University and Assembly Grounds are located four miles from Penn Yan, the northern terminus of the Lake. Here, during the summer months, the great assembly is held, and during the remainder of the year, with the exception of the summer vacation, Keuka College is filled with students. The location is accessible, beautiful and healthy, on the west shore of Lake Keuka, and comprises some 250 acres of land, twenty of which are occupied by the college and campus, thirty acres of natural grove, several acres of streets, and the remainder by cottages.

Lake Keuka's grapes have a national reputation, while its champagnes are only rivalled by those of foreign vintages. Over 20,000 tons of grapes are annually grown, and many million gallons of still wines and bottles of champagne are produced. The wine cellars are well worth coming miles to see, and "the hospitality extended to the visitor is as broad as the sky."

The steamboat service upon the Lake is unexcelled. The Lake Keuka Navigation

LAKE KEUKA.

Company recently added to its fleet the steamer "Mary Bell," 150 feet long, built of steel, and designed through her light draft and powerful machinery to make the distance of 22 miles between Hammondsport and Penn Yan in about one hour. She has triple expansion engines, two boilers and twin screws, and capacity of accommodating 1,000 passengers. In addition to the "Mary Bell," the steamers of The Lake Keuka Navigation Company are the "Halsey," "Urbana," "Holmes," "West Branch," and "Lulu," and hardly an hour passes but that the summer sojourner upon the Lake can, if he will, take a boat to some point of interest or "make train connections." Round trip from Hammondsport to Penn Yan, fifty cents.

Lake Keuka is nicely located for little excursion trips during one's outing. Niagara Falls is but three hours ride via the Delaware, Lackawanna & Western Railroad, while Watkin's Glen is but twenty miles distant. The New York State Soldiers' and Sailors' Home at Bath is reached in thirty minutes, and the beautiful drives along Lake Keuka's shores touch picturesque little hamlets, while the Lake and surrounding country as viewed by a drive along the brow of its hills present a panorama unrivalled.

Those wishing a more detailed description of Lake Keuka and its environments should address The Lake Keuka Navigation Company, Hammondsport, N. Y., for their illustrated book, which will be mailed free.

EXCURSION NO. 6.—HAMMONDSPORT AND RETURN (LAKE KEUKA).

Delaware, Lack. & Western R. R...to Bath.
Bath & Hammondsport R. R......to Hammondsport.
Returning via same route.

THROUGH RATES.

New York	$12 50	Water Gap	$9 05
Paterson	12 00	Stroudsburg	8 90
Newark	12 25	Scranton	6 55
Morristown	11 50	Pittston	6 55
Dover	11 00	Kingston	6 75
Hackettstown	10 30	Wilkesbarre	6 75
Washington	9 90	Binghamton	4 30
Greene	5 05	Waverly	2 70
Oxford	5 60	Elmira	1 90
Norwich	5 90	Corning	1 30
Sherburne	6 35	Atlanta	1 30
Waterville	7 25	Wayland	1 55
Richfield Springs	8 40	Dansville	1 85
Utica	8 10	Mount Morris	2 45
Owego	3 95	Buffalo	4 90
Ithaca	3 95		

EXCURSION S. T. 5.—BATH TO HAMMONDSPORT (LAKE KEUKA).

Bath & Hammondsport R. R.... { to Hammondsport and return.

Sold only in connection with Summer Excursion Ticket passing through Bath.
Rate..............50 cents.

EXCURSION NO. 34.—GROVE SPRING, GIBSON'S OR KEUKA AND RETURN.

Del., Lack. & Western R. R....to Bath.
Bath & Hammondsport R. R...to Hammondsport.
Lake Keuka Navigation Co.'s to Grove Spring, Gibson's or Keuka.
Steamers ....
Returning via same route.

THROUGH RATES.

New York	$12 80	Norwich	$6 20
Paterson	12 30	Sherburne	6 65
Newark	12 55	Waterville	7 55
Morristown	11 80	Richfield Springs	8 70
Dover	11 30	Buffalo	5 20
Hackettstown	11 60	Utica	8 40
Washington	10 20	Owego	3 75
Water Gap	9 35	Ithaca	4 25
Stroudsburg	9 20	Waverly	3 00
Scranton	6 85	Elmira	2 20
Pittston	6 85	Corning	1 60
Kingston	7 05	Atlanta	1 60
Wilkesbarre	7 05	Wayland	1 85
Binghamton	4 60	Dansville	2 15
Greene	5 35	Mount Morris	2 75
Oxford	5 90		

EXCURSION NO. 389.—OGAYAGO, UNIVERSITY OR PENN YAN AND RETURN.

Del., Lack. & Western R. R....to Bath.
Bath & Hammondsport R. R...to Hammondsport.
Lake Keuka Navigation Co.'s to Ogayago, University Steamers.......... or Penn Yan.
Returning via same route.

THROUGH RATES.

New York	$12 65	Norwich	$6 35
Paterson	12 35	Sherburne	6 80
Newark	12 65	Waterville	7 65
Morristown	11 90	Richfield Springs	8 80
Dover	11 40	Utica	8 50
Hackettstown	10 70	Owego	3 90
Washington	10 40	Ithaca	4 40
Water Gap	9 45	Waverly	3 15
Stroudsburg	9 30	Elmira	2 40
Scranton	7 15	Corning	1 75
Pittston	7 15	Atlanta	1 80
Kingston	7 25	Wayland	2 05
Wilkesbarre	7 25	Dansville	2 35
Binghamton	4 70	Mount Morris	2 95
Greene	5 50	Buffalo	5 10
Oxford	6 00		

EXCURSION NO. 72.—PENN YAN AND RETURN.

Del., Lack. & Western R. R ......to Corning.
Fall Brook Ry. (via W'k's Glen)...to Penn Yan.
Lake Keuka Nav. Co.'s Steamers..to Hammondsport.
Bath & Hammondsport R. R......to Bath.
Del., Lack. & Western R. R.......to starting point.

EXCURSION NO. 73.—REVERSE OF THE PRECEDING.

THROUGH RATES.

New York	$13 00	Norwich	$6 65
Paterson	12 70	Sherburne	7 10
Newark	13 00	Waterville	7 95
Morristown	12 20	Richfield Springs	9 15
Dover	11 75	Utica	8 80
Hackettstown	11 00	Owego	4 20
Washington	10 60	Waverly	3 45
Water Gap	9 75	Elmira	2 55
Stroudsburg	9 60	Corning	2 05
Scranton	7 50	Bath	2 05
Pittston	7 85	Atlanta	2 90
Kingston	8 15	Wayland	3 10
Wilkesbarre	8 15	Dansville	3 40
Binghamton	5 05	Mount Morris	3 95
Greene	5 80	Buffalo	6 50
Oxford	6 35		

EXCURSION NO. 424 —PENN YAN AND RETURN.

Del., Lack. & Western R. R............to Corning.
Fall Brook Ry .. ..to Penn Yan.

THROUGH RATES.

New York	$12 65	Stroudsburg	$9 30
Paterson	12 35	Scranton	7 15
Newark	12 65	Pittston	7 55
Morristown	11 90	Kingston	7 85
Dover	11 40	Wilkesbarre	7 85
Hackettstown	10 70	Binghamton	4 70
Washington	10 30	Greene	5 50
Water Gap	9 45	Oxford	6 00

SUMMER EXCURSION ROUTES AND RATES.

Norwich	$ 6 35	Elmira	$ 2 40	
Sherburne	6 75	Bath	2 60	
Waterville	7 65	Atlanta	3 40	
Richfield Springs	8 85	Wayland	3 65	
Utica	8 50	Dansville	3 95	
Owego	3 90	Mount Morris	4 50	
Waverly	3 15	Buffalo	7 00	

LAKEWOOD, N. J.

EXCURSION 340 Y.—LAKEWOOD, N. J., AND RETURN.

Limited to six (6) months from date of sale.
Delaware, Lack. & Western R. R......to New York.
Central R. R. of N. J. (via Red Bank)..to Lakewood.
Returning via same route.

THROUGH RATES.

Summit	$ 3 15	Richfield Springs	$13 10	
Morristown	3 60	Utica	11 60	
Dover	4 10	Cortland	12 35	
Hackettstown	4 80	Syracuse	12 35	
Washington	5 20	Fulton	12 35	
Stroudsburg	6 20	Oswego	12 35	
Scranton	8 35	Owego	11 20	
Pittston	8 75	Ithaca	12 85	
Kingston	9 15	Waverly	11 95	
Wilkesbarre	9 20	Elmira	12 60	
Montrose	10 55	Corning	13 25	
Binghamton	10 35	Bath	14 10	
Greene	11 15	Atlanta	15 35	
Oxford	11 35	Wayland	15 55	
Norwich	11 35	Dansville	16 05	
Sherburne	11 60	Mount Morris	16 05	
Waterville	11 60	Buffalo	18 35	

LONG BRANCH, N. J.

*EXCURSION NO. 173.—LONG BRANCH AND RETURN.

Delaware, Lack. & Western R. R...to New York.
Pennsylvania Railroad............to Long Branch.
Returning via same route.

*EXCURSION NO. 18.—LONG BRANCH AND RETURN.

Del., Lack. & Western R. R....to New York.
Central R. R. of N. J. Steamers..to Sandy Hook.
Central Railroad of N. J ......to East Long Branch.
Returning via same route.

EXCURSION NO. 19.—LONG BRANCH AND RETURN.

Delaware, Lack & Western R. R....to New York.
Central Railroad of N. J............to Perth Amboy.
N. Y. & Long Branch R. R..........to Long Branch.
Returning via same route.

THROUGH RATES FOR EITHER EXCURSION.

Morristown	$ 2 75	Kingston	$8 65	
Dover	3 25	Wilkesbarre	8 70	
Hackettstown	3 95	Plymouth	8 55	
Washington	4 35	Nanticoke	8 70	
Water Gap	5 20	Shickshinny	9 10	
Stroudsburg	5 35	Berwick	9 50	
Scranton	7 50	Bloomsburg	10 00	
Pittston	7 90	Danville	10 20	
Binghamton	9 50	Ithaca	12 00	
Greene	10 30	Waverly	11 10	
Oxford	10 50	Elmira	11 75	
Norwich	10 50	Corning	12 40	
Sherburne	11 20	Bath	13 25	
Waterville	11 50	Atlanta	14 40	
Cortland	11 50	Wayland	14 70	
Syracuse	11 50	Dansville	15 20	
Oswego	11 50	Mount Morris	15 20	
Owego	10 35	Buffalo	17 50	

* Good for passage between New York and Long Branch either via the boat and trains of the Sandy Hook route, or the trains of either the Central Railroad of New Jersey or the Pennsylvania Railroad.

EXCURSION NO. 17.—LONG BRANCH AND RETURN.

Delaware, Lack. & Western R. R...to New Hampton.
Central Railroad of New Jersey....to Perth Amboy.
New York & Long Branch R. R....to Long Branch.
Returning via same route.

THROUGH RATES.

Water Gap	$ 4 35	Sherburne	$11 20	
Stroudsburg	4 50	Waterville	11 50	
Scranton	6 65	Cortland	10 85	
Pittston	7 00	Syracuse	11 50	
Kingston	7 30	Oswego	11 50	
Wilkesbarre	7 30	Owego	11 10	
Plymouth	7 45	Ithaca	12 00	
Nanticoke	7 60	Waverly	11 10	
Shickshinny	7 95	Elmira	11 75	
Berwick	8 40	Corning	12 40	
Bloomsburg	8 90	Bath	13 25	
Danville	9 35	Atlanta	14 40	
Binghamton	9 50	Wayland	14 70	
Greene	9 90	Dansville	15 20	
Oxford	10 45	Mount Morris	15 20	
Norwich	10 50	Buffalo	17 50	

LURAY CAVERNS, VA.

Those who have visited these wonderful and recently discovered subterranean caverns testify that they form wonderful examples of nature's handiwork. Words cannot adequately describe them; they must be studied to be thoroughly realized. The vestibule of this subterranean mansion is attained by descending the stone steps of the cave, and once there, the first sensation experienced by the visitor is one of awe, at the fearful stillness that reigns supreme, and this is in no way enlivened by the grotesque forms surrounding. Once mastered, however, these emotions turn to wonder. From an entrance hall, elaborate with stalactite decoration, numerous avenues lead into unknown depths. One of the corridors leads to the Fish Market, or rather to a cave which, to all appearances, is hung with row upon row of fish, so natural is the form of the pendants from above. The crystal lake with its unruffled ice-cold surface; the vegetable garden with ever erratic, but none the less vegetable like hangings. Numerous chambers, every one known from a striking resemblance to too easily recognized objects, and each filled with the quaint subterranean creations are connected one to the other by lanes, which appear as though covered by some giant hand; grottoes, elaborated with the richest ornamentation; sparkling waterfalls, and figures and forms of indefinite shape inspire emotions of wonder, which grow with each new revelation. Here we find a Cathedral, with its ever noiseless organ; a hall of giants relieved by fluted columns and arches innumerable. A plateau-like spot, commonly known as the Elfin Ramble, together with Hades, Horey's Hall and Pluto's Chasm, and a variety of other equally fine attractions form but a limit to the marvelous sights these caverns contain. Here, nature has fashioned itself in its own erratic style. Nothing in the way of artificial

DELAWARE, LACKAWANNA & WESTERN R. R.

adornment has been done here by man. These caves may be examined without much difficulty, as the obstructions are few, and may be easily surmounted by the anxious and ever daring explorer.

EXCURSION 338 Y.—LURAY, VA., AND RETURN.

Limited to six (6) months from date of sale.

Del., Lack. & Western R. R.....to Northumberland.
Pennsylvania Railroad......... to Harrisburg.
Cumberland Valley Railroad....to Hagerstown.
Norfolk & Western Railroad....to Luray.

Returning *via* same route.

THROUGH RATES.

Paterson	$15 10	Bloomsburg	$10 60
Boonton	15 10	Danville	10 10
Morristown	15 10	Montrose	15 35
Dover	15 10	Binghamton	15 50
Hackettstown	15 10	Greene	16 30
Washington	15 10	Oxford	16 90
Stroudsburg	15 10	Norwich	17 25
Scranton	13 05	Sherburne	17 65
Pittston	12 55	Waterville	18 50
Kingston	12 20	Richfield Springs	19 70
Wilkesbarre	12 20	Utica	19 35
Plymouth	12 05	Cortland	17 25
Nanticoke	11 90	Syracuse	18 70
Shickshinny	11 50	Fulton	19 70
Berwick	11 10	Oswego	19 75

EXCURSION 339 Y.—LURAY, VA., AND RETURN.

Limited to six (6) months from date of sale.

Delaware, Lack.& Western R. R....to Easton.
Lehigh Valley Railroad..... .....to Allentown.
Philadelphia & Reading Railroad....to Harrisburg.
Cumberland Valley Railroad...... to Hagerstown.
Norfolk & Western Railroad..........to Luray.

Returning *via* same route.

THROUGH RATES.

New York	$15 35	Morristown	$15 10
Newark	15 10	Dover	14 30
Paterson	15 10	Hackettstown	13 40
Boonton	15 10	Washington	12 80

EXCURSION 349 Y.—LURAY, VA., AND RETURN.

Limited to six (6) months from date of sale.

Delaware, Lack. & Western R. R....to Elmira.
Pennsylvania Railroad..............to Harrisburg.
Cumberland Valley Railroad.........to Hagerstown.
Norfolk & Western Railroad..........to Luray.

Returning *via* same route.

THROUGH RATES.

Binghamton	$15 50	Atlanta	$17 65
Owego	15 50	Wayland	18 15
Ithaca	16 20	Dansville	18 45
Waverly	14 35	Mount Morris	18 75
Corning	15 30	Buffalo	21 00
Bath	16 55		

MARION, MASS.

EXCURSION NO. 284.—MARION AND RETURN.

Delaware, Lack. & Western R. R......to New York.
Fall River Line Steamers..... ....to Fall River.
Old Colony Railroad................to Marion.

Returning *via* same route.

THROUGH RATES.

Morristown	$ 8 25	Waterville	$17 00
Dover	8 75	Cortland	17 00
Hackettstown	9 45	Syracuse	17 00
Washington	9 85	Oswego	17 00
Water Gap	10 70	Owego	15 85
Stroudsburg	10 85	Ithaca	17 50
Scranton	13 00	Waverly	16 60
Pittston	13 40	Elmira	17 25
Kingston	14 15	Corning	17 90
Wilkesbarre	14 20	Bath	18 75
Binghamton	15 00	Atlanta	19 90
Greene	15 80	Wayland	20 25
Oxford	16 00	Dansville	20 70
Norwich	16 00	Mount Morris	20 70
Sherburne	16 70	Buffalo	23 00

MATTAPOISETT, MASS.

EXCURSION NO. 285.—MATTAPOISETT AND RETURN.

Delaware, Lack. & Western R. R....to New York.
Fall River Line Steamers..... ....to Fall River.
Old Colony Railroad .. ..to Mattapoisett.

Returning *via* same route.

THROUGH RATES.

Morristown	$ 8 50	Waterville	$17 25
Dover	9 00	Cortland	17 25
Hackettstown	9 70	Syracuse	17 25
Washington	10 10	Oswego	17 25
Water Gap	10 95	Owego	16 10
Stroudsburg	11 10	Ithaca	17 75
Scranton	13 25	Waverly	16 85
Pittston	13 65	Elmira	17 50
Kingston	14 40	Corning	18 15
Wilkesbarre	14 45	Bath	19 00
Binghamton	15 25	Atlanta	20 15
Greene	16 05	Wayland	20 50
Oxford	16 25	Dansville	20 95
Norwich	16 25	Mount Morris	20 95
Sherburne	16 95	Buffalo	23 25

MAUCH CHUNK, PA.

Mauch Chunk is situated in the picturesque gorge or cañon formed by the hand of nature for the passage of the Lehigh River through the mountains. Besides being unique in its site, it possesses a wealth of beauty in its surroundings that has given it a prominent place among the mountain cities of the world. The scenery in every direction is superb. Every prospect is replete with wild beauty; every emotion excited by the outlook is one of admiration. Leading up from the city to the top of Mt. Pisgah is the celebrated Switchback Railroad, which lifts the passengers to an elevation of eighteen hundred feet above the waters of the river. The ascent though absolutely safe is exciting, and the view, both from the car and from the mountain's top, is magnificent. Within a few minutes' ride up the Lehigh is the beautiful Glen Onoko.

EXCURSION No 138.—MAUCH CHUNK AND RETURN.

Del. Lack. & Western Railroad....to Pittston.
Lehigh Valley Railroad ....to Mauch Chunk.

Returning *via* same route.

SUMMER EXCURSION ROUTES AND RATES.   135

THROUGH RATES.

Water Gap	$5 30	Sherburne	$7 60
Stroudsburg	5 10	Waterville	8 40
Scranton	3 60	Richfield Springs	9 60
Binghamton	5 50	Utica	9 30
Greene	6 25	Cortland	7 20
Oxford	6 80	Syracuse	8 65
Norwich	7 15	Oswego	10 05

EXCURSION NO. 139.—MAUCH CHUNK AND RETURN.

Del., Lack. & Western Railroad . .to Kingston.
Wilkesbarre & Kingston St. Rail'y,to Wilkesbarre.
Lehigh Valley Railroad........... to Mauch Chunk.
Returning *via* same route.

THROUGH RATES.

Water Gap	$5 35	Sherburne	$7 65
Stroudsburg	5 15	Waterville	8 45
Scranton	3 65	Richfield Springs	9 65
Binghamton	5 55	Utica	9 35
Greene	6 30	Cortland	7 25
Oxford	6 85	Syracuse	8 70
Norwich	7 20	Oswego	10 10

EXCURSION NO. 140.—MAUCH CHUNK AND RETURN.

Delaware, Lack. & Western R. R...to Pittston.
Lehigh Valley Railroad.............to Mauch Chunk.
Lehigh Valley Railroad ....to Wilkesbarre.
Wilkesbarre & Kingston St. Rail'y. to Kingston.
Delaware, Lack. & Western R. R.. to starting point

EXCURSION NO. 141.—REVERSE OF THE PRECEDING.

THROUGH RATES.

Water Gap	$5 35	Sherburne	$7 65
Stroudsburg	5 15	Waterville	8 45
Scranton	3 65	Richfield Springs	9 65
Binghamton	5 55	Utica	9 35
Greene	6 30	Cortland	7 25
Oxford	6 85	Syracuse	8 70
Norwich	7 20	Oswego	10 10

*EXCURSION NO. 142.—MAUCH CHUNK AND RETURN.

Delaware, Lack. & Western R. R...to Pittston.
Lehigh Valley Railroad .. .... .to Mauch Chunk.
Lehigh Valley Railroad........ ....to New York.
From New York........$6 80.

*EXCURSION NO. 143.—MAUCH CHUNK AND RETURN.

Delaware, Lack. & Western R. R...to Kingston.
Wilkesbarre & Kingston Railway...to Wilkesbarre.
Lehigh Valley Railroad.............to Mauch Chunk.
Lehigh Valley Railroad   ....to New York.
From New York........$6 85.

*NOTE.—Excursions Nos. 142 and 143 may be sold from any Line Station between New York and Scranton (inclusive) at the same rates as from New York. To make up the round trip from such Line Stations, agents will issue in connection with these tickets Form " C E " reading from " New York to Station Stamped on Back." Agents north of Scranton may issue these forms (142 and 143) in the same manner as stations south of that point, but will charge, in addition to the rate from New York, as follows :

Binghamton	$2 50	Cortland	$4 20
Greene	3 30	Syracuse	5 70
Oxford	3 80	Oswego	7 10
Norwich	4 20	Owego	3 35
Sherburne	4 60	Ithaca	4 70
Waterville	5 45	Waverly	4 10
Richfield Springs	6 65	Elmira	4 80
Utica	6 30		

EXCURSION NO. 166.—MAUCH CHUNK AND RETURN.

Delaware, Lack. & Western R. R...to Phillipsburg.
Lehigh Valley Railroad....... . ...to Mauch Chunk.
Returning *via* same route.

EXCURSION NO. 167.—MAUCH CHUNK AND RETURN.

Delaware, Lack. & Western R. R...to Easton.
Central Railroad of N. J...............to Mauch Chunk.
Returning *via* same route.

THROUGH RATES FOR EITHER EXCURSION.

New York	$5 55	Dover	$4 00
Paterson	4 95	Hackettstown	3 25
Newark	5 30	Washington	2 90
Morristown	4 45		

MAUCH CHUNK SWITCHBACK, PA.

EXCURSION S. T. 26.—UPPER MAUCH CHUNK TO SUMMIT HILL AND RETURN.

Mauch Chunk & Summit Hill } to Summit Hill and
Railroad.   ....} return.
Sold only in connection with Summer Excursion Ticket to, or passing through Mauch Chunk.
Rate............75 cents.

MONTREAL, P. Q.

Is situated upon the southeast side of a triangular island formed by the mouths of the Ottawa, where, after a course of 600 miles, it flows into the St. Lawrence. Population, 200,000.

Back of the city, but within its limits, rises Mount Royal (700 feet), on the summit of which is a fine park. The city is on about the same spot, where the Indian village Hockelaga existed when Carter visited this neighborhood early in the sixteenth century.

It has been under English rule since 1761 —prior to which it was in possession of the French.

EXCURSION NO. 91 A.—TO MONTREAL.

Delaware, Lack. & Western R. R...to Buffalo.
N Y. Central & Hudson R. R. R...to Niagara Falls.
N. Y. Central & Hudson R. R. R....to Lewiston.
Niagara Pacific Railway Co.'s Steamer..to Toronto.
Canadian Pacific Railway... ....to Ottawa.
Canadian Pacific Railway, or Ottawa River Navi. Co.'s Steamer... } to Montreal.

EXCURSION NO. 92 A.—TO MONTREAL.

Delaware, Lack. & Western R. R...to Buffalo.
N. Y. Central & Hudson R. R R...to Niagara Falls.
N. Y. Central & Hudson R. R....to Lewiston.
Niagara Navigation Co.'s Steamer to Toronto
Canadian Pacific Railway..........to Ottawa.
Canadian Pacific Railway ....to Prescott.
Grand Trunk R'lway, or Richelieu } to Montreal.
& Ontario Nav. Co.'s Steamer . }

EXCURSION NO. 93 A.—TO MONTREAL.

Delaware, Lack. & Western R. R...to Buffalo.
N. Y. Central & Hudson R. R. R....to Niagara Falls.
N. Y. Central & Hudson R. R. R ..to Lewiston.
Niagara Navigation Co.'s Steamer..to Toronto.
Grand Trunk R'lway, or Richelieu } to Kingston.
& Ontario Nav. Co.'s Steamer ...}
Grand Trunk R'lway, or Richelieu } to Prescott.
& Ontario Nav. Co.'s Steamer.....}
Grand Trunk R'lway, or Richelieu } to Montreal.
& Ontario Nav. Co.'s Steamer.....}

EXCURSION No. 250 A.—TO MONTREAL.

Del. Lack. & Western R. R....to Buffalo.
N. Y., L. E. & W. R. R........to Suspension Bridge.
Grand Trunk Railway........to Port Dalhousie.
Steamer "Empress of India"..to Toronto.
Canadian Pacific Railway.....to Ottawa.
Can. Pac. Railway. or Ottawa } to Montreal.
River Nav. Co.'s Steamer.... }

EXCURSION No. 251 A.—TO MONTREAL.

Del., Lack. & Western R. R...to Buffalo.
N. Y., L. E. & Western R. R...to Suspension Bridge.
Grand Trunk Railway.........to Port Dalhousie.
Steamer "Empress of India"..to Toronto.
Canadian Pacific Railway......to Ottawa.
Canadian Pacific Railway......to Prescott.
Grand Trunk Railway or }
Richelieu & Ontario Navi- } to Montreal.
gation Co.'s Steamer..... }

EXCURSION No. 252 A.—TO MONTREAL.

Del., Lack. & Western R. R....to Buffalo.
N. Y., L. E. & W. R. R........to Suspension Bridge.
Grand Trunk Railway.........to Port Dalhousie.
Steamer "Empress of India"..to Toronto.
Grand Trunk Railway, or }
Richelieu & Ontario Navi- } to Kingston.
gation Co.'s Steamer....... }
Grand Trunk Railway, or }
Richelieu & Ontario Navi- } to Prescott.
gation Co.'s Steamer ...... }
Grand Trunk Railway or }
Richelieu & Ontario Navi- } to Montreal.
gation Co.'s Steamer....... }

EXCURSION No. 94 A.—TO MONTREAL.

Delaware. Lack. & Western R. R.. to Buffalo.
N. Y. Central & Hudson R. R. R...to Niagara Falls.
Grand Trunk Railway...............to Toronto.
Grand Trunk R'lway, or Richelieu } to Kingston.
& Ontario Nav. Co.'s Steamer.. }
Grand Trunk R'lway or Richelieu } to Prescott.
& Ontario Nav. Co.'s Steamer }
Grand Trunk R'lway, or Richelieu } to Montreal.
& Ontario Nav. Co.'s Steamer.. }

EXCURSION No. 136 A.—TO MONTREAL.

Delaware, Lack. & Western R. R.to Buffalo.
N. Y. Central & Hudson R. R. to Niagara Falls.
N. Y. Central & Hudson R. R. R..to Lewiston.
Rome, Watertown & Ogdbg R. R.to Clayton.
Richelieu & Ont. Nav. Co.'s Str...to Alexandria Bay.
Richelieu & Ont. Nav. Co.'s Str...to Montreal.
(Good until October 1st.)

THROUGH RATES FOR EXCURSIONS 91A, 92A, 93A, 94A, 136A, 250A, 251A AND 252A.

New York........	$19 50	Bloomsburg.......	$18 50
Paterson..........	19 50	Danville.........	18 75
Newark...........	19 50	Binghamton......	16 25
Morristown.......	19 50	Greene...........	16 55
Dover............	19 50	Oxford...........	16 80
Hackettstown.....	19 15	Norwich..........	16 95
Washington.......	18 95	Cortland.........	17 00
Water Gap........	18 55	Owego............	15 70
Stroudsburg.......	18 45	Ithaca............	16 40
Scranton	17 35	Waverly..........	15 30
Pittston..........	17 55	Elmira............	14 95
Kingston..........	17 70	Corning..........	14 90
Wilkesbarre.......	17 70	Bath..............	14 75
Plymouth.........	17 80	Atlanta...........	14 20
Nanticoke.........	17 85	Wayland..........	14 10
Shickshinny.......	18 05	Dansville.........	13 90
Berwick...........	18 25	Mount Morris.....	13 55

EXCURSION No. 96 A.—TO MONTREAL.

Delaware, Lack. & Western R. R..to Utica.
Rome, Watertown & Ogdbg. R. R..to Clayton.
Richelieu & Ont. Nav. Co.'s Str... to Alexandria Bay.
Richelieu & Ont. Nav. Co.'s Str...to Montreal.
(Good until October 1st.)

THROUGH RATES.

New York........	$13 50	Bloomsburg.......	$12 80
Paterson..........	13 50	Danville.........	13 00
Newark...........	13 50	Binghamton......	10 40
Morristown.......	13 50	Greene...........	10 05
Dover............	13 50	Oxford...........	9 75
Hackettstown.....	13 40	Norwich..........	9 60
Washington.......	13 25	Sherburne.........	9 40
Water Gap........	12 80	Waterville........	8 95
Stroudsburg.......	12 70	Richfield Springs..	9 25
Scranton..........	11 65	Cortland..........	10 85
Pittston..........	11 85	Owego............	10 85
Kingston..........	12 00	Ithaca............	11 50
Wilkesbarre.......	12 00	Waverly..........	11 20
Plymouth.........	12 10	Elmira............	11 55
Nanticoke.........	12 15	Corning..........	11 80
Shickshinny.......	12 30	Bath..............	12 30
Berwick...........	12 55		

EXCURSION No. 97 A.—TO MONTREAL.

Del., Lack. & Western R. R....to Richfield Springs.
Del., Lack. & Western R. R....to Utica.
Rome, W't'n & Ogdbg. R. R....to Clayton.
R. & O. Nav. Co.'s Steamers... to Alexandria Bay.
R. & O. Nav. Co.'s Steamers...to Montreal.
(Good until October 1st.)

THROUGH RATES.

New York........	$14 40	Berwick..........	$13 45
Paterson..........	14 40	Bloomsburg.......	13 70
Newark...........	14 40	Dansville.........	13 90
Morristown.......	14 40	Binghamton......	11 30
Dover............	14 40	Greene...........	10 95
Hackettstown.....	14 30	Oxford...........	10 65
Washington.......	14 15	Norwich..........	10 50
Water Gap........	13 70	Sherburne.........	10 30
Stroudsburg.......	13 60	Waterville........	9 85
Scranton..........	12 55	Cortland..........	11 75
Pittston..........	12 75	Owego............	11 75
Kingston..........	12 90	Ithaca............	12 40
Wilkesbarre.......	12 90	Waverly..........	12 10
Plymouth.........	13 00	Elmira............	12 45
Nanticoke.........	13 05	Corning..........	12 80
Shickshinny.......	13 20	Bath..............	13 20

EXCURSION No. 183 A.—TO MONTREAL

Delaware, Lack. & Western R. R.to Syracuse.
Rome, W't'n & Ogdbg. R. R .. ..to Clayton.
R. & O. Nav. Co's Steamers......to Alexandria Bay.
R. & O. Nav. Co.'s Steamers...to Montreal.
(Good until October 1st.)

THROUGH RATES.

New York........	$14 40	Nanticoke.........	$11 95
Paterson	14 10	Shickshinny......	12 15
Newark....	14 30	Berwick..........	12 35
Morristown.......	13 80	Bloomsburg.......	12 65
Dover............	13 65	Danville.........	12 85
Hackettstown.....	13 25	Binghamton......	10 25
Washington.......	13 05	Greene...........	10 20
Water Gap........	12 65	Oxford...........	10 45
Stroudsburg.......	12 55	Norwich..........	10 65
Scranton..........	11 50	Cortland..........	9 40
Pittston..........	11 70	Owego............	10 65
Kingston..........	11 85	Waverly..........	10 80
Wilkesbarre.......	11 85	Elmira............	10 80
Plymouth.........	11 90		

EXCURSION No. 156 A.—TO MONTREAL.

Delaware, Lack. & Western R. R.to Oswego.
Rome, Watert'n & Ogdbg. R. R..to Clayton.
R. & O. Nav. Co.'s Steamers......to Alexandria Bay.
R. & O. Nav. Co.'s Steamers. to Montreal.
(Good until October 1st.)

THROUGH RATES.

New York........	$14 70	Scranton..........	$11 80
Paterson	14 40	Pittston	12 00
Newark...........	14 60	Kingston	12 15
Morristown	14 15	Wilkesbarre.......	12 15
Dover............	13 95	Plymouth.........	12 20
Hackettstown.....	13 95	Nanticoke.........	12 25
Washington.......	13 35	Shickshinny.......	12 45
Water Gap........	12 95	Berwick..........	12 65
Stroudsburg.......	12 85	Bloomsburg.......	12 95

SUMMER EXCURSION ROUTES AND RATES.

Danville	$13 15	Cortland	$9 70
Binghamton	10 55	Syracuse	8 95
Greene	10 50	Owego	10 95
Oxford	10 75	Waverly	11 20
Norwich	10 95	Elmira	11 20

EXCURSION S. T. 34.—ALEXANDRIA BAY TO MONTREAL AND RETURN.

Richelieu & Ontario Navigation Co.'s Steamers................ } to Montreal and return.
(Good until October 1st.)
Sold only in connection with Summer Excursion Ticket to, or passing through Alexandria Bay.
Rate............$8 50

ROUTES RETURNING FROM MONTREAL.

(Issued only in connection with routes to Montreal.)

To make round trip rates from New York, add the fare from New York to Montreal to that from Montreal to New York, via the desired route.

The round trip rates from any Line Station on Morris & Essex Division, Main Line or Buffalo Division, for routes via Buffalo and Niagara Falls, will be the same as those made from New York. For example, the round trip rate to Montreal and return via route of Excursion No. 91 A to Montreal, and that of Excursion No. 109 X from Montreal, would be $29.50 ($19.50+10) from New York, and would be the same from Elmira for a ticket made up of the same forms, but starting from Elmira and returning via New York to Elmira,

Round trip rates from any Line Station on the Morris & Essex Division, Main Line, or Utica Division, for routes going via Utica, and from any Line Station on the Morris & Essex Division, Main Line, Syracuse, Binghamton and New York Division, or Oswego and Syracuse Division, for routes going via Syracuse or Oswego, can be made in the same manner as for routes going via Buffalo and Niagara Falls.

Round trip rates from other stations will be as follows For routes going via Buffalo and Niagara Falls: Pittston, 40c.; Kingston, 80c.; Wilkesbarre, 85c.; Plymouth, 90c.; Nauticoke, $1 05; Shickshinny, $1 45; Berwick, $1.85; Bloomsburg, $2 35; Danville, $2.85; Greene, 80c.; Oxford, $1.35; Norwich, $1.65; Cortland, $1.70, and Ithaca, $1.40 more than the round trip rate from New York.

For routes going via Utica: Pittston, 40c.; Kingston, 80c.; Wilkesbarre, 85c.; Plymouth, 90c.; Nauticoke, $1.05; Shickshinny, $1.45; Berwick, $1.85; Bloomsburg, $2 35; Danville, $2 85; Cortland, $1 70; Owego, 85c.; Ithaca, $2.20; Waverly, $1.60; Elmira, $2.25 Corning, $2.90; and Bath, $3.75 more than the round trip rate from New York.

For routes going via Syracuse: Pittston, 40c.; Kingston, 80c.; Wilkesbarre, 85c.; Plymouth, 90c.; Nauticoke, $1.05; Shickshinny, $1.45; Berwick, $1 85; Bloomsburg, $2.35; Danville, $2.85; Owego, 85c.; Waverly, $1 60; and Elmira, $2.25 more than the round trip rate from New York.

For routes going via Oswego: Pittston, 40c.; Kingston, 80c.; Wilkesbarre 85c.; Plymouth, 90c.; Nauticoke, $1.05; Shickshinny, $1.45; Berwick, $1.85; Bloomsburg, $2.35; Danville, $2.85; Greene, 40c.; Oxford, 90c.; Norwich, $1.20; Owego, 85c.; Waverly, $1.60, and Elmira, $2.25 more than the round trip rate from New York.

To make up such round trip tickets through Montreal from Line Stations, agents will issue Form C. E., reading via Delaware, Lackawanna & Western Railroad, " New York to Station stamped on back," which, in connection with the form to Montreal and that from Montreal to New York, makes a complete round trip from starting point.

*EXCURSION NO. 109 X.—MONTREAL TO NEW YORK.

Grand Trunk Railway............to Rouse's Point.
Del. & Hudson Canal Co.'s Lines.to Plattsburg.
Del. & Hudson Canal Co.'s Lines or Lake Champlain Steamer. } to Ft. Ticonderoga.
Del. & Hudson Canal Co.'s Lines.to Saratoga.
Del. & Hudson Canal Co.'s Lines..to Troy.
N. Y. Central & Hudson R. R. R..to New York.
Rate............$10.00

*EXCURSION NO. 110 X.—MONTREAL TO NEW YORK.

Via same route as 109 X to Saratoga, thence Delaware & Hudson Canal Co.'s Lines..to Albany.
Day Line Hudson River Steamers......to New York.
Rate........$9.65

*EXCURSION NO. 111 X.—MONTREAL TO NEW YORK.

Via same route as 109 X to Saratoga, thence Delaware & Hudson Canal Co.'s Lines..to Albany.
People's (Night)Line H. R. Steamers..to New York.
Rate.........$9.15

*EXCURSION NO. 112 X.—MONTREAL TO NEW YORK.

Grand Trunk Railway............to Rouse's Point.
Del. & Hudson Canal Co.'s Line..to Plattsburg.
Del. & Hud. Canal Co.'s Lines,or Lake Champlain Steamer....} to Ft. Ticonderoga.
Del. & Hudson Canal Co.'s Lines..to Baldwin.
Lake George Steamer............to Caldwell.
Del. & Hudson Canal Co.'s Lines.to Saratoga.
Del. & Hudson Canal Co.'s Lines.to Troy.
N. Y. Central & Hudson R. R. R..to New York.
Rate............$11.50

*EXCURSION NO. 113 X.—MONTREAL TO NEW YORK.

Via same route as 112 X to Saratoga, thence Del. & Hudson Canal Co.'s Lines..to Albany.
Day Line Hudson River Steamers.....to New York.
Rate............$11.15

*EXCURSION NO. 114 X.—MONTREAL TO NEW YORK.

Via same route as 112 X to Saratoga, thence Del. & Hudson Canal Co.'s Lines.......to Albany.
People's (Night) Line H. R. Steamers..to New York.
Rate.........$10.65

*EXCURSION NO. 298 X.—MONTREAL TO NEW YORK.

Grand Trunk Railway..........to St. John's.
Central Vermont Railroad......to Burlington.
Lake Champlain Steamer......to Ft. Ticonderoga.
Del. & Hud. Canal Co.'s Lines.to Baldwin.
Lake George Steamer..........to Caldwell.
Del. & Hud. Canal Co.'s Lines..to Saratoga.
Del. & Hud. Canal Co.'s Lines .to Troy.
N. Y. Central & Hud. R. R. R....to New York.
Rate $11.50

*EXCURSION NO. 299 X.—MONTREAL TO NEW YORK.

Via same route as 298 X to Saratoga, thence Del. & Hudson Canal Co.'s Lines..to Albany.
Day Line Hudson River Steamers.....to New York.
Rate............$11.15.

*EXCURSION NO. 300 X.—MONTREAL TO NEW YORK.

Via same route as 298 X to Saratoga, thence Del. & Hudson Canal Co.'s Lines..to Albany.
People's (Night) Line H. R. Steamers..to New York.
Rate............$10.65

DELAWARE, LACKAWANNA & WESTERN R. R.

*Excursion No. 386 X.—Montreal to New York.

N. Y. Central & Hudson R. R. R...to New York.
Rate $10.00
* Not to be sold in connection with tickets to Montreal *via* the Canadian Pacific Railway.

*Excursion No. 115 X.—Montreal to New York.

Grand Trunk Railway..............to St. John's
Central Vermont Railrond ....to Windsor.
Vermont Valley Railroad ....to Brattleboro.
Central Vermont Railroad.........to South Vernon.
Connecticut River Railroad........to Springfield.
N. Y., New Haven & H. R. R.......to New York.
Rate...........$10.00

*Excursion No. 116 X.—Montreal to New York.

Grand Trunk Railway..............to St. John's.
Central Vermont Railroad.........to White River Jc.
Boston & Maine Railroad (Lowell System)........................ } to Concord.
Concord Railroad ....to Nashua.
Boston & Maine Railroad (Lowell System)........................ } to Boston.
Old Colony Railroad.............to Fall River.
Fall River Line Steamers........to New York.
Rate........ $13.50

†Excursion No. 117 X.—Montreal to New York.

Canadian Pacific Railway...... } to Newport, Vt. (Lake Memphremagog.)
Boston & Maine Railroad (Passumpsic Division)............ } to Wells River.
Concord & Montreal Railroad....to Nashua.
Boston & Main Railroad (Lowell System)......................... } to Boston.
Old Colony Railroad.............to Fall River.
Fall River Line Steamers .....to New York.
Rate $13.50

†Excursion No. 119 X.—Montreal to New York.

Canadian Pacific Railway...... } to Newport, Vt. (Lake Memphremagog.)
Boston & Maine Railroad (Passumpsic Division)............ } to St. Johnsbury.
St. Johnsbury & L. Cham. R. R...to Scott's.
Concord & Montreal Railroad ...to Fabyan's.
Concord & Montreal Railroad....to Concord.
Concord & Montreal Railroad....to Nashua.
Boston & Maine R. R (Lowell System)......................... } to Boston.
Fall River Line Steamers.........to New York.
Rate $13.50

*Excursion No. 301 X.—Montreal to New York.

Grand Trunk Railway..............to St. John's.
Central Vermont Railroad........to Montpelier.
Montpelier & Wells River R. R...to Wells River.
Concord & Montreal Railroad....to Fabyan's.
Concord & Montreal Railroad....to Concord.
Concord & Montreal Railroad....to Nashua.
Boston & MainRailroad (Lowell System) .... } to Boston
Fall River Line Steamers ....to New York.
Rate $13 50

†Excursion No. 120 X.—Montreal to New York.

Canadian Pacific Railway....... } to Newport, Vt. (Lake Memphremagog.)
Boston & Maine Railroad (Passumpsic Division)............ } to St. Johnsbury.

St. Johnsonsbury L. Cham. R, R..to Scott's.
Concord & Montreal Railroad.....to Fabyan's.
Maine Central Railroad (White Mountains Line)............... } to Crawford House.
Maine Central Railroad (White Mountains Line)............... } to North Conway.
Boston & Maine Railroad........to Boston.
Old Colony Railroad.... ....to Fall River.
Fall River Line Steamers........,....to New York.
Rate...... ....$13.50

*Excursion No. 302 X.—Montreal to New York.

Grand Trunk Railway.......... to St. John's.
Central Vermont Railroad....... to Montpelier.
Montpelier & Wells River R. R...to Wells River.
Concord & Montreal Railroad....to Fabyan's.
Maine Central Reilroad (White Mountains Line .... } to Crawford House.
Maine Central Railroad (White Mountains Line............... } to North Conway.
Boston & Maine Railroad........to Boston.
Old Colony Railroad..........to Fall River.
Fall River Line Steamers ....to New York.
Rate $13.50

* Not to be sold in connection with tickets to Montreal *via* the Canadian Pacific Railway
† Not to be sold in connection with tickets to Montreal *via* the Grand Trunk Railway.

†Excursion No. 147 X.—Montreal to New York.

Canadian Pacific Railway....... } to Newport, Vt. (Lake Memphremagog.)
Boston & Maine Railroad (Passumpsic Division)............ } to St. Johnsbury.
St. Johnsbury & Lake Champlain R R .... } to Scott's.
Concord & Montreal R R...... ....to Fabyan's.
Maine Central Railroad (White Mountains Line............... } to Portland.
Boston & Maine Railroad ....to Boston.
Old Colony Railroad ....to Fall River.
Fall River Line Steamers.........to New York.
Rate............... $13 50

*Excursion No 303 X.—Montreal to New York.

Grand Trunk Railway.............to St. John's.
Central Vermont Railroad........ to Montpelier.
Montpelier & Wells River R. R....to Wells River.
Concord & Montreal Railroad.....to Fabyan's.
Maine Central Railroad (White Mountains Line) .... } to Portland.
Boston & Maine Railroad..........to Boston.
Old Colony Railroad.. ....to Fall River.
Fall River Line Steamers..........to New York.
Rate...................$14.50

†Excursion No. 118 X.—Montreal to New York.

Canadian Pacific Railway...... } to Newport, Vt. (Lake Memphremagog.)
Boston & Maine Railroad (Passumpsic Division............ } to St. Johnsbury.
St Johns'y & Lake Cham. R. R.to Scott's.
Concord & Montreal R. R......to Fabyan's.
Concord & Montreal R R......to Base Mt. Wash'n.
Mount Washington Railroad.....to Summit.
Milliken's Stage Line ....to Glen House.
Milliken's Stage Line. .... to Glen Station.
Maine Central Railroad (White Mountains Line)............. } to North Conway.
Boston & Maine Railroad........to Boston.
Old Colony Railroad.............to Fall River.
Fall River Line Steamers ....to New York.
Rate...........$23.00

* Not to be sold in connection with tickets to Montreal *via* the Canadian Pacific Railway.
† Not to be sold in connection with tickets to Montreal *via* the Grand Trunk Railway.

SUMMER EXCURSION ROUTES AND RATES.

MONTROSE, PA.

LOCAL EXCURSION.

(Good for continuous passage only.)

THROUGH RATES.

‡New York	$8 20	Shickshinny	$3 70
Passaic	7 95	Berwick	4 10
Paterson	7 80	Bloomsburg	4 60
Boonton	7 25	Danville	5 10
‡Newark	8 20	Great Bend	1 10
‡Roseville Ave	8 20	Binghamton	1 65
Orange	8 10	Greene	2 45
Mountain	7 95	Oxford	3 00
South Orange	7 90	Norwich	3 30
Milburn	7 75	Sherburne	3 75
Short Hills	7 70	Waterville	4 60
Summit	7 70	Richfield Springs	5 80
Chatham	7 50	Utica	5 45
Madison	7 40	Cortland	3 40
Morristown	7 25	Syracuse	4 80
Dover	6 75	Oswego	6 20
Andover	6 35	Owego	2 50
Newtown	6 75	Ithaca	3 85
Franklin	7 25	Waverly	3 20
Hackettstown	6 05	Elmira	3 95
Washington	5 65	Corning	4 60
Scranton	2 30	Bath	5 40
Pittston	2 60	Atlanta	6 20
Kingston	3 05	Wayland	6 40
Wilkesbarre	3 05	Dansville	6 75
Plymouth	3 20	Mount Morris	7 30
Nanticoke	3 45	Buffalo	9 75

‡ Tickets Good until used.

MOUNT POCONO, PA.

LOCAL EXCURSION.

(Good for continuous passage only.)

THROUGH RATES.

‡New York	$4 65	Shickshinny	$3 15
Passaic	4 35	Berwick	3 45
Paterson	4 20	Bloomsburg	3 75
Boonton	3 65	Danville	4 10
‡Newark	4 65	Great Bend	3 30
‡Roseville Ave	4 65	Binghamton	3 85
Orange	4 45	Greene	4 65
Mountain	4 35	Oxford	5 20
South Orange	4 30	Norwich	5 50
Milburn	4 15	Sherburne	5 95
Short Hills	4 10	Waterville	6 80
Summit	4 10	Richfield Springs	8 00
Chatham	3 90	Utica	7 65
Madison	3 80	Cortland	5 60
Morristown	3 65	Syracuse	7 00
Dover	3 15	Oswego	8 40
Andover	2 95	Owego	4 70
Newton	3 15	Ithaca	6 05
Franklin	3 65	Waverly	5 40
Hackettstown	2 45	Elmira	6 15
Washington	2 05	Corning	6 80
Scranton	1 85	Bath	7 60
Pittston	2 25	Atlanta	8 40
Kingston	2 60	Wayland	8 60
Wilkesbarre	2 60	Dansville	8 95
Plymouth	2 75	Mount Morris	9 50
Nanticoke	2 90	Buffalo	12 00

‡ Tickets good until used.

MOUNT TABOR, N. J.

Special Excursion Tickets issued on account of the Mount Tabor Camp Meeting Association. On sale from June 1st until October 31st.

RATES.

*New York	$1 40	Chatham	$ 55
*Hoboken	1 40	Madison	45
Kingsland	1 15	Morristown	30
Passaic	1 00	Morris Plains	20
Clifton	90	Rockaway	15
Paterson	80	Dover	25
West Paterson	80	Pt. Oram	35
Little Falls	75	Succasunna	55
Mountain View	60	Ironia	60
Lincoln Park	50	Chester	75
Boonton	25	Mt. Arlington	50
Harrison	1 15	Hopatcong Station	60
Newark	1 15	Stanhope	65
Roseville Ave	1 10	Waterloo	75
Grove St	1 00	Andover	1 05
East Orange	1 00	Newton	1 25
Brick Church	1 00	Lafayette	1 40
Orange	90	Branchville	1 60
Highland Ave	90	Franklin	1 75
Mountain	90	Hackettstown	1 00
South Orange	90	Pt. Murray	1 25
Maplewood	85	Washington	1 40
Wyoming, N. J	80	Broadway	1 60
Milburn	80	Stewartsville	1 75
Short Hills	75	Phillipsburg	1 50
Huntly	70	Easton	1 95
Summit	65	New Hampton	1 60
Murray Hill	85	Oxford Furnace	1 60
Stirling	1 05	Bridgeville	1 75
Basking Ridge	1 20	Delaware	1 90
Bernardsville	1 25	Portland	2 00
Far Hills	1 45	Water Gap	2 20
Gladstone	1 55	Stroudsburg	2 40

* Tickets good until used.

MOUNT WASHINGTON, N. H. (WHITE MOUNTAINS.)

The summit of this well known mountain is six thousand two hundred and ninety-three feet above the sea level, with a railroad running to the top, and also a carriage road connecting the Summit House with the Glen Mountain House. It is a most popular diversion for tourists who pass through, as well as for those who spend the summer, to make the ascent to witness the rugged surroundings, the beautiful cloud views and the unequalled pictures at sunrise and sunset.

EXCURSION S T 43.—FABYAN'S TO MOUNT WASHINGTON AND RETURN

Concord & Montreal Railroad..........to Base Station.
Mount Washington Railway..........to Summit.
Returning via same route.
Sold only in connection with Summer Excursion Ticket to, or passing through Fabyan's.
Rate.............$6.00

Trains will commence running regularly for the summer season to and from summit of Mt. Washington on Monday, July 2d, and the sale of tickets can therefore be resumed on that date.

MUSKOKA LAKES, ONT.

Gravenhurst—reached from Toronto via the Northern and Northwestern Division of the Grand Trunk Railway, is properly called the Gateway to Muskoka, which latter is located at the foot of Muskoka Lake.

Gravenhurst is quite a town, and of growing importance. The several lakes, such as Joseph, Rosseau, afford rare opportunities for the sportsman, as they abound in salmon, trout, black bass, perch, and speckled trout.

EXCURSION S T 23.—NIAGARA FALLS TO GRAVENHURST, TOUR OF LAKES OF MUSKOKA AND RETURN.

N. Y. Central & Hudson River R. R...to Lewiston
Niagara Navigation Co.'s Steamers..to Toronto.
Grand Trunk Railway...............to Gravenhurst.
Muskoka & Geo. Bay Navigation } through Lake
  Company....................... }   Muskoka.
Lake Rosseau & Lake Jos. & return...to Gravenhurst.
Returning *via* same route.
Sold only in connection with Summer Excursion Ticket to, or passing through Niagara Falls.
Rate.............$8.90

EXCURSION S T 24.—TORONTO TO GRAVENHURST, TOUR OF LAKES OF MUSKOKA AND RETURN.

Grand Trunk Railway...............to Gravenhurst.
Muskoka and Geo. Bay Navigation } through Lake
  Company....................... }   Muskoka.
Lake Ros. & Lake Joseph & return...to Gravenhurst.
Returning *via* same route.
Sold only in connection with Summer Excursion Ticket to or passing through Toronto.
Rate.............$7.50

NANTUCKET, MASS.

Is about twenty miles long and "away out at sea." Its quaint, old-fashioned character and its peculiar social and physical aspects, prove very interesting to the new comer, as well as charming to the frequent visitor.

The town is full of reminders of a prosperity of the past.

Fishing, sailing, and like aquatic sports are here to be enjoyed.

EXCURSION NO. 21.—NANTUCKET AND RETURN.

Delaware Lack. & Western R. R.....to New York.
Fall River Line Steamers ....to Fall River.
Old Colony Railroad................to New Bedford.
New Bedford, Vineyard, Nantucket } to Nantucket.
  & Cape Cod S. B. Line............ }
Returning *via* same route.

THROUGH RATES.

Morristown.......	$ 9 50	Waterville.........	$18 25
Dover...........	10 00	Cortland.........	18 25
Hackettstown.....	10 70	Syracuse.........	18 25
Washington......	11 10	Oswego...........	18 25
Water Gap.......	11 95	Owego............	17 10
Stroudsburg......	12 10	Ithaca............	18 75
Scranton.........	14 25	Waverly..........	17 85
Pittston	14 65	Elmira............	18 50
Kingston.........	15 40	Corning..........	19 15
Wilkesbarre......	15 45	Bath..............	20 00
Binghamton,.....	16 25	Atlanta...........	21 15
Greene...........	17 05	Wayland..........	21 45
Oxford	17 25	Dansville.........	21 95
Norwich.........	17 25	Mount Morris....	21 95
Sherburne	17 95	Buffalo...........	24 25

NARRAGANSETT PIER, R. I.

The very best of bathing facilities are to be found at this fashionable ocean resort.

The extended reputation it now enjoys is of comparatively recent date, but the quality of its attractions had only to be demonstrated to move "The Pier" into the very first of leading sea-side places.

It is directly on the ocean, with a smooth beach about a mile in extent.

EXCURSION No. 69.—NARRAGANSETT PIER AND RETURN.

Del., Lack. & Western R. R....to New York.
Stonington Line Steamers. ...to Stonington.
N. Y., Providence & Boston R. R.to Kingston.
Narragansett Pier Railroad to Narragansett Pier.
Returning *via* same route.

THROUGH RATES.

Morristown.......	$ 6 25	Waterville.........	$15 00
Dover...........	6 75	Cortland	15 00
Hackettstown....	7 45	Syracuse..........	15 00
Washington......	7 85	Oswego	15 00
Water Gap.......	8 70	Owego	13 85
Stroudsburg......	8 85	Ithaca............	15 50
Scranton.........	11 00	Waverly..........	14 60
Pittston.........	12 45	Elmira............	15 25
Kingston	12 15	Corning..........	15 90
Wilkesbarre.....	12 20	Bath..............	16 75
Binghamton..	13 00	Atlanta...........	17 90
Greene	13 80	Wayland..........	18 20
Oxford...........	14 00	Dansville.........	18 70
Norwich..........	14 00	Mount Morris.....	18 70
Sherburne....	14 70	Buffalo...........	21 00

NEW BEDFORD, MASS.

New Bedford glories in the possession of one of the finest, as well as the most picturesque, harbors of the Atlantic coast. The entrance to the harbor, lying between Clark's Neck and Sconticut Point, is strongly fortified, and the wharf frontage extends along the broad Acushnet for two miles. Fairhaven, on the opposite shore of the river, is connected with the city by a long bridge. The city rises gradually from the water's edge, and the streets are shaded and beautified by fine old elms. A public driveway extending along the coast for five miles presents excellent views of the ocean and the islands which dot its surface. The various industries of New Bedford attract people of all nationalities, and an idle hour may be well passed in studying the various types of its inhabitants.

New Bedford is the starting point for the steamer ride to Nantucket, Martha's Vineyard, and Cottage City.

It has pleasant neighbors in the pretty summer towns of Fairhaven, Mattapoisett, Marion, and Nonquit.

EXCURSION No. 286.—NEW BEDFORD AND RETURN.

Delaware, Lack. and Western R. R..to New York.
Fall River Line Steamers............to Fall River.
Old Colony Railroad........ ....to New Bedford.
Returning *via* same route.

THROUGH RATES.

Morristown.......	$ 7 50	Waterville.........	$16 25
Dover...........	8 00	Cortland	16 25
Hackettstown ...	8 70	Syracuse.........	16 25
Washington......	9 10	Oswego...........	16 25
Water Gap.......	9 95	Owego............	15 10
Stroudsburg......	12 10	Ithaca............	16 75
Scranton.........	12 25	Waverly..........	15 85
Pittston ....., ..	12 65	Elmira............	16 50
Kingston.........	13 40	Corning	17 15
Wilkesbarre......	13 45	Bath..............	18 00
Binghamton	14 25	Atlanta...........	19 15
Greene...........	15 05	Wayland..........	19 50
Oxford	15 25	Dansville.........	19 95
Norwich.........	15 25	Mount Morris.....	19 95
Sherburne	15 95	Buffalo............	22 25

NEWPORT, R. I.

This fashionable watering place probably takes first place in that it out-ranks all other of our resorts in age and in the social scale. "Nature has lavished her riches on the spot. There is rare beauty in the land, its grass and shrubs; there is a surpassing charm in air and sky, and a fascination in the sea and its blue waters with gem-like isles."

The city is of itself a beautiful place; its habitations costly and elaborate. Its drives are world famous, particularly the cliff road, which, in the season, presents a magnificent array of gorgeous equipages and richly dressed people.

EXCURSION No. 64.—NEWPORT, R. I. AND RETURN.

Delaware, Lack. & Western R. R........to New York.
Fall River Line Steamers..............to Newport.
Returning *via* same route.

THROUGH RATES.

Morristown	$7 25	Waterville	$16 00
Dover	7 75	Cortland	16 00
Hackettstown	8 45	Syracuse	16 00
Washington	8 85	Oswego	16 00
Water Gap	9 70	Owego	14 85
Stroudsburg	11 85	Ithaca	16 50
Scranton	12 00	Waverly	15 60
Pittston	12 40	Elmira	16 25
Kingston	13 15	Corning	16 90
Wilkesbarre	13 20	Bath	17 75
Binghamton	14 00	Atlanta	18 90
Greene	14 80	Wayland	19 20
Oxford	15 00	Dansville	19 70
Norwich	15 00	Mount Morris	19 70
Sherburne	15 70	Buffalo	22 00

NIAGARA-ON-THE-LAKE, ONT.

EXCURSION S T 51.—NIAGARA FALLS TO NIAGARA-ON THE-LAKE AND RETURN.

N. Y. C. & Hud. River R. R..to Lewiston.
Niagara Nav. Co.'s Strs......to Niagara-on-the-Lake.
Returning *via* same route.
Sold only in connection with Summer Excursion Tickets to, or passing through Niagara Falls.
Rate ....80 cents.

NIAGARA FALLS, N. Y.

This magnificent cataract, the grandeur of which has been but inadequately dwelt upon by many celebrated writers, calls for far more elaborate treatment than in our limited space, even if we had words at command to do this wonder of Nature justice, we can allot to it. We are only able to hint at few of its marvels and to dilate a little on the unrivalled beauty of the ceaseless roaring "Thunder of Waters."

To the aborigines, this wonderful cataract was called "Ony-a-ka-ra" and "Og-na-kar-ra" "Thunder of Waters," and thus it will be seen that even they, in all their simplicity, realized what a mighty work Nature had here accomplished. Niagara Falls never becomes monotonous to the visitor. Any one gazing upon it realizes how hard it is to be able to describe it adequately, for any attempt at word painting of this rolling flood would prove but a poor travesty of the work of Almighty God.

Three distinct falls comprise the whole. These are the "Horse Shoe" on the Canadian side, "American" on the Niagara or United States side, and "Central" which descends between Luna and Goat Islands. Three thousand feet is the entire breadth of the combined falls.

Niagara ranks as the foremost of the world's wonders, and is visited annually by hundreds of thousands from all parts. Indeed many a newly married couple will spend their honeymoon there.

It has been stated that the sound of the falling waters can be heard at a distance of 24 miles, and that from eighteen to twenty-one millions of cubic feet of water descend per minute from the river above. The lakes and streams that find an outlet in the Niagara River drain five hundred thousand or more square miles of land, and the lakes and tributaries themselves cover a surface of one hundred and fifty thousand square miles.

The river in its onward flow to Lake Ontario has a fall of 334 feet. It dashes heedlessly on over rocks and islets, and is lashed into foam all the way to Lewiston. No craft yet built —yes, one, the *Maid of the Mist*, on June 15, 1861, was successfully taken from the foot of the falls, through the rapids and whirlpool, and finally delivered on Lake Ontario— even were the water of sufficient depth, could sail the rapids. Several daring adventurers have sacrificed their lives to win fame and money by braving the rapids, and foremost among these was Captain Webb.

The State of New York having secured the rights to the lands adjacent to the Falls, has incorporated them into Niagara Park, which embraces the greatest points of interest on the American side. The park is open to the public free of charge. Goat Island, connected with this park by a bridge, offers the best view of the falls, and from Prospect Park, on the mainland, the scenery is magnificent. The drive along the Canadian shore affords a splendid view of the gorge and rapids.

Connected with the falls are innumerable points of interest, principal among which are the Cave of the Winds, Three Sisters Island, Burning Spring, the Whirlpool Rapids, Suspension and Cantilever Bridges. A sensational trip is that made across the river below the falls in a little steamer, the modern *Maid of the Mist*.

The drives around Niagara are very interesting, and the village itself, with its pretty homes, fine streets and great number of large well-kept hotels, should be explored by visitors.

EXCURSION NO. 36—NIAGARA FALLS AND RETURN

Delaware, Lack. & Western R. R.... to Buffalo.
N. Y. Cent. & Hudson River R. R....to Niagara Falls.
Returning via same route.

THROUGH RATES.

New York	$16 00	Danville	$13 50
Paterson	16 00	Binghamton	9 00
Newark	16 00	Greene	9 95
Morristown	16 00	Oxford	10 45
Dover	15 90	Norwich	10 80
Hackettstown	15 15	Sherburne	11 25
Washington	14 75	Waterville	12 10
Water Gap	13 95	Vestal	8 65
Stroudsburg	13 75	Owego	8 00
Scranton	11 20	Ithaca	8 55
Pittston	11 20	Waverly	7 25
Kingston	11 35	Elmira	6 50
Wilkesbarre	11 35	Corning	6 25
Plymouth	11 50	Bath	5 25
Nanticoke	11 75	Atlanta	4 60
Shickshinny	12 30	Wayland	4 25
Berwick	12 90	Dansville	4 00
Bloomsburg	13 50	Mount Morris	3 50

*EXCURSION NO. 37.—NIAGARA FALLS AND RETURN.

Delaware, Lack. & Western R. R .to Buffalo.
N. Y. Central & Hudson River R. R.to Niagara Falls.
N. Y. Central & Hudson River R. R.to New York.
From New York...........$17.00

*EXCURSION NO. 46.—NIAGARA FALLS AND RETURN.

Delaware, Lack. & Western R. R....to Buffalo.
N. Y. Lake Erie & Western R. R....to Niagara Falls.
N. Y. Lake Erie & Western R. R ...to New York.
From New York...........$16.00

*EXCURSION NO. 315.—NIAGARA FALLS AND RETURN.

Delaware, Lack. & Western R. R.... to Buffalo.
N. Y. Lake Erie & Western R. R....to Niagara Falls.
West Shore Railroad................to New York.
From New York...........$16.00

EXCURSION NO. 387.—NIAGARA FALLS AND RETURN.

Del., Lack. & Western R. R ... to Corning.
Fall Brook Ry. Co (via Watkins),to Penn Yan.
Lake Keuka Nav. Co.'s Steamers to Hammondsport
Bath & Hammondsport R. R..... to Bath.
Delaware, Lack. & Western R. R.to Buffalo.
N. Y. Central & Hud River R. R.to Niagara Falls.
N. Y. Central & Hud River R. R..to Buffalo
Delaware, Lack. & Western R. R.to Starting point.

EXCURSION NO. 388.—REVERSE OF THE PRECEDING

THROUGH RATES.

New York	$17 00	Binghamton	$10 40
Paterson	17 00	Greene	11 20
Newark	17 00	Oxford	11 75
Morristown	17 00	Norwich	12 05
Dover	17 00	Sherburne	12 30
Hackettstown	16 40	Waterville	13 35
Washington	16 00	Owego	9 60
Water Gap	15 15	Waverly	8 80
Stroudsburg	15 00	Elmira	8 10
Scranton	12 85	Atlanta	7 50
Pittston	13 25	Wayland	7 50
Kingston	13 55	Dansville	7 50
Wilkesbarre	13 55	Mount Morris	7 50

*EXCURSION NO. 44.—NIAGARA FALLS AND RETURN.

Delaware, Lack. & Western R. R ..to Buffalo.
N. Y. Central & Hud River R. R...to Niagara Falls.
N. Y. Central & Hud. River R. R...to Albany.
Day Line Hudson River Steamers. to New York.
From New York..... .. $16.15

*EXCURSION NO. 45.—NIAGARA FALLS AND RETURN.

Delaware, Lack. & Western R. R...to Buffalo.
N. Y. Central & Hud. River R. R...to Niagara Falls.
N. Y. Central & Hud. River R. R....to Schenectady.
Delaware & Hudson Canal Co......to Saratoga.
Delaware & Hudson Canal Co......to Troy
N. Y. Central & Hud.River R. R....to New York.
From New York..........$18.70

*EXCURSION NO. 316.—NIAGARA FALLS AND RETURN.

Delaware, Lack. & Western R. R...to Buffalo.
N. Y. Central & Hud. River R. R...to Niagara Falls.
N. Y. Central & Hud. River R. R....to Schenectady.
Delaware & Hudson Canal Co.......to Saratoga.
Delaware & Hudson Canal Co.... ..to Albany.
West Shore Railroad................to New York.
From New York..........$18.80

*EXCURSION NO. 317.—NIAGARA FALLS AND RETURN.

Delaware, Lack, & Western R. R...to Buffalo.
N. Y. Central & Hud. River R. R....to Niagara Falls.
N. Y. Central & Hud. River R. R ...to Schenectady.
Delaware & Hudson Canal Co......to Saratoga.
Delaware & Hudson Canal Co... ...to Albany.
Day Line Hudson River Steamers..to New York.
From New York............$17.70

*EXCURSION NO. 318 —NIAGARA FALLS AND RETURN.

Delaware, Lack., & Western R R. to Buffalo.
N. Y. Central & Hud. River R. R. to Niagara Falls.
N. Y. Central & Hud. River R. R to Lewiston.
Rome, Watert'n & Ogdenb'g R. R. to Clayton.
Thousand Island Steamboat Co....to Alexandria Bay
Thousand Island Steamboat Co... to Clayton.
Rome, Watert'n & Ogdenb'g R. R.to Utica.
N. Y. Central & Hud. River R. R...to New York.
From New York........... $23.60

*EXCURSION NO. 319.—NIAGARA FALLS AND RETURN.

Delaware, Lack. & Western R. R.to Buffalo.
N. Y. Central & Hud. River R. R.to Niagara Falls.
N. Y. Central & Hud. River R. R.to Lewiston.
Rome, Watert'n & Ogdenb'g R. R. to Clayton.
Thousand Island Steamboat Co....to Alexandria Bay.
Thousand Island Steamboat Co...to Clayton.
Rome, Water'n & Ogdenb'g R. R. to Utica.
West Shore Railroad..............to New York.
From New York..........$23.60.

* NOTE.—Excursions Nos. 37, 44, 45, 46, 315, 316, 317, 318, and 319, may be sold from any Line Station on the Morris and Essex Division, Main Line or Buffalo Division, at the same rates as from New York. To make up round-trip tickets from such Line Stations agents will issue in connection with these tickets Form C E, reading from " New York to Station stamped on Back," which, in connection with the tickets ending in New York, will make the complete round trip from the starting point.
These Form tickets may be issued from other Line Stations in the same manner, but agents will charge in addition to the rates from New York, as follows : Pittston, 40c.; Kingston, 80c.; Wilkesbarre, 85c.; Plymouth, 90c.; Nanticoke, $1.05; Shickshinny, $1 45; Berwick, $1.85; Bloomsburg, $2.35; Danville, $2.85; Greene, 80c ; Oxford, $1.40; Norwich, $1.70; Cortland, $1.75 ; and Ithaca, $1.40.

EXCURSION NO. 40.—NIAGARA FALLS AND RETURN.

Del. Lack. & Western R. R .. .to Buffalo.
N. Y. Cen, & Hud. River R. R.. to Niagara Falls.
N. Y. Cen. & Hud River R. R. to Utica.
Del. Lack. & Western R. R.....to Richfield Springs.
Del. Lack. & Western R. R.....to starting point.

SUMMER EXCURSION ROUTES AND RATES. 143

EXCURSION No. 41.—REVERSE OF THE PRECEDING.
THROUGH RATES.
New York	$19 15	Binghamton	$11 65
Paterson	19 15	Greene	11 65
Newark	19 15	Oxford	11 65
Morristown	18 85	Norwich	11 65
Dover	18 45	Sherburne	11 65
Hackettstown	17 65	Waterville	11 65
Washington	17 25	Owego	11 65
Water Gap	16 45	Ithaca	13 00
Stroudsburg	16 25	Waverly	11 65
Scranton	14 10	Elmira	11 65
Pittston	14 50	Corning	11 65
Kingston	14 80	Bath	11 65
Wilkesbarre	14 80		

EXCURSION No. 42.—NIAGARA FALLS AND RETURN.
Delaware, Lack. & Western R. R ...to Buffalo.
N. Y. Central & Hudson River R. R.to Niagara Falls
N. Y. Central & Hud. River R. R....to Utica.
Delaware, Lack. & Western R. R....to starting point.

EXCURSION No. 47.—REVERSE OF THE PRECEDING.
THROUGH RATES.
New York	$18 25	Binghamton	$10 75
Paterson	18 25	Greene	10 75
Newark	18 25	Oxford	10 75
Morristown	17 95	Norwich	10 75
Dover	17 45	Sherburne	10 75
Hackettstown	16 75	Waterville	10 75
Washington	16 35	Owego	10 75
Water Gap	15 55	Ithaca	12 10
Stroudsburg	15 35	Waverly	10 75
Scranton	13 20	Elmira	10 75
Pittston	13 60	Corning	10 75
Kingston	13 90	Bath	10 75
Wilkesbarre	13 90		

EXCURSION No. 149 —NIAGARA FALLS AND RETURN.
Delaware, Lack. & Western R. R...to Buffalo.
N. Y. Central & Hud. River R. R....to Niagara Falls.
N. Y. Central & Hud. River R. R....to Syracuse.
Delaware, Lack. & Western R R....to starting point.

EXCURSION No. 150.—REVERSE OF THE PRECEDING.
THROUGH RATES.
New York	$16 00	Stroudsburg	$13 95
Paterson	16 00	Scranton	11 80
Newark	16 00	Pittston	12 20
Morristown	16 00	Kingston	12 50
Dover	16 00	Wilkesbarre	12 50
Hackettstown	15 30	Binghamton	9 35
Washington	14 95	Cortland	9 35
Water Gap	14 10		

EXCURSION No. 38.—NIAGARA FALLS AND RETURN.
Delaware, Lack. & Western R. R...to Buffalo.
N. Y. Central & Hud. River R. R....to Niagara Falls.
N. Y. Central & Hud River R. R. } to Cayuga.
(via Clifton Springs) ....
Cayuga Lake Steamer ....to Ithaca.
Delaware, Lack. & Western R. R... to starting point.

EXCURSION No. 39.—REVERSE OF THE PRECEDING.
THROUGH RATES.
New York	$17 00	Wilkesbarre	$12 70
Paterson	17 00	Binghamton	0 50
Newark	17 00	Greene	10 35
Morristown	16 80	Oxford	11 10
Dover	16 30	Norwich	11 25
Hackettstown	15 60	Sherburne	11 75
Washington	15 20	Waterville	12 55
Water Gap	14 35	Owego	8 70
Stroudsburg	14 20	Waverly	8 70
Scranton	12 10	Elmira	8 70
Pittston	12 40	Corning	8 70
Kingston	12 70	Bath	8 70

EXCURSION No. 48.—NIAGARA FALLS AND RETURN.
Delaware, Lack. & Western R. R....to Buffalo.
N. Y. Central & Hud. River R. R....to Niagara Falls.
N. Y. Central & Hud River R. R....to Geneva.
Seneca Lake steamer..................to Watkins
Penn. R. R. (via Haven Glen).......to Elmira.
Delaware, Lack. & Western R. R ...to starting point.

EXCURSION No. 49.—REVERSE OF THE PRECEDING.
THROUGH RATES.
New York	$17 00	Binghamton	$9 75
Paterson	17 00	Greene	10 55
Newark	17 00	Oxford	11 05
Morristown	16 75	Norwich	11 45
Dover	16 25	Sherburne	11 90
Hackettstown	15 50	Waterville	12 75
Washington	15 15	Owego	8 85
Water Gap	14 35	Ithaca	10 25
Stroudsburg	14 15	Waverly	7 85
Scranton	12 00	Elmira	7 00
Pittston	12 35	Corning	7 00
Kingston	12 65	Bath	7 00
Wilkesbarre	12 65		

EXCURSION No. 134.—NIAGARA FALLS AND RETURN.
Del. Lack. & Western R. R......to Buffalo.
N. Y. Cent. & Hud. River R. R...to Niagara Falls.
N. Y. Cent. & Hud. River R. R...to Lewiston.
Rome, Watert'n & Ogdenb'g R. R.to Clayton.
Thousand Island Steamboat Co...to Clayton.
Thousand Island Steamboat Co...to Alexandria Bay.
Thousand Island Steamboat Co...to Clayton.
Rome, Watert'n & Ogdenb'g R. R.to Utica.
Del. Lack. & Western R. R ......to starting point.

EXCURSION No. 135.—REVERSE OF THE PRECEDING.
THROUGH RATES.
New York	$23 60	Oxford	$17 15
Paterson	23 60	Norwich	17 15
Newark	23 60	Sherburne	17 15
Morristown	23 60	Waterville	17 15
Dover	23 60	Owego	17 15
Hackettstown	23 15	Waverly	17 15
Washington	22 75	Elmira	17 15
Water Gap	21 95	Corning	17 15
Stroudsburg	21 75	Bath	17 15
Scranton	19 60	Atlanta	17 15
Pittston	20 05	Wayland	17 15
Kingston	20 30	Dansville	17 15
Wilkesbarre	20 30	Mount Morris	17 15
Binghamton	17 15	Buffalo	17 15
Greene	17 15		

EXCURSION No. 51.—NIAGARA FALLS AND RETURN.
Delaware, Lack. & Western R. R..to Bath.
Bath & Hammondsport Railroad.to Hammondsport.
Lake Keuka Nav. Co.'s Steamers .to Penn Yan.
Pennsylvania Railroad............to Canandaigua.
N. Y. Cent. & Hud. River R R....to Niagara Falls.
N. Y. Cent. & Hud. River R. R....to Buffalo.
Delaware, Lack. & Western R. R.to starting point.

EXCURSION No. 50.—REVERSE OF THE PRECEDING.
THROUGH RATES.
New York	$17 00	Wilkesbarre	$12 85
Paterson	17 00	Binghamton	9 70
Newark	17 00	Greene	10 55
Morristown	17 00	Oxford	11 10
Dover	16 50	Norwich	11 40
Hackettstown	15 55	Sherburne	11 85
Washington	15 35	Waterville	12 70
Water Gap	14 55	Owego	8 80
Stroudsburg	14 35	Ithaca	10 30
Scranton	12 25	Waverly	7 80
Pittston	12 55	Elmira	6 95
Kingston	12 25	Corning	6 95

EXCURSION NO. 161.—NIAGARA FALLS AND
RETURN.
Delaware, Lack. & Western R. R....to Buffalo.
N. Y. Central & Hud. River R. R....to Niagara Falls.
N. Y. Central & Hud. River R. R....to Geneva.
F. B. C. Co.'s R. R. (*via* Watk's Glen)to Corning.
Del. Lack. & Western R. R..........to starting point.

EXCURSION NO. 162.—REVERSE OF THE
PRECEDING.

THROUGH RATES.

New York	$17 30	Binghamton	$9 80
Paterson	17 30	Greene	10 60
Newark	17 30	Oxford	11 10
Morristown	17 00	Norwich	11 45
Dover	16 50	Sherburne	11 90
Hackettstown	15 80	Waterville	12 75
Washington	15 40	Owego	9 00
Water Gap	14 55	Ithaca	10 35
Stroudsburg	14 40	Waverly	8 20
Scranton	12 25	Elmira	7 50
Pittston	12 65	Corning	6 90
Kingston	12 95	Bath	6 90
Wilkesbarre	12 95		

EXCURSION NO. 163.—NIAGARA FALLS AND
RETURN.
Delaware, Lack. & Western R. R....to Buffalo.
N. Y. Cent. & Hud. River R R.......to Niagara Falls.
N. Y. Cent. & Hud. River R. R......to Canadaigua.
Pennsylvania Railroad...............to Penn Yan.
F. B. C. Co, R. R.(*via* Wat. Glen)....to Corning.
Del.. Lack. & Western R. R.........to starting point

EXCURSION NO. 164.—REVERSE OF THE
PRECEDING.

THROUGH RATES

New York	$17 60	Binghamton	$9 65
Paterson	17 60	Greene	10 45
Newark	17 60	Oxford	10 95
Morristown	16 85	Norwich	11 30
Dover	16 40	Sherburne	11 75
Hackettstown	15 65	Waterville	12 60
Washington	15 25	Owego	8 85
Water Gap	14 40	Ithaca	10 20
Stroudsburg	14 25	Waverly	8 10
Scranton	12 10	Elmira	7 40
Pittston	12 50	Corning	6 75
Kingston	12 80	Bath	6 75
Wilkesbarre	12 80		

NORTH CONWAY, N. H. (WHITE MOUNTAINS).

This village is situated on a terrace just above the intervale of the Saco. The valley is bounded on the west by the long Mote Mountain, on the East by the Rattlesnake Ridge, while to the North the Mountains part sufficiently to enable one to see the whole White Mountain range.

EXC. S T 44.—BOSTON TO NORTH CONWAY
AND RETURN.
Boston & Maine R. R....to North Conway and return
Sold only in connection with summer Excursion
Ticket to, or passing through Boston.
Rate..............$6.50

OAK BLUFFS, MASS.
(See COTTAGE CITY, MASS.)

OCEAN GROVE (Asbury Park), N. J.

What is now the resort of hundreds of thousands of summer visitors was originally (and that but a few years since) a camp ground of members of the Methodist church. To-day it is a splendid summer city by the sea. The rules prohibiting the sale of intoxicating liquors at any time, and forbidding driving, boating, bathing, etc., on Sunday are strictly enforced, and that a resting place with such moral observances is very popular with a large proportion of the people is amply attested by the unparalleled prosperity to be witnessed at Ocean Grove.

*EXCURSION NO. 172.—OCEAN GROVE AND
RETURN.
Delaware, Lack. & Western R. R ...to New York.
Pennsylvania Railroad..............to Ocean Grove.
Returning *via* same route.

*EXCURSION NO. 23.—OCEAN GROVE AND
RETURN
Delaware, Lack. & Western R. R....to New York.
Central R. R. of New Jersey Strs.....to Sandy Hook.
Central Railroad of New Jersey......to West End.
New York & Long Branch R. R......to Ocean Grove.
Returning *via* same route.

*EXCURSION NO. 24.—OCEAN GROVE AND
RETURN.
Delaware, Lack & Western R. R .. to New York.
Central Railroad of New Jersey.....to Perth Amboy.
New York & Long Branch R R . to Ocean Grove.
Returning *via* same route.

THROUGH RATES FOR EITHER EXCURSION.

Morristown	$3 10	Oxford	$10 85
Dover	3 60	Norwich	10 85
Hackettstown	4 30	Sherburne	11 85
Washington	4 70	Waterville	11 85
Water Gap	5 55	Cortland	11 85
Stroudsburg	5 70	Syracuse	11 85
Scranton	7 75	Oswego	11 85
Pittston	8 25	Owego	10 70
Kingston	8 80	Ithaca	12 35
Wilkesbarre	8 85	Waverly	11 45
Plymouth	8 85	Elmira	12 10
Nanticoke	8 75	Corning	12 75
Shickshinny	9 20	Bath	13 60
Berwick	9 55	Atlanta	14 75
Bloomsburg	9 90	Wayland	15 05
Danville	10 05	Dansville	15 55
Binghamton	9 85	Mount Morris	15 55
Greene	10 65	Buffalo	17 85

EXCURSION NO. 22.—OCEAN GROVE AND
RETURN.
Del. Lack. & Western R. R.........to New Hampton.
Central Railroad of New Jersey.....to Perth Amboy.
New York & Long Branch R. R.   to Ocean Grove.
Returning *via* same route.

THROUGH RATES.

Water Gap	$4 70	Sherburne	$11 55
Stroudsburg	4 85	Waterville	11 85
Scranton	7 00	Cortland	11 20
Pittston	7 35	Syracuse	11 85
Kingston	7 65	Oswego	11 85
Wilkesbarre	7 65	Owego	11 45
Plymouth	7 80	Ithaca	12 35
Nanticoke	7 95	Waverly	11 45
Shickshinny	8 30	Elmira	12 10
Berwick	8 75	Corning	12 75
Bloomsburg	9 25	Bath	13 60
Danville	9 70	Atlanta	14 75
Binghamton	9 85	Wayland	15 05
Greene	10 25	Dansville	15 55
Oxford	10 80	Mount Morris	15 55
Norwich	10 85	Buffalo	17 85

SUMMER EXCURSION ROUTES AND RATES. 145

EXCURSION NO. 30.—OCEAN GROVE AND RETURN.

Del. Lack. & Western R. R........to New Hampton.
Central Railroad of New Jersey . to Perth Amboy.
New York & Long Branch R. R....to Ocean Grove.
New York & Long Branch R. R....to Perth Amboy.
Central Railroad of New Jersey....to New York.
Del. Lack. & Western R R ....to starting point.

*EXCURSION NO. 274.—REVERSE OF THE PRECEDING.

THROUGH RATES.

Water Gap.......	$ 5 20	Syracuse...........	$12 00
Stroudsburg.......	5 35	Oswego..........	13 40
Scranton..........	7 50	Owego...........	10 80
Pittston..........	7 85	Ithaca...........	12 15
Kingston.........	8 15	Waverly..........	11 50
Wilkesbarre.......	8 15	Elmira...........	12 20
Binghamton.......	9 95	Corning..........	12 85
Greene...........	10 75	Bath............	13 70
Oxford...........	11 30	Atlanta..........	14 50
Norwich..........	11 60	Wayland.........	14 70
Sherburne........	12 05	Dansville........	15 00
Waterville........	12 90	Mount Morris.....	15 60
Cortland.........	11 70	Buffalo..........	18 10

*Good for passage between Ocean Grove and New York, either *via* the boat and trains of the Sandy Hook route, or the trains of either the Central Railroad of New Jersey or the Pennsylvania Railroad.

OLD ORCHARD BEACH, ME.

The name is derived from an old apple orchard a few miles from Saco, Me. The beach, however, is the great attraction, being rated the finest in New England. Having an average width of three hundred feet at low tide, and extending about ten miles in length, it offers not only splendid bathing facilities but a charming drive.

EXCURSION S. T. 12.—BOSTON TO OLD ORCHARD BEACH AND RETURN.

Boston & Maine Railroad { to Old Orchard Beach and return.

Sold only in connection with Summer Excursion Ticket to, or passing through Boston.
Rate.................$4.00

OLD POINT COMFORT, VA.
(Fortress Monroe.)

Peace has here erected monumental reminders of her victories in the Soldier's Home, National Normal School, etc., interesting accompaniments to a sojourner, whether he hies him here to rest and recreation from business cares or in search of restored health. A mammoth hotel, of the first-class, supplies every creature comfort; the broad bay offers diversions that are competed for by the picturesque precincts of the fortress.

Music, the dance, bright uniforms, ships of war and peace, add life to the splendid picture, and though far away from the everyday activity of city life, monotony is unknown.

EXCURSION NO. 170 Y.—OLD POINT COMFORT, VA.

Limited to three (3) months from date of sale.

Del., Lack. & Western R. R....to Manunka Chunk.
Pennsylvania Railroad........to Delmar.
N. Y. Phila. & Norfolk R. R ...to Old Point Comfort.
Returning *via* same route.

EXCURSION NO. 168 Y.—OLD POINT COMFORT, VA.

Limited to three(3) months from date of sale.

Del. Lack. & Western R. R....to Manunka Chunk.
Pennsylvania Railroad .....to Baltimore.
Baltimore Steam Packet Co.....to Old Point Comfort.
Returning *via* same route.

THROUGH RATES.

Stroudsburg........	$15 30	Syracuse.........	$21 45
Scranton..........	15 30	Fulton...........	22 45
Pittston...........	15 30	Oswego..........	22 85
Kingston..........	15 30	Owego...........	18 70
Wilkesbarre.......	15 30	Ithaca...........	20 05
Montrose..........	17 60	Waverly..........	18 70
Binghamton.......	17 80	Elmira...........	18 70
Greene............	18 60	Corning..........	19 65
Oxford............	19 15	Bath.............	20 90
Norwich...........	19 50	Atlanta...........	22 00
Sherburne........	19 95	Wayland..........	22 40
Waterville.........	20 80	Dansville.........	22 80
Richfield Springs...	21 95	Mount Morris.....	23 00
Utica	21 60	Buffalo...........	25 00
Cortland..........	19 55		

EXCURSION 171 Y.—OLD POINT COMFORT, VA.

Limited to three (3) months from date of sale.

Del. Lack. & Western R. R ...to New York.
Pennsylvania Railroad ...to Delmar.
N. Y. Phila. & Norfolk R. R...to Old Point Comfort.
Returning *via* same route.

EXCURSION 169 Y.—OLD POINT COMFORT, VA.

Limited to three (3) months from date of sale.

Del. Lack. & Western R. R....to New York.
Pennsylvania Railroad........to Baltimore.
Baltimore Steam Packet Co....to Old Point Comfort.
Returning *via* same route.

THROUGH RATES.

Summit..........	$16 40	Richfield Springs..	$26 35
Morristown.......	16 85	Utica............	24 85
Dover	17 35	Cortland.........	25 60
Hackettstown.....	18 05	Syracuse.........	25 60
Washington.......	18 45	Fulton...........	25 60
Stroudsburg.......	19 45	Oswego..........	25 60
Scranton..........	21 60	Owego...........	24 45
Pittston..........	22 00	Ithaca...........	25 60
Kingston.........	22 40	Waverly..........	25 20
Wilkesbarre......	22 00	Elmira...........	25 85
Montrose.........	23 80	Corning..........	26 50
Binghamton......	23 20	Bath............	27 35
Greene...........	24 40	Atlanta..........	28 50
Oxford...........	24 60	Wayland.........	28 80
Norwich..........	24 60	Dansville.........	29 30
Sherburne........	24 85	Mount Morris.....	29 30
Waterville........	24 85	Buffalo...........	31 60

EXCURSION 382 Y.—OLD POINT COMFORT, VA.

Limited to three (3) months from date of sale.

Del. Lack. & Western R. R....to Manunka Chunk.
Pennsylvania Railroad..... .to Washington.
Norfolk & Wash. D.C Steam-} to Old Point Comfort.
boat Co.........
Returning *via* same route.

DELAWARE, LACKAWANNA & WESTERN R. R.

THROUGH RATES.

Stroudsburg....... $15 30	Syracuse........... $21 00	Summit........... $20 80	Richfield Springs.. $30 75
Scranton.......... 15 30	Fulton............. 22 00	Morristown 21 25	Utica............. 29 25
Pittston.......... 15 30	Oswego............ 22 40	Dover............. 21 75	Cortland.......... 30 00
Kingston......... 15 30	Owego............. 18 70	Hackettstown...... 22 45	Syracuse.......... 30 00
Wilkesbarre...... 15 30	Ithaca............. 20 05	Washington....... 22 85	Fulton............ 30 00
Montrose......... 17 60	Waverly........... 18 70	Stroudsburg....... 23 85	Oswego........... 30 00
Binghamton...... 17 80	Elmira............. 18 70	Scranton.......... 26 00	Owego............ 28 85
Greene........... 18 60	Corning............ 19 65	Pittston........... 26 35	Ithaca............ 30 50
Oxford........... 19 15	Bath............... 20 90	Kingston.......... 26 80	Waverly........... 29 60
Norwich.......... 19 50	Atlanta............ 22 00	Wilkesbarre....... 26 85	Elmira............ 30 25
Sherburne........ 19 95	Wayland........... 22 40	Montrose.......... 28 20	Corning........... 30 90
Waterville........ 20 80	Dansville.......... 22 80	Binghamton 28 00	Bath.............. 31 75
Richfield Springs.. 21 95	Mount Morris 23 00	Greene........... 28 80	Atlanta........... 32 90
Utica............. 21 60	Buffalo............ 25 00	Oxford............ 29 00	Wayland.......... 33 20
Cortland.......... 19 55		Norwich........... 29 00	Dansville......... 33 70
		Sherburne......... 29 25	Mount Morris..... 33 70
		Waterville......... 29 25	Buffalo............ 36 00

EXCURSION 383 Y.—OLD POINT COMFORT, VA.

Limited to three (3) months from date of sale.

Del. Lack. & Western R. R....to New York.
Pennsylvania Railroad........to Washington.
Norfolk & Wash. D. C. Steamboat Co. .... } to Old Point Comfort.
Returning *via* same route.

THROUGH RATES.

Summit........... $16 40	Richfield Springs.. $26 35	New York......... $21 25	Berwick........... $20 05
Morristown....... 16 85	Utica.............. 24 85	Paterson.......... 21 25	Bloomsburg....... 20 60
Dover............ 17 35	Cortland.......... 25 60	Newark........... 21 25	Danville.......... 21 00
Hackettstown..... 18 05	Syracuse.......... 25 60	Morristown 21 25	Binghamton...... 15 80
Washington...... 18 45	Fulton............. 25 60	Dover............. 21 25	Greene........... 15 05
Stroudsburg...... 19 45	Oswego........... 25 60	Hackettstown..... 21 25	Oxford........... 14 50
Scranton......... 21 60	Owego............ 24 45	Washington...... 21 25	Norwich.......... 14 20
Pittston.......... 22 00	Ithaca............. 26 10	Water Gap 20 60	Sherburne........ 13 75
Kingston......... 22 40	Waverly........... 25 20	Stroudsburg...... 20 40	Waterville........ 12 90
Wilkesbarre...... 22 45	Elmira............. 25 85	Scranton......... 18 30	Richfield Springs.. 13 50
Montrose......... 23 80	Corning........... 26 50	Pittston.......... 18 70	Owego............ 16 65
Binghamton...... 23 60	Bath.............. 27 35	Kingston......... 19 00	Waverly.......... 17 40
Greene........... 24 40	Atlanta............ 28 50	Wilkesbarre...... 19 00	Elmira............ 18 10
Oxford........... 24 60	Wayland........... 28 80	Plymouth......... 19 15	Corning........... 18 60
Norwich.......... 24 60	Dansville.......... 29 30	Nanticoke......... 19 25	Bath.............. 19 60
Sherburne........ 24 85	Mount Morris..... 29 30	Shickshinny....... 19 60	
Waterville........ 24 85	Buffalo............ 31 60		

EXCURSION 384 Y.—OLD POINT COMFORT, VA.

Limited to three (3) months from date of sale.

Del. Lack. & Western R. R....to Manunka Chunk.
Pennsylvania Railroad........to Quantico.
Rich. Fred. & P. R. R........to Richmond.
Ches. & Ohio R. R............to Old Point Comfort.
Returning *via* same route.

THROUGH RATES.

Stroudsburg....... $21 45	Syracuse........... $27 10		
Scranton.......... 21 45	Fulton............. 28 10		
Pittston.......... 21 45	Oswego............ 28 50		
Kingston......... 21 45	Owego............. 24 85		
Wilkesbarre...... 21 45	Ithaca............. 26 25		
Montrose......... 23 75	Waverly........... 24 85		
Binghamton 23 95	Elmira............. 24 85		
Greene........... 24 70	Corning........... 25 80		
Oxford........... 25 25	Bath.............. 27 05		
Norwich.......... 25 60	Atlanta............ 28 20		
Sherburne........ 26 05	Wayland........... 28 55		
Waterville........ 26 90	Dansville.......... 28 95		
Richfield Springs.. 28 05	Mount Morris..... 29 65		
Utica............. 27 75	Buffalo............ 31 45		
Cortland.......... 25 65			

EXCURSION 385 Y.—OLD POINT COMFORT, VA.

Limited to three (3) months from date of sale.

Del. Lack. & Western R. R....to New York.
Pennsylvania Railroad........to Quantico.
Rich. Fred. & P. R. R........to Richmond.
Ches. & Ohio R. R............to Old Point Comfort.
Returning *via* same route.

OTTAWA, ONT.

EXCURSION No. 320.—OTTAWA AND RETURN.

Del. Lack. & Western R. R........to Utica.
Rome, Watert'n & Ogdenb'g R. R.to Clayton.
R. & O. Navi. Co.'s Steamers......to Alexandria Bay.
R. & O. Navi. Co.'s Steamers..... to Prescott.
Canadian Pacific R. R............to Ottawa.
Returning *via* same route.
(Good until October 1st.)

EXCURSION No. 321.—OTTAWA AND RETURN.

Del. Lack. & Western R. R..... to Syracuse.
Rome, Watert'n & Ogdenb'g R. R to Clayton.
R. & O. Navi. Co.'s Steamers.....to Alexandria Bay.
R. & O. Navi. Co.'s Steamers.....to Prescott.
Canadian Pacific Railway.......to Ottawa.
Returning *via* same route.
(Good until October 1st.)

THROUGH RATES.

New York......... $21 25	Wilkesbarre....... $18 35		
Paterson.......... 21 25	Plymouth.......... 18 50		
Newark 21 25	Nanticoke......... 18 05		
Morristown 21 25	Shickshinny....... 19 00		
Dover............. 21 25	Berwick........... 19 40		
Hackettstown..... 21 20	Bloomsburg....... 19 95		
Washington...... 20 80	Danville.......... 20 40		
Water Gap........ 20 00	Binghamton...... 15 20		
Stroudsburg..... 19 80	Cortland.......... 13 50		
Scranton......... 17 70	Owego............ 16 00		
Pittston.......... 18 05	Waverly........... 16 50		
Kingston......... 18 35	Elmira............ 16 50		

EXCURSION S. T. 14.—PRESCOTT TO OTTAWA AND RETURN.

Canadian Pacific Railway.......to Ottawa and return.
Sold only in connection with Summer Excursion.
Ticket to, or passing through Prescott.
Rate $3.50

SUMMER EXCURSION ROUTES AND RATES. 147

PLATTSBURG, N. Y. (Lake Champlain.)

EXCURSION S. T. 47.—SARATOGA TO PLATTSBURG AND RETURN.

Delaware & Hudson Canal Co.....to Ft. Ticonderoga.
Delaware & Hudson Canal Co. or }
Lake Champlain Steamer . } to Plattsburg.
Returning via same route.
Rate...............$7.80

EXCURSION S. T. 48.—SARATOGA TO PLATTSBURG AND RETURN.

Delaware & Hudson Canal Co.....to Ft. Ticonderoga.
Delaware & Hudson Canal Co or }
Lake Champlain Steamer ... } to Plattsburg.
Delaware & Hudson Canal Co.or }
Lake Champlain Steamer.... } to Ft. Ticonderoga.
Delaware & Hudson Canal Co...to Baldwin.
Lake George Steamer.........to Caldwell.
Delaware & Hudson Canal Co.....to Saratoga.

EXCURSION S. T. 49.—REVERSE OF THE PRECEDING.

Rate for either Excursion........$10.15

PLYMOUTH, MASS.

EXCURSION NO. 287.—PLYMOUTH AND RETURN.

Del. Lack., & Western R. R............to New York.
Fall River Line Steamers............to Fall River.
Old Colony Railroad.................to Plymouth.
Returning via same route.

THROUGH RATES.

Morristown........$ 9 25	Waterville.........$18 00
Dover............. 9 75	Cortland.......... 18 00
Hackettstown..... 10 45	Syracuse.......... 18 00
Washington....... 10 85	Oswego............ 18 00
Water Gap........ 11 70	Owego............. 16 85
Stroudsburg....... 11 85	Ithaca............ 18 50
Scranton 14 00	Waverly........... 17 60
Pittston.......... 14 40	Elmira............ 18 25
Kingston.......... 15 15	Corning........... 18 90
Wilkesbarre....... 15 20	Bath.............. 19 75
Binghamton....... 16 00	Atlanta............ 20 90
Greene............ 16 80	Wayland........... 21 25
Oxford............ 17 00	Dansville.......... 21 70
Norwich........... 17 00	Mount Morris...... 21 70
Sherburne......... 17 70	Buffalo............ 24 00

POCASSET, MASS.

EXCURSION NO. 288.—POCASSET AND RETURN.

Del., Lack. & Western R. R............to New York.
Fall River Line Steamers............to Fall River.
Old Colony Railroad..................to Pocasset.
Returning via same route.

THROUGH RATES.

Morristown........$ 8 25	Waterville.........$17 00
Dover 8 75	Cortland.......... 17 00
Hackettstown..... 9 45	Syracuse.......... 17 00
Washington....... 9 85	Oswego............ 17 00
Water Gap........ 10 70	Owego 15 85
Stroudsburg....... 10 85	Ithaca............ 17 50
Scranton 13 00	Waverly........... 16 60
Pittston.......... 13 40	Elmira............ 17 25
Kingston.......... 14 15	Corning........... 17 90
Wilkesbarre....... 14 20	Bath.............. 18 75
Binghamton....... 15 00	Atlanta............ 19 90
Greene............ 15 80	Wayland........... 20 35
Oxford............ 16 00	Dansville.......... 20 70
Norwich........... 16 00	Mount Morris...... 20 70
Sherburne......... 16 70	Buffalo............ 23 00

POCONO SUMMIT, PA.

LOCAL EXCURSION.
(Good for continuous passage only.)

THROUGH RATES.

*New York.........$4 65	Shickshinny........$3 00
Passaic........... 4 50	Berwick............ 3 30
Paterson.......... 4 35	Bloomsburg........ 3 60
Boonton 3 80	Danville........... 3 95
*Newark........... 4 65	Great Bend........ 3 20
*Roseville Ave..... 4 65	Binghamton....... 3 80
Orange........... 4 60	Greene............ 4 55
Mountain 4 50	Oxford............. 5 10
South Orange..... 4 45	Norwich........... 5 40
Milburn........... 4 30	Sherburne.......... 5 85
Short Hills........ 4 25	Waterville 6 70
Summit........... 4 25	Richfield Springs.. 7 90
Chatham 4 05	Utica.............. 7 60
Madison.......... 3 95	Cortland........... 5 50
Morristown........ 3 80	Syracuse........... 6 95
Dover............. 3 30	Oswego............ 8 35
Andover........... 3 10	Owego............. 4 60
Newton........... 3 30	Ithaca 5 95
Franklin.......... 3 80	Waverly........... 5 35
Hackettstown...... 2 60	Elmira............ 6 05
Washington....... 2 20	Corning........... 6 65
Scranton 1 70	Bath............... 7 50
Pittston.......... 2 10	Atlanta............ 8 30
Kingston.......... 2 45	Wayland........... 8 55
Wilkesbarre....... 2 45	Dansville.......... 8 80
Plymouth 2 60	Mount Morris...... 9 40
Nauticoke......... 2 75	Buffalo............11 90

* Tickets good until used.

PROFILE HOUSE, N. H. (White Mountains.)

The Profile House is the principal resort in the Franconia range, the feature in the locality being Mt. Lafayette (5,585 feet), Cannon, Bald, Liberty, Pleasant and others. Other peculiarities are Echo Lake, Eagle Cliff, Old Man of the Mountain, Profile Lake, the Plume, Pool, etc., etc. The house, though immense in size and placed at an elevation of 2,000 feet above sea level, is sunk into comparative insignificance, so small is it compared with the almost perpendicular mountains which rise up from its doors.

What is particularly striking here is the magnitude of everything. The air is, of course, pure as can be obtained; the drives are perfect in their roadbed and penetrate romantic regions.

EXCURSION S. T. 45.—BETHLEHEM JUNCTION TO PROFILE HOUSE AND RETURN.

Profile & Franconia Notch (to Profile House and
Railroad.......................{ return.
Sold only in connection with Summer Excursion Ticket to, or passing through Bethlehem Junction.
Rate...............$3.00

QUEBEC, P. Q.

Quebec, a great city of 75,000 inhabitants, is the only walled city in this country. It is triangular in form (St. Charles and St. Lawrence Rivers, and Plains of Abraham being the lines). There are really two towns—

DELAWARE, LACKAWANNA & WESTERN R. R.

upper and lower—the former being strongly fortified and elevated nearly four hundred feet above the latter.

It is quaint and antique in the extreme and strangers are naturally surprised to find so ancient a city in this part of the world. The citadel attracts every visitor to Quebec. Within the battlements there are more than forty acres, the wall surrounding which is about three miles long.

EXCURSION NO. 100 A.—TO QUEBEC.

Delaware, Lack. & Western R. R...to Buffalo.
N. Y. Central & Hud. River R. R...to Niagara Falls.
N. Y. Central & Hud. River R. R....to Lewiston.
Niagara Navigation Co.'s Steamer..to Toronto.
Canadian Pacific Railway............to Ottawa.
Canadian Pacific R'way, or Ottawa } to Montreal.
River Navi. Co.'s Steamer......
Grand Trunk Ry., or Richelieu & } to Quebec.
Ontario Nav. Co.'s Steamer....

EXCURSION NO. 101 A.—TO QUEBEC.

Delaware, Lack. & Western R. R...to Buffalo.
N. Y. Central & Hud. River R. R...to Niagara Falls.
N. Y. Central & Hud. River R. R .to Lewiston.
Niagara Navigation Co.'s Steamer..to Toronto.
Canadian Pacific Railway............to Ottawa.
Canadian Pacific Railway ....to Prescott.
Grand Trunk Ry., or Richelieu & } to Montreal.
Ontario Nav. Co.'s Steamer.....)
Grand Trunk Ry., or Richelieu & } to Quebec.
Ontario Nav. Co.'s Steamer.....)

EXCURSION NO. 102 A.—TO QUEBEC.

Delaware Lack., & Western R. R...to Buffalo.
N. Y. Central & Hud. River R. R....to Niagara Falls.
N. Y. Central & Hud. River R. R .to Lewiston.
Niagara Navigation Co.'s Steamer..to Toronto.
Grand Trunk Ry., or Richelieu & } to Kingston.
Ontario Nav. Co.,s Steamer.....)
Grand Trunk Ry., or Richelieu & } to Prescott.
Ontario Nav. Co.'s Steamer ..)
Grand Trunk Ry., or Richelieu & } to Montreal.
Ontario Nav. Co.'s Steamer.....)
Grand Trunk Ry., or Richelieu & } to Quebec.
Ontario Nav. Co.'s Steamer.....)

EXCURSION NO. 253 A.—TO QUEBEC.

Del., Lack. & Western R. R...to Buffalo.
N. Y. Lake Erie & W R. R.... to Suspension Bridge.
Grand Trunk Railway.........to Port Dalhousie.
Steamer "Empress of India "..to Toronto.
Canadian Pacific Railway........to Ottawa.
Canadian Pacific Ry., or Otta- } to Montreal.
wa River Nav. Co.'s Steamer)
Grand Trunk Ry., or Rich. & } to Quebec.
Ontario Nav. Co.'s Str.......)

EXCURSION NO. 254 A.—TO QUEBEC.

Del., Lack. & Western R. R...to Buffalo.
N. Y. Lake Erie & W. R. R....to Suspension Bridge.
Grand Trunk Railway.... .to Port Dalhousie.
Steamer "Empress of India "..to Toronto.
Canadian Pacific Railway ....to Ottawa.
Canadian Pacific Railway.....to Prescott.
Grand Trunk Ry., or Rich. & } to Montreal.
Ontario Nav. Co.'s Str .....)
Grand Trunk Ry., or Rich. & } to Quebec.
Ontario Nav. Co.'s Str.....)

EXCURSION NO. 255 A.—TO QUEBEC.

Del., Lack & Western R. R...to Buffalo.
N. Y. Lake Erie & W. R. R....to Suspension Bridge.
Grand Trunk Railway.........to Port Dalhousie.
Steamer "Empress of India "..to Toronto.
Grand Trunk Ry., or Rich. & } to Kingston.
Ontario Nav. Co.'s Str ....)
Grand Trunk Ry., or Rich. & } to Prescott.
Ontario Nav. Co.'s Str.....)

Grand Trunk Ry., or Rich., & } to Montreal.
Ontario Nav. Co.'s Str......)
Grand Trunk Ry , or Rich. & } to Quebec.
Ontario Nav. Co.'s Str......)

EXCURSION NO. 103 A.—TO QUEBEC.

Delaware Lack. & Western R. R....to Buffalo.
N. Y Central & Hud. River R. R.. to Niagara Falls.
Grand Trunk Railway......... to Toronto.
Grand Trunk Ry., or Richelieu & } to Kingston.
Ontario Nav. Co.'s Str ....)
Grand Trunk Ry., or Richelieu & } to Prescott.
Ontario Nav. Co.'s Str ....)
Grand Trunk Ry., or Richelieu & } to Montreal.
Ontario Nav. Co.'s Str... ...)
Grand Trunk Ry., or Richelieu & } to Quebec.
Ontario Nav. Co 's Str..........)

EXCURSION NO. 137 A.—TO QUEBEC.

Del., Lack. & Western R. R ...to Buffalo.
N. Y. Central & Hud. River R. R..to Niagara Falls.
N. Y. Central & Hud. River R. R..to Lewiston.
Rome, Watertown & Ogdbg. R. R.to Clayton.
Rich. & Ontario Nav. Co.'s Strs...to Alexandria Bay.
Rich. & Ontario Nav. Co.'s Strs...to Montreal.
Grand Trunk Ry.,or Richelieu & } to Quebec.
Ontario Nav. Co.'s Strs........)
(Good until October 1st.)

THROUGH RATES.

FOR EXCURSIONS 100 A, 101 A, 102 A, 103 A, 137 A, 253 A, 254 A AND 255 A.

New York.........$22 50	Bloomsburg........$21 50
Paterson..... ..... 22 50	Danville......... 21 75
Newark 22 50	Binghamton..... 19 25
Morristown 22 50	Greene 19 55
Dover............. 22 50	Oxford........... 19 80
Hackettstown 22 15	Norwich.......... 19 95
Washington........ 21 95	Cortland......... 20 00
Water Gap......... 21 55	Owego........... 18 70
Stroudsburg....... 21 45	Ithaca 19 40
Scranton 20 35	Waverly......... 18 30
Pittston............ 20 55	Elmira 17 95
Kingston........... 20 70	Corning.......... 17 90
Wilkesbarre....... 20 70	Bath............. 17 75
Plymouth 20 80	Atlanta.. .... 17 20
Nanticoke......... 20 85	Wayland........ 17 10
Shickshinny........ 21 05	Dansville........ 16 90
Berwick 21 25	Mount Morris..... 16 55

EXCURSION NO. 105 A.—TO QUEBEC.

Del. Lack. & Western R. R.......to Utica.
Rome, Watertown & Ogdbg. R. R.to Clayton.
Rich. & Ontario Nav. Co.'s Strs....to Alexandria Bay.
Rich. & Ontario Nav. Co.'s Strs....to Montreal.
Grand Trunk Ry., or Richelieu & } to Quebec.
Ontario Nav. Co.'s Strs........)
(Good until October 1st.)

THROUGH RATES.

New York.........$16 50	Bloomsburg........$15 80
Paterson......... 16 50	Danville 16 00
Newark 16 50	Binghamton..... 13 40
Morristown........ 16 50	Greene 13 05
Dover............. 16 50	Oxford........... 12 75
Hackettstown...... 16 40	Norwich......... 12 60
Washington....... 16 25	Sherburne....... 12 40
Water Gap........ 15 80	Waterville....... 11 95
Stroudsburg....... 15 70	Richfield Springs... 12 25
Scranton 11 65	Cortland......... 13 85
Pittston........... 14 85	Owego........... 13 85
Kingston.......... 15 00	Ithaca 14 50
Wilkesbarre....... 15 00	Waverly......... 14 20
Plymouth 15 10	Elmira 14 30
Nanticoke......... 15 15	Corning 14 30
Shickshinny.. ... 15 30	Bath............ 14 90
Berwick 15 55

EXCURSION NO. 106 A.—TO QUEBEC.

Del., Lack. & Western R. R ... to Richfield Springs.
Del., Lack. & Western R. R....to Utica.
Rome, Watert'n & Ogdbg. R. R.to Clayton.
Rich. & Ontario Nav. Co.'s Strs..to Alexandria Bay.
Rich. & Ontario Nav. Co.'s Strs..to Montreal.
Grand Trunk Ry., or Rich. & } to Quebec.
Ontario Nav. Co.'s Strs.....)
(Good until October 1st.)

SUMMER EXCURSION ROUTES AND RATES.

THROUGH RATES.

From	Rate	To	Rate
New York	$17 40	Berwick	$16 45
Paterson	17 40	Bloomsburg	16 70
Newark	17 40	Danville	16 90
Morristown	17 40	Binghamton	14 30
Dover	17 40	Greene	13 95
Hackettstown	17 30	Oxford	13 65
Washington	17 15	Norwich	13 50
Water Gap	16 70	Sherburne	13 30
Stroudsburg	16 60	Waterville	12 85
Scranton	15 55	Cortland	14 75
Pittston	15 75	Owego	14 75
Kingston	15 90	Ithaca	15 40
Wilkesbarre	15 90	Waverly	15 10
Plymouth	16 00	Elmira	15 45
Nanticoke	16 10	Corning	15 80
Shickshinny	16 20	Bath	16 20

EXCURSION No. 185 A.—TO QUEBEC.

Del., Lack. & Western R. R......to Syracuse.
Rome, Watertown & Ogdb'g R. R.to Clayton.
R. & O. Navi. Co.'s Steamers ... ,to Alexandria Bay.
R. & O. Navi. Co.'s Steamers......to Montreal.
Grand Trunk Ry., or Richelieu & } to Quebec.
Ontario Navi. Co.'s Steamers... }
Good until October 1st.

THROUGH RATES.

From	Rate	To	Rate
New York	$17 40	Nanticoke	$14 95
Paterson	17 10	Shickshinny	15 15
Newark	17 30	Berwick	15 35
Morristown	16 80	Bloomsburg	15 65
Dover	16 65	Danville	15 85
Hackettstown	16 25	Binghamton	13 25
Washington	16 05	Greene	13 20
Water Gap	15 65	Oxford	13 45
Stroudsburg	15 55	Norwich	13 65
Scranton	14 50	Cortland	12 40
Pittston	14 70	Owego	13 30
Kingston	14 85	Waverly	13 30
Wilkesbarre	14 85	Elmira	13 30
Plymouth	14 90		

EXCURSION No. 157 A.—TO QUEBEC.

Del., Lack. & Western R. R......to Oswego.
Rome, Watert'n & Ogdenb'g R. R. to Clayton.
R. & O. Navi. Co.'s Steamers.....to Alexandria Bay.
R & O. Navi. Co.'s Steamers......to Montreal.
Grand Trunk Ry.,or Richelieu & } to Quebec.
Ontario Navi. Co 's Steamers.. }
(Good until October 1st.)

THROUGH RATES.

From	Rate	To	Rate
New York	$17 70	Nanticoke	$15 25
Paterson	17 40	Shickshinny	15 45
Newark	17 60	Berwick	15 65
Morristown	17 50	Bloomsburg	15 95
Dover	16 95	Danville	16 15
Hackettstown	16 55	Binghamton	13 55
Washington	16 35	Greene	13 50
Water Gap	15 95	Oxford	13 75
Stroudsburg	15 85	Norwich	13 95
Scranton	14 80	Cortland	12 70
Pittston	15 00	Syracuse	11 95
Kingston	15 15	Owego	13 70
Wilkesbarre	15 15	Waverly	13 70
Plymouth	15 20	Elmira	13 70

EXCURSION S. T. 6.—MONTREAL TO QUEBEC AND RETURN.

Grand Trunk Ry., or Richelieu & } to Quebec and re-
Ont. Navi. Co.'s Steamers ....} turn.
Sold only in connection with Summer Excursion Ticket passing through Montreal.
Rate............$5.00

ROUTES RETURNING FROM QUEBEC.

Issued only in connection with routes to Quebec.
(See note to Routes returning from Montreal.)

*EXCURSION No. 304 X.—QUEBEC TO NEW YORK.

Ferry................to Point Levi.
Grand Trunk Railway.........to Rouse's Point.
Del. & Hud. Canal Co.'s Lines...to Plattsburg.
Del. & Hud. C. Co.'s Lines, or } to Ft. Ticonderoga.
Lake Champlain Steamer.... }
Del. & Hud. Canal Co.'s Lines....to Saratoga.
Del. & Hud. Canal Co.'s Lines....to Troy.
N. Y. Central & Hud. Riv. R. R...to New York.
Rate...................$12.00

*EXCURSION No. 305 X.—QUEBEC TO NEW YORK.

via same route as 304 X to Saratoga, thence
Delaware & Hudson Canal Co.'s Lines..to Albany.
Day Line Hudson River Steamers......to New York.
Rate....................$11.60

*EXCURSION No. 306 X.—QUEBEC TO NEW YORK.

via same route as 304 X to Saratoga, thence
Delaware & Hudson Canal Co.'s Lines..to Albany.
People's (Night) Line Hud. Riv. Strs...to New York.
Rate.....................$10.95

EXCURSION No. 307 X.—QUEBEC TO NEW YORK.

Ferry. ....to Point Levi.
Grand Trunk Railway..........to Rouse's Point.
Del., & Hud. Canal Co 's Lines..to Plattsburg.
or Lake Champlain Steamer } to Ft. Ticonderoga.
Del. & Hud Canal Co.'s Lines..to Baldwin.
Lake George Steamer..........to Caldwell.
Del. & Hud. Canal Co 's Lines....to Saratoga.
Del. & Hud. Canal Co 's Lines ...to Troy.
N. Y. Central & Hud. Riv. R. R..to New York.
Rate $13.50

*EXCURSION No. 308 X.—QUEBEC TO NEW YORK.

via same route as 307 X to Saratoga, thence
Delaware & Hudson Canal Co.'s Lines to Albany.
Day Line Hudson River Steamers......to New York.
Rate..................... $13.10

*EXCURSION No. 309 X.—QUEBEC TO NEW YORK.

via same route as 307 X to Saratoga, thence
Delaware & Hudson Canal Co.'s Lines.to Albany.
People's (Night) Line Hud. Riv. Strs....to New York.
Rate............... ....$12.45

*EXCURSION No. 310 X.—QUEBEC TO NEW YORK.

Ferry............................to Point Levi.
Grand Trunk Railway.......to St. John's.
Central Vermont Railroad.......to Burlington.
Lake Champlain Steamer ....to Ft. Ticonderoga.
Del & Hud. Canal Co.'s Lines...to Baldwin.
Lake George Steamer.........to Caldwell.
Del., & Hud. Canal Co.'s Lines...to Saratoga.
Del. & Hud Canal Co.'s Lines...to Troy.
N. Y. Central & Hud. Riv. R. R..to New York.
Rate.......................$13 50
*Not to be sold in connection with tickets to Quebec via the Canadian Pacific Railroad.

*EXCURSION No. 311 X.—QUEBEC TO NEW YORK.

via same route as 310 X to Saratoga, thence
Delaware & Hudson Canal Co.'s Lines..to Albany.
Day Line Hudson River Steamers......to New York.
Rate........................$13.10

*EXCURSION No.312 X.—QUEBEC TO NEW YORK.

via same route as 310 X to Saratoga, thence
Delaware & Hudson Canal Co.'s Lines.to Albany.
People's (Night) Line Hud. Riv. Strs....to New York.
Rate $12 45

DELAWARE, LACKAWANNA & WESTERN R. R.

*EXCURSION NO. 121 X.—QUEBEC TO NEW YORK.

Ferry.................................to Point Levi.
Grand Trunk Railway............to Sherbrooke.
Boston & Maine Railroad (Passumpsic Division)............ } to White River Jnc.
Central Vermont Railroad........ to Windsor.
Vermont Valley Railroad......... to Brattleboro.
Central Vermont Railroad........to South Vernon.
Connecticut River Railroad......to Springfield.
N. Y., N. Hav. & Hartford R. R....to New York.
Rate.....................$12.00

*EXCURSION NO. 122 X.—QUEBEC TO NEW YORK.

Ferry.................................to Point Levi.
Grand Trunk Railway............to Sherbrooke.
Boston & Maine Railroad (Passumpsic Division)............ } to St. Johnsbury.
St. Johnsbury & Lake Champl'n Railroad........................ } to Scott's.
Concord & Montreal Railroad.....to Fabyan's.
Concord & Montreal Railroad.....to Concord.
Concord & Montreal Railroad.....to Nashua.
Boston & Maine Railr'd (Lowell System)........................ } to Boston.
Old Colony Railroad............. to Fall River.
Fall River Line Steamers..........to New York.
Rate.................$15.50

EXCURSION NO. 123 X.—QUEBEC TO NEW YORK.

Ferry.................................to Point Levi.
Grand Trunk Railway............to Sherbrooke.
Boston & Maine Railroad (Passumpsic Division) via Newp't Vt. } to St. Johnsbury.
St. Johnsbury & Lake Champl'n Railroad........................ } to Scott's
Concord & Montreal Railroad......to Fabyan's.
Maine Central Railroad (White Mountains Line)............... } toCrawfordHouse.
Maine Central Railroad (White Mountains Line)............... } to North Conway.
Boston & Maine Railroad.........to Boston
Old Colony Railroad.............to Fall River.
Fall River Line Steamers ....to New York.
Rate.....................$15.50

*EXCURSION NO. 124 X.—QUEBEC TO NEW YORK.

Same as Excursion 123 X to Fabyan's, thence
Concord & Montreal Railroad.. } to Base Mount Washington.
Mount Washington Railway......to Summit.
Milliken's Stage Line...........to Glen House.
Milliken's Stage Line ....to Glen Station.
Maine Central Railroad (White Mountains Line)............... } to North Conway.
Boston & Maine Railroad.........to Boston.
Old Colony Railroad.............to Fall River.
Fall River Line Steamers..... .. .to New York.
Rate.................$24.00

*EXCURSION NO. 148 X.—QUEBEC TO NEW YORK.

Same as Excursion 123 X to Fabyan's, thence
Maine Central Railroad (White Mountains Line)............... } to Portland.
Boston & Maine Railroad.........to Boston.
Old Colony Railroad.............to Fall River.
Fall River Line Steamers..........to New York.
Rate.................$15.50

*EXCURSION NO. 391 X.—QUEBEC TO NEW YORK.

Ferry.................................to Levis
Quebec Central Railway...........to Sherbrooke.
Bos. & Me R. R. (Passumpsic Div.).to White River Jc.
Central Vermont Railroad ....to Windsor.
Vermont Valley Railroad..........to Brattleboro.
Central Vermont Railroad........ to South Vernon.
Connecticut River Railroad.......to Springfield.
N. Y. N. Hav. & Hartford R. R....to New York.
Rate.................$12.00

*EXCURSION NO. 392 X.—QUEBEC TO NEW YORK.

Ferry.................................to Levis.
Quebec Central Railway...........to Sherbrooke.
Boston & Maine Railroad.........to Concord.
Concord & Montreal Railroad.....to Nashua.
Boston & Maine Railr'd (Lowell System)........................ } to Boston.
Old Colony Railroad............. to Fall River.
Fall River Line Steamers..........to New York.
Rate.................$15.50

*EXCURSION NO. 394 X.—QUEBEC TO NEW YORK.

Ferry.................................to Levis.
Quebec Central Railway...........to DudswellJunc.
Maine Central Railroad...........to North Conway.
Boston & Maine Railroad.........to Boston.
Old Colony Railroad............. to Fall River.
Fall River Line Steamers..........to New York.
Rate.................$15.50

*EXCURSION NO. 393 X.—QUEBEC TO NEW YORK.

Ferry.................................to Levis.
Quebec Central Railway.. ....to Dudswell Junc.
Maine Central Railroad ....to Portland.
Boston & Maine Railroad.........to Boston.
Old Colony Railroad............. to Fall River.
Fall River Line Steamers..........to New York.
Rate.................$15.50

*Not to be sold in connection with tickets to Quebec *via* the Canadian Pacific Railway.

RICHFIELD SPRINGS, N. Y.

LOCAL EXCURSION.

(Good for continuous passage only)

THROUGH RATES.

**New York	$10 75	Kingston	$7 35
Passaic	10 75	Wilkesbarre	7 35
Paterson	10 75	Plymouth	7 45
Boonton	10 75	Nanticoke	7 60
**Newark	10 50	Shickshinny	8 00
Roseville	10 50	Berwick	8 40
Orange	10 50	Bloomsburg	8 90
Mountain	10 50	Danville	9 40
South Orange	10 50	Great Bend	4 75
Milburn	10 50	Binghamton	4 00
Short Hills	10 50	Greene	3 40
Summit	10 50	Oxford	2 85
Chatham	10 50	Norwich	2 55
Madison	10 50	Sherburne	2 05
Morristown	10 50	Waterville	1 20
Dover	10 50	†Utica	1 50
Andover	10 60	*Utica	2 00
Newton	10 80	Cortland	5 00
Franklin	11 30	Owego	5 00
Hackettstown	10 15	Ithaca	6 35
Washington	9 80	Waverly	5 75
Portland	9 15	Elmira	6 45
Water Gap	8 95	Corning	7 10
Stroudsburg	8 80	Bath	7 90
Scranton	6 65	Atlanta	8 70
Pittston	7 00		

†Rate for Excursion Tickets good for two days only, except that tickets purchased on a Saturday are good to return on the following Monday.
* Rate for Excursion Tickets good until October 31st.
** Good for stop-over.

EXCURSION S. T. 4.—UTICA TO RICHFIELD SPRINGS AND RETURN.

Del., Lack. & Western R. R. } to Richfield Springs and return.

Sold only in connection with Summer Excursion Ticket passing through Utica.

Rate.............$2.00

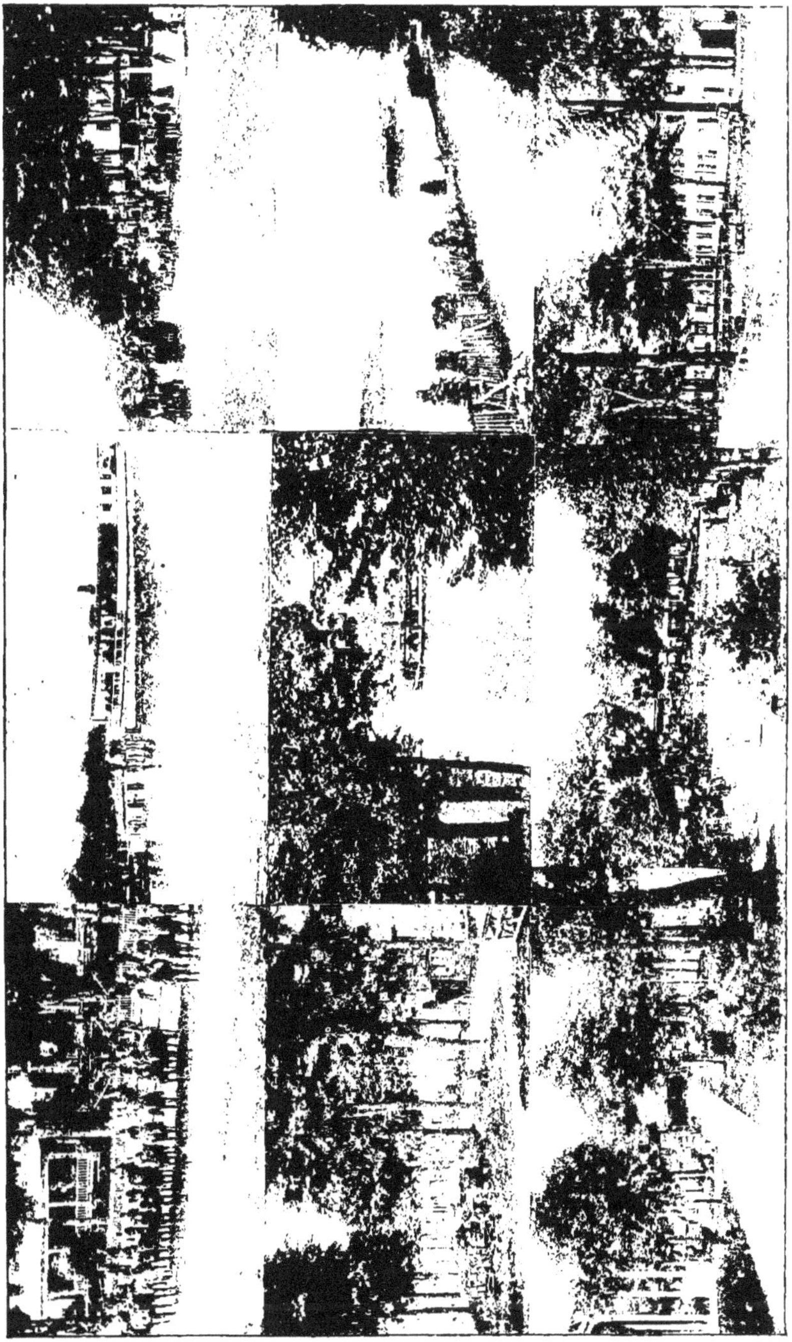

SCENES IN AND AROUND RICHFIELD SPRINGS, N. Y.

EXCURSION S. T. 27.—RICHFIELD JUNCTION TO RICHFIELD SPRINGS AND RETURN.

Del., Lack. & Western R. R... } to Richfield Springs and return
Sold only in connection with Summer Excursion Ticket passing through Richfield Junction.
Rate........ ......90 cents

SARATOGA SPRINGS, N. Y.

Originally famous for the curative quality of its waters, Saratoga Springs has long been a leading resort for fashion.

The hotels are mammoth in their proportions, and on their piazzas and in their gardens the highest social figures of the day congregate to participate in the gayeties, which here are never ceasing. Justly celebrated for having the largest hotels in the world, conveying the idea of prohibitory rates to those of modest income, it should be understood that accommodations may be had in the town at rates satisfactory to all purses.

EXCURSION NO. 5.—SARATOGA AND RETURN.

Delaware, Lack. & Western R. R....to Binghamton
Del. & Hud. C. Co. (via Howe's Cave).to Saratoga.
Returning via same route.

THROUGH RATES.

Washington.......$ 12 90	Waverly............$ 8 85
Water Gap........ 12 10	Elmira 9 55
Stroudsburg....... 11 90	Corning 10 10
Scranton 9 25	Bath................ 10 85
Pittston 9 70	Atlanta............ 11 60
Kingston.......... 10 05	Wayland 11 95
Wilkesbarre....... 10 05	Dansville.......... 12 40
Owego,........... 8 10	Mount Morris. ... 12 95
Ithaca............. 9 50	Buffalo 14 35

EXCURSION NO. 144.—SARATOGA AND RETURN.

Delaware, Lack. & Western R. R....to Utica.
New York Central & Hudson R. R...to Schenectady
Delaware & Hudson Canal Co..... .to Saratoga.
Returning via same route.

THROUGH RATES.

Washington........$14 15	Richfield Springs..$ 6 25
Water Gap........ 13 35	Cortland........... 9 35
Stroudsburg....... 13 15	Owego............. 9 35
Scranton 11 00	Ithaca............. 10 75
Pittston.......... 11 40	Waverly........... 10 15
Kingston......... 11 70	Elmira 10 80
Wilkesbarre...... 11 70	Corning........... 11 45
Binghamton....... 8 55	Bath................ 12 30
Greene 7 75	Atlanta............ 13 10
Oxford 7 20	Wayland 13 35
Norwich.......... 6 90	Dansville.......... 13 60
Sherburne......... 6 45	Mount Morris..... 14 15
Waterville........ 5 60	Buffalo 15 65

EXCURSION NO. 145.—SARATOGA AND RETURN.

Delaware, Lack. & Western R. R..to Utica.
N. Y. Central & Hud. River R. R....to Schenectady.
Delaware & Hudson Canal Co........to Saratoga.
D. & H.Canal Co.(via Howe's Cave).to Binghamton.
Delaware, Lack. & Western R. R..to starting point.

EXCURSION NO. 146.—REVERSE OF THE PRECEDING.

THROUGH RATES.

Washington........$13 55	Owego.............$ 8 75
Water Gap........ 12 70	Ithaca............ 10 10
Stroudsburg.. .... 12 50	Waverly........... 9 50
Scranton 10 35	Elmira 10 20
Pittston.......... 10 75	Corning.......... 10 80
Kingston......... 11 05	Bath. 11 65
Wilkesbarre....... 11 05	Atlanta........... 12 40
Binghamton....... 7 90	Wayland.......... 12 65
Greene........... 7 90	Dansville... ..... 12 95
Oxford 7 90	Mount Morris..... 13 50
Norwich.......... 7 90	Buffalo........... 16 00
Cortland.......... 9 20	

EXCURSION NO. 158.—SARATOGA AND RETURN.

Delaware, Lack. & Western R. R...to New York.
People s (N'g't)Line Hud. R. Strs...to Albany.
Delaware, & Hudson Canal Co.....to Saratoga.
Delaware & Hudson Canal Co......to Albany.
Day Line Hudson River Steamers..to New York.
Delaware, Lack. & Western R. R...to starting point.

EXCURSION NO. 159.—GOING *via* DAY LINE AND RETURNING *via* NIGHT LINE.

THROUGH RATES FOR EITHER EXCURSION.

Morristown ....$ 7 00	Greene............$14 55
Dover 7 50	Oxford 14 75
Hackettstown..... 8 20	Norwich........... 14 75
Washington....... 8 60	Sherburne......... 15 45
Water Gap........ 9 45	Cortland.......... 15 75
Stroudsburg...... 9 60	Syracuse 15 75
Scranton 11 75	Oswego........... 15 75
Pittston 12 15	Owego............ 14 60
Kingston......... 12 90	Ithaca 16 25
Wilkesbarre...... 12 95	Waverly...... .... 15 35
Binghamton....... 13 75	Elmira 16 00

EXCURSION NO. 181.—SARATOGA AND RETURN.

Delaware, Lack. & Western R. R..to New York.
N. Y. Central & Hud. River R. R....to Troy
Delaware & Hudson Canal Co......to Saratoga.
Delaware & Hudson Canal Co......to Troy.
N. Y. Central & Hud. River R. R...to New York.
Delaware, Lack. & Western R.R. .to starting point.

THROUGH RATES.

Morristown .... $ 8 75	Greene............$16 30
Dover............. 9 25	Oxford 16 50
Hackettstown..... 9 95	Norwich........... 16 50
Washington..... .. 10 35	Sherburne......... 17 20
Water Gap..... ... 11 20	Cortland..... ..... 17 50
Stroudsburg....... 11 35	Syracuse 17 50
Scranton 13 50	Oswego........... 17 50
Pittston........... 13 90	Owego............ 16 35
Kingston......... 14 65	Ithaca............. 18 00
Wilkesbarre....... 14 70	Waverly........... 17 10
Binghamton...... 15 50	Elmira............ 17 75

SHARON SPRINGS, N. Y.

EXCURSION NO. 1.—SHARON SPRINGS AND RETURN.

Del., Lack. & Western R. R......to Binghamton.
Delaware & Hudson Canal Co   to Sharon Springs.
Returning via same route.

THROUGH RATES.

New York..........$12 80	Cortland........,.....$ 6 25
Paterson.. .... 12 20	Syracuse 7 70
Newark 12 65	Owego............. 5 45
Morristown 11 75	Ithaca............. 6 70
Dover 11 30	Waverly........... 6 20
Hackettstown..... 10 10	Elmira............ 6 90
Washington...... 10 10	Corning........... 7 45
Water Gap........ 9 30	Bath................ 8 20
Stroudsburg....... 9 10	Atlanta............ 8 95
Scranton 6 40	Wayland........... 9 30
Pittston.......... 6 85	Dansville.......... 9 60
Kingston......... 7 25	Mount Morris..... 10 15
Wilkesbarre....... 7 25	Buffalo 12 25

SUMMER EXCURSION ROUTES AND RATES

EXCURSION S. T. 13.—COBLESKILL TO SHARON SPRINGS AND RETURN.

Del. & Hud. Canal Co..to Sharon Springs and return.
Sold only in connection with Summer Excursion Ticket passing through Cobleskill.
Rate.................80 cents

SHELDRAKE, N. Y.

Cayuga Lake is one of the finest inland lakes that make Central New York so famous as a summer resort It is forty miles long and reposes between high hills that stretch along its entire length, and far beyond to the south. It is, also, one of the most magnificent lakes in this country, being clear and of great depth; it abounds in most entrancing scenery. Lake fishing, which is always a delightful pastime, is here indulged in every season by many enthusiastic fishermen, who invariably catch sufficient trout, bass, etc., to convince one that old Cayuga Lake is the vertible Mecca of anglers.

At Sheldrake, a little hamlet situated on the shore of the lake fifteen miles from Ithaca, is the Cayuga Lake House, cut of which can be seen on page 161. This hotel accommodates 200 guests, has all modern improvements, including electric lights and elevator. The nights in this locality are cool and dry. Water is noted for its purity and medicinal qualities. Winding roads, under shade trees on the very shore of the lake, make this country noted for its drives.

Sheldrake can be reached by Robert L. Darragh's line of excursion steamers which run at frequent intervals between Sheldrake and Ithaca. These boats are new and have a speed of 18 knots an hour.

EXCURSION NO. 397.—SHELDRAKE AND RETURN.

Delaware, Lack. & Western R. R........to Ithaca.
Steamer "Laura A. Darragh".........to Sheldrake.
Returning via same route.

THROUGH RATES.

New York..........	$11 00	Plymouth...........	$6 00
Paterson..........	10 40	Nanticoke.........	6 15
Newark...........	11 00	Shickshinny........	6 50
Orange............	10 80	Berwick...........	6 95
Summit...........	10 30	Bloomsburg........	7 45
Morristown.......	9 90	Danville...........	7 90
Dover.............	9 45	Binghamton.......	2 70
Hackettstown.....	8 70	Greene............	3 50
Washington......	8 50	Oxford............	4 05
Water Gap.......	7 50	Norwich...........	4 35
Stroudsburg......	7 30	Sherburne.........	4 80
Scranton..........	5 50	Waterville.........	5 70
Pittston..........	5 50	Utica..............	6 50
Kingston..........	5 90	Richfield Springs...	6 85
Wilkesbarre......	5 90		

SILVER LAKE, N. Y.

Silver Lake, famous for a brief, glorious period, a generation ago, because of its fabled sea serpent, has gained a less transitory fame in these latter days in that it has its devoted band of those who worship at Nature's shrine along its gravelly shores. Here, as at Conesus and Keuka and Seneca, yes, and as at Lake George, the cottage builder has adorned the leafy shores with his gay bungalow, and the tents of the campers gleam far across the sleeping waters.

The Geneseo Conference Camp Ground Association has thirty acres of improved grounds enclosed, on which are erected about sixty cottages, and the Silver Lake Temperance Assembly has a very extensive rendezvous upon the lake, meeting here annually.

Taken altogether, the grounds and surroundings are the handsomest to be found in Western New York, and are annually visited by over 30,000 people. There is a cabin, the first one of the kind ever erected in the United States, as a Pioneer Log Cabin Museum, and the collection within its walls could never be replaced should it by any means be destroyed.

EXCURSION NO. 245.—SILVER LAKE AND RETURN.

Del., Lack. & Western R. R. } to Buffalo, Rochester & Pittsburg Junction.
Buff., Roch. & Pittsburg R. R..to Silver Lake.
Returning via same route.

THROUGH RATES.

Corning..............	$3 70	Danville.....	$2 30
Bath.................	3 60	Groveland..........	2 00
Kanona..............	3 45	Mount Morris.......	1 75
Avoca...............	3 30	Leicester...........	1 60
Wallace.............	3 20	Alexander..........	1 50
Cohocton............	3 00	Darien..............	1 70
Atlanta..............	2 80	Alden..............	2 00
Wayland.............	2 60	Lancaster..........	2 35
Perkinville..........	2 50	Buffalo.............	2 35

EXCURSION NO. 245 L.—SILVER LAKE AND RETURN.

Same route as Excursion No. 245.
Limited to 30 days.

THROUGH RATES.

Bath........	$2 65	Cohocton..........	$2 65
Kanona	2 65	Bloods.............	2 65
Avoca	2 65	Wayland...........	2 55
Wallace	2 05		

SPRAGUEVILLE, PA.

LOCAL EXCURSION.

(Good for continuous passage only.)

THROUGH RATES.

*New York........	$4 05	Dover	$2 45
Passaic............	3 65	Andover...........	2 25
Paterson	3 50	Newton............	2 45
Boonton..........	2 95	Franklin...........	2 95
*Newark...........	3 95	Hackettstown......	1 75
*Roseville.........	3 95	Washington.......	1 35
Orange............	3 75	Scranton	2 55
Mountain	3 65	Pittston...........	2 95
South Orange.....	3 60	Kingston..........	3 10
Milburn...........	3 45	Wilkesbarre........	3 30
Short Hills........	3 40	Plymouth	3 45
Summit............	3 40	Nanticoke.........	3 60
Chatham...........	3 25	Shickshinny	3 85
Madison...........	3 10	Berwick............	4 15
Morristown	2 95	Bloomsburg........	4 45

DELAWARE, LACKAWANNA & WESTERN R. R.

Danville	$4 80	Oswego	$9 00
Great Bend	3 90	Owego	5 30
Binghamton	4 45	Ithaca	6 65
Greene	5 25	Waverly	6 00
Oxford	5 80	Elmira	6 75
Norwich	6 10	Corning	7 40
Sherburne	6 55	Bath	8 20
Waterville	7 40	Atlanta	9 00
Richfield Springs	8 60	Wayland	9 20
Utica	8 25	Dansville	9 55
Cortland	6 20	Mount Morris	10 10
Syracuse	7 60	Buffalo	12 55

* Tickets good until used.

STANHOPE, N. J.
(Station for Budd's Lake.)
LOCAL EXCURSION.
(Good for continuous passage only.)
THROUGH RATES.

*New York	$2 10	Morristown	$ 90
Passaic	1 55	Dover	50
Paterson	1 40	Andover	50
Boonton	85	Newton	70
*Newark	2 00	Franklin	1 20
*Roseville	2 00	Hackettstown	40
Orange	1 80	Washington	80
Mountain	1 70	Phillipsburg	1 35
South Orange	1 65	Easton	1 45
Milburn	1 50	Portland	1 50
Short Hills	1 40	Water Gap	1 70
Summit	1 35	Stroudsburg	1 90
Chatham	1 20	Scranton	3 90
Madison	1 10		

* Tickets good until used.

STROUDSBURG, PA.
LOCAL EXCURSION.
(Good for continuous passage only.)
THROUGH RATES.

*New York	$3 85	Shickshinny	$4 05
Passaic	3 45	Berwick	4 35
Paterson	3 30	Bloomsburg	4 65
Boonton	2 75	Danville	5 00
*Newark	3 65	Great Bend	4 05
*Roseville	3 75	Binghamton	4 60
Orange	3 55	Greene	5 40
Mountain	3 45	Oxford	5 95
South Orange	3 40	Norwich	6 30
Milburn	3 25	Sherburne	6 75
Short Hills	3 20	Waterville	7 60
Summit	3 20	Richfield Springs	8 80
Chatham	3 00	Utica	8 45
Madison	2 90	Cortland	6 35
Morristown	2 75	Syracuse	7 80
Dover	2 25	Oswego	9 20
Andover	2 05	Owego	5 45
Newton	2 25	Ithaca	6 80
Franklin	2 75	Waverly	6 20
Hackettstown	1 55	Elmira	6 90
Washington	1 15	Corning	7 55
Scranton	2 75	Bath	8 40
Pittston	3 15	Atlanta	9 20
Kingston	3 50	Wayland	9 40
Wilkesbarre	3 50	Dansville	9 70
Plymouth	3 65	Mount Morris	10 25
Nanticoke	3 80	Buffalo	12 75

* Tickets good until used.

TAUGHANNOCK FALLS, N. Y.

Halsey Creek has its rise upon the ridge dividing Seneca and Cayuga Lakes, and, flowing down the easterly watershed, finally reaches the latter by a prodigious plunge into a wild and romantic chasm, thus forming the Falls of Taughannock, the highest single cascade in the State, having a direct fall of two hundred and fifteen feet. The gorge is plainly visible from the decks of passing steamers, but its creamy headlong cataract is deeply hidden by the environing foliage. About ten miles from Ithaca.

EXCURSION No. 133.—TAUGHANNOCK FALLS AND RETURN.

Del., Lack. & Western R. R..to Ithaca.
Cayuga Lake Steamer.... . to Taughannock Falls.
Returning *via* same route.

THROUGH RATES.

New York	$11 00	Scranton	$5 50
Paterson	10 40	Binghamton	2 70
Newark	11 00	Greene	3 50
Morristown	9 80	Oxford	4 05
Dover	9 45	Norwich	4 35
Hackettstown	8 70	Sherburne	4 80
Washington	8 30	Waterville	5 70
Water Gap	7 50	Owego	2 00
Stroudsburg	7 30		

TOBYHANNA, PA.
LOCAL EXCURSION.
(Good for continuous passage only.)
THROUGH RATES.

*New York	$4 95	Shickshinny	$2 65
Passaic	4 85	Berwick	2 95
Paterson	4 70	Bloomsburg	3 25
Boonton	4 15	Danville	3 60
*Newark	4 95	Great Bend	3 00
*Roseville	4 95	Binghamton	3 60
Orange	4 95	Greene	4 35
Mountain	4 85	Oxford	4 90
South Orange	4 80	Norwich	5 20
Milburn	4 65	Sherburne	5 65
Short Hills	4 60	Waterville	6 50
Summit	4 60	Richfield Springs	7 70
Chatham	4 40	Utica	7 40
Madison	4 30	Cortland	5 30
Morristown	4 15	Syracuse	6 75
Dover	3 65	Oswego	8 15
Andover	3 45	Owego	4 40
Newton	3 65	Ithaca	5 75
Franklin	4 15	Waverly	5 15
Hackettstown	2 95	Elmira	5 85
Washington	2 55	Corning	6 50
Scranton	1 35	Bath	7 35
Pittston	1 75	Atlanta	8 10
Kingston	2 10	Wayland	8 35
Wilkesbarre	2 10	Dansville	8 60
Plymouth	2 25	Mount Morris	9 20
Nanticoke	2 40	Buffalo	11 70

* Tickets good until used.

TORONTO, ONT.

EXCURSION S. T. 15.—NIAGARA FALLS TO TORONTO AND RETURN.

N. Y. Central & Hud River Railroad....to Lewiston.
Niagara Navigation Co.'s Steamer......to Toronto.
Returning *via* same route.
Sold only in connection with Summer Excursion Ticket to, or passing through Niagara Falls.
Rate.................$2.25

EXCURSION S. T. 36.—NIAGARA FALLS TO TORONTO AND RETURN.

New York, Lake Erie and Western Railroad ..... } to Suspension Bridge.
Grand Trunk Railway....... to Port Dalhousie.
Steamer "Empress of India" to Toronto.
Returning *via* same route.
Sold only in connection with Summer Excursion Ticket to, or passing through Niagara Falls.
Rate.................$2.25

TRENTON FALLS, N. Y.

Are on West Canada Creek, which flows into the Mohawk River—about fifteen miles north of Utica.

Slanting Water the Indians called them (Kuyahora).

A series of cascades—five in number—descend within a distance of two miles, over 300 feet. Deep channels have been worn in the limestone hills. The ravine formed by this incessant flow is very narrow, but deep, in some portions being two hundred feet below the level of the surrounding country. The names given to the principal falls are Sherman, High Mill-Dam, Alhambra and Rocky-Heart.

EXCURSION NO. 25.—TRENTON FALLS AND RETURN.

Delaware, Lackawanna & Western Railroad............................ } to Utica.
Rome, Watertown & Ogdensburg Railroad............................ } to Trenton Falls.
Returning *via* same route.

THROUGH RATES.

New York..........	$10 25	Binghamton........	$4 80
Paterson..........	10 25	Greene............	4 05
Newark............	10 25	Oxford............	3 50
Morristown........	10 25	Norwich...........	3 20
Dover.............	10 25	Sherburne.........	2 75
Hackettstown......	10 25	Waterville........	1 90
Washington........	10 25	Richfield Springs.	2 50
Water Gap	9 60	Owego.............	5 65
Stroudsburg.......	9 40	Waverly...........	6 40
Scranton	7 30	Elmira............	7 10
Pittston	7 70	Corning...........	7 75
Kingston..........	8 00	Bath..............	8 60
Wilkesbarre,......	8 00		

EXCURSION S. T. 3.—UTICA TO TRENTON FALLS AND RETURN.

Rome, Waterown & Ogdensburg } to Trenton Falls.
Railroad............................ { and return.
Sold only in connection with Summer Excursion Ticket passing through Utica.
Rate............ ......$1.00

TULLY LAKE PARK, N. Y.

EXCURSION NO. 351 L.—TULLY LAKE PARK AND RETURN.

(Good for continuous passage only.)
Del., Lack. & Western Railroad..to Tully.
Tully Lake Park Transfer........to Tully Lake Park.
Returning *via* same route.

THROUGH RATES.

Binghamton........	$2 60	Homer.....	$ 75
Chenango Bridge...	2 40	Onativia...........	60
Chenango Forks ...	2 10	Jamesville.........	90
Whitney's Point....	1 75	Syracuse...........	1 15
Lisle..............	1 65	Baldwinsville......	1 65
Killawog...........	1 50	Lamsous............	1 85
Marathon	1 40	Fulton.............	2 10
Messengerville.....	1 25	Oswego.............	2 55
Cortland...........	85		

WATCH HILL, R. I.

Years ago this charming site was selected as a site by a few families for their summer homes, but it was not long before others, appreciating the exceptional advantages and its picturesque situation, located here, until now Watch Hill, R. I., is as well known as any summer resort along the coast. It is situated on elevated ground, at the south-western extremity of the State; while on the mainland it enjoys all the advantages of being out at sea. Eleven lighthouses and one lightship are visible from the town.

EXCURSION No. 70.—WATCH HILL, R. I., AND RETURN.

Delaware, Lack. & Western R. R....to New York.
Stonington Line Steamers..... .....to Stonington.
Steamer................ .... to Watch Hill.
Returning *via* same route.

EXCURSION No. 71.—WATCH HILL R. I., AND RETURN.

Delaware, Lack, & Western R. R....to New York.
Norwich Line Steamers,............ to New London.
Steamer Block Island ....to Watch Hill.
Returning *via* same route.

THROUGH RATES FOR EITHER EXCURSION.

Morristown......	..$ 4 65	Waterville.........	$13 40
Dover	5 15	Cortland...........	13 40
Hackettstown.....	5 85	Syracuse...........	13 40
Washington.......	6 25	Oswego.............	13 40
Water Gap.......	7 10	Owego..............	12 25
Stroudsburg......	7 25	Ithaca.............	13 90
Scranton	9 40	Waverly............	13 00
Pittston	9 80	Elmira.............	13 65
Kingston.........	10 55	Corning............	14 30
Wilkesbarre......	10 60	Bath...............	15 15
Binghamton	11 40	Atlanta............	16 30
Greene...........	12 20	Wayland............	16 60
Oxford	12 40	Dansville..........	17 10
Norwich..........	12 40	Mount Morris.......	17 10
Sherburne........	13 10	Buffalo............	19 40

WATKINS GLEN, N. Y.

Here Dame Nature, outdoing herself, perfected a work that would reflect nothing but credit upon herself, for this wonderful piece of earthen architecture fills all humanity with amazement.

Of all places visited by those who go to enjoy themselves, and who love to investigate the wonders of this land, none has won such well-merited fame as Watkins Glen. From the very entrance of the Glen to its extreme limit there is something charming to be seen.

The Glen is situated in the village of Watkins, Schuyler County, at the head of Seneca Lake. The village in itself is a pretty spot, but the Glen, of course, is the main attraction.

This Glen consists of a series of cascades, galleries and weird caves, and here and there silver cascades are to be found that impart a wonderfully romantic appearance to this romantic spot.

Here human art stepped in to assist Nature in exhibiting her marvelous store of wonders to the best advantage. Before any explorations could be made by tourists it became necessary to erect ladders, by means of which ascents could be made from one steep incline to another, and to cut pathways in the rock. This was done by the proprietor of the Glen Mountain House, who owns the Glen, and offers the best facilities of inspection to his guests.

Probably the most beautiful of the attractions of this spot is Rainbow Falls, so called because at particular seasons when the sun is in a certain position, it shines through the mist which emanates from the waterfall, causing it to assume all the colors of the rainbow. The other great attractions are Entrance Cascade, Trout Pool, Glen Alpha, Stillwater Gorge, Minnehaha Cascade, Fairy Cascade, Neptune's Pool, Cavern Cascade, Cavern Gorge and the Labyrinth.
A delightful feature of the chasm is the wonderful coolness of the air. The sun never shines here, and very often on the hottest day a light wrap becomes a necessary adjunct to a tour of inspection.

EXCURSION NO. 32.—WATKINS AND HAVANA GLENS AND RETURN.

Delaware, Lackawanna & Western R. R.to Elmira.
Pennsylvania R. R. (via Havana Glen)..to Watkins.
Returning via same route.

THROUGH RATES.

New York	$11 15	Norwich	$4 85
Paterson	10 65	Sherburne	5 30
Newark	10 90	Waterville	6 15
Morristown	10 40	Richfield Springs	7 35
Dover	9 90	Utica	7 00
Hackettstown	9 20	Owego	2 75
Washington	8 80	Ithaca	2 95
Water Gap	8 00	Waverly	1 75
Stroudsburg	7 80	Corning	1 75
Scranton	5 45	Bath	2 70
Pittston	5 45	Atlanta	3 50
Kingston	5 75	Wayland	3 75
Wilkesbarre	5 75	Dansville	3 85
Binghamton	3 65	Mount Morris	4 30
Greene	4 00	Buffalo	6 25
Oxford	4 50		

EXCURSION NO. 244.—WATKINS GLEN AND RETURN.

Delaware, Lackawanna & Western R. R.to Corning.
Fall Brook Railway.......to Watkins.
Returning via same route.

THROUGH RATES.

New York	$11 65	Oxford	$5 00
Paterson	11 35	Norwich	5 30
Newark	11 80	Sherburne	5 75
Morristown	10 90	Waterville	6 65
Dover	10 40	Richfield Springs	7 85
Hackettstown	9 70	Utica	7 50
Washington	9 30	Owego	2 90
Water Gap	8 45	Ithaca	3 45
Stroudsburg	8 30	Waverly	2 15
Scranton	5 95	Bath	1 60
Pittston	5 95	Atlanta	2 40
Kingston	6 35	Wayland	2 65
Wilkesbarre	6 35	Dansville	2 95
Binghamton	3 70	Mount Morris	3 50
Greene	4 50	Buffalo	6 00

EXCURSION S. T. 1.—ELMIRA TO WATKINS GLEN AND RETURN.

Pennsylvania Railroad..to Watkins Glen and return.
Sold only in connection with Summer Excursion Ticket passing through Elmira.
Rate............90 cents

EXCURSION S. T. 35—CORNING TO WATKINS GLEN AND RETURN.

Fall Brook Railway.....to Watkins Glen and return
Sold only in connection with Summer Excursion Ticket passing through Corning.
Rate............75 cents

WEST BARNSTABLE, MASS.

EXCURSION NO. 289.—WEST BARNSTABLE AND RETURN.

Del., Lack. & Western R. R......to New York.
Fall River Line Steamers........to Fall River.
Old Colony Railroad..............to West Barnstable.
Returning via same route.

THROUGH RATES.

Morristown	$8 85	Waterville	$17 60
Dover	9 35	Cortland	17 60
Hackettstown	10 05	Syracuse	17 60
Washington	10 45	Oswego	17 60
Water Gap	11 30	Owego	16 45
Stroudsburg	11 45	Ithaca	18 10
Scranton	13 60	Waverly	17 20
Pittston	14 40	Elmira	17 85
Kingston	14 75	Corning	18 50
Wilkesbarre	14 80	Bath	19 35
Binghamton	15 60	Atlanta	20 50
Greene	16 40	Wayland	20 85
Oxford	16 60	Dansville	21 30
Norwich	16 60	Mount Morris	21 30
Sherburne	17 30	Buffalo	23 60

WINOLA LAKE, PA.

EXCURSION NO. 344.—LAKE WINOLA AND RETURN.

Delaware, Lack. & Western R. R....to Factoryville.
N. A. Gardner's Stage Line..........to Lake Winola.
Returning via same route.

THROUGH RATES.

New York	$8 15	Dover	$6 40
Paterson	7 45	Hackettstown	5 60
Newark	7 90	Washington	5 30
Morristown	6 90	Water Gap	4 35
Stroudsburg	4 15	Oswego	7 20
Scranton	1 35	Owego	3 50
Binghamton	2 65	Ithaca	4 90
Greene	3 45	Waverly	4 20
Oxford	3 95	Elmira	4 95
Norwich	4 30	Corning	5 55
Sherburne	4 75	Bath	6 40
Waterville	5 60	Atlanta	7 20
Richfield Springs	6 75	Wayland	7 40
Utica	6 45	Dausville	7 75
Cortland	4 35	Mount Morris	8 30
Syracuse	5 80	Buffalo	10 75

The above Excursion Tickets to Winola Lake go on sale July 1st. Sale to be discontinued August 31st.

YARMOUTH, MASS.

EXCURSION NO. 290.—YARMOUTH AND RETURN.

Delaware, Lack. & Western R. R......to New York.
Fall River Line Steamers..............to Fall River.
Old Colony Railroad...................to Yarmouth.
Returning via same route.

THROUGH RATES.

Morristown	$9 15	Waterville	$17 90
Dover	9 65	Cortland	17 90
Hackettstown	10 35	Syracuse	17 90
Washington	10 75	Oswego	17 90
Water Gap	11 60	Owego	16 75
Stroudsburg	11 75	Ithaca	18 40
Scranton	13 90	Waverly	17 50
Pittston	14 30	Elmira	18 15
Kingston	15 05	Corning	18 80
Wilkesbarre	15 10	Bath	19 65
Binghamton	15 90	Atlanta	20 80
Greene	16 70	Wayland	21 15
Oxford	16 90	Dansville	21 60
Norwich	16 90	Mount Morris	21 60
Sherburne	17 60	Buffalo	23 90

BONDS OF SURETYSHIP
FOR EMPLOYEES IN POSITIONS OF TRUST.
NO OTHER BUSINESS.

THE ORIGINAL COMPANY. — — — — — — ESTABLISHED 1872.

THE GUARANTEE COMPANY
OF NORTH AMERICA.

Assets and Resources, January, 1894, — $1,196,282.56
Deposits and Assets in the U. S., — — 540,047.48

HEAD OFFICE, - - MONTREAL.
EDWARD RAWLINGS, PRESIDENT AND MANAGING DIRECTOR.

NEW YORK DIRECTORS.

H. W. CANNON, W. B. DUNCAN, HORACE PORTER, JOHN PATON,
J. E. PULSFORD, E. F. WINSLOW.

NEW YORK OFFICE, - 111 BROADWAY,
D. J. TOMPKINS, SECRETARY.

THEODORE IRWIN, President   GEO. B. SLOAN, JR., Sec'y and Treas.

EDWARD CLIFF, Superintendent

NATIONAL RAILWAY SPRING CO.
OSWEGO, N. Y.

MANUFACTURERS OF

ELLIPTIC AND SPIRAL CAR SPRINGS

SPECIAL SPRINGS MADE TO SPECIFICATIONS

NEW YORK OFFICE, 115 BROADWAY

LIST OF HOTELS, BOARDING AND FARM HOUSES TAKING SUMMER BOARDERS

ON OR NEAR THE LINES OF THE

DELAWARE, LACKAWANNA & WESTERN RAILROAD

Post Office.	Railway Station.	Hotel or Boarding House	Name of Proprietor.	Miles from Station.	Capacity	Price per Day.	Price per Week.	Altitude above Sea.	How Reached from Railway Station.
Paterson, N. J.	Paterson	U. S. Hotel	A. A. Van Voorhees	—	75	—	Europ. plan.	—	Electric cars.
Boonton, N. J.	Boonton	Mansion House	D. Bowden	—	55	2.00	8.00 to 12.00	411 ft.	
Netcong, Morris Co., N. J.	Stanhope	Rockland Farm House	A. Chamberlain	1	15	1.00	6.00	1200 "	Stages meet all trains, fare 15c.
Budd's Lake, N. J.	"	Forrest House	F. M. Duryea	2	250	2.50	8.00 to 12.00	1200 "	Hotel stages meet all trains.
Newton, Sussex Co., N. J.	Newton	Ward House	S. R. Jenson	¼	40	2.00	7.00 to 10.00	—	Special rates to commercial men.
Washington, Warren Co. N. J.	Washington	Washington H'se	E. Hoover	—	—	2.00	—	—	Opposite D. L. & W. Depot.
Delaware, Warren Co., N. J.	Delaware	Farm House	John Myers	¼	50	1.00	7.00	1500 "	Carriage if notified.
Delaware Water Gap, Monroe Co., Pa.	Water Gap	The Kittatiny	W. A. Broadhead & Sons	¾	350	3.00 to 4.00	16.00 to 27.00	800 "	Hotel stages meet all trains.
" "	"	Cataract House	L. M. Tucker	2	100	2.00	7.00 to 10.00	1600 "	" "
" "	"	River Farm H'se	E. T. Croasdale	1	35	2.00	8.00 to 10 00	500 "	Carriages if notified.
" "	"	Woodside Cott'ge	A. J. Doughty	¼	15	1.00	6.00	616 "	" "
" "	"	The Central	S. D. Oserfield	¼	75	2.00	8.00 to 10.00	1600 "	Hotel stages meet all trains.
" "	"	Mountain House	Mrs. Theo. Hauser & Son	⅛	80	2.00	10.00 to 12.00	800 "	" "
" "	"	River View	Mrs. T L. LeBarre	—	25	—	7.00 to 9.00	500 "	One minutes walk from station.
" "	"	Glenwood	Johnson Bros.	½	200	2.00 to 2.50	8.00 to 14.00	—	See ad. on page 163.
" "	"	The Arlington	Louise A. Dutot	⅛	60	2.00	8.00 to 10.00	1600 "	Carriage meets all trains.
Minsi, Monroe Co., Pa.	"	Gap View	Samuel Overfield	1½	50	2.00	7.00 to 10.00	—	Carriages if notified.
Swift Water, Monroe Co. Pa.	Mt. Pocono	The Swift Water	The Swift Water	—	125	3.00 to 3.50	12.00 to 20.00	1800 "	References exchanged with strangers.
Mt. Pocono, " "	"	The Wiscasset	I. D. Iverson, Manager.	1¼	125	3.50	14.00 to 22.50	1700 "	References requested of strangers.
Tobyhanna Mills, " "	Tobyhanna	Tobyhanna Ho'se	J. W. Cornish	⅛	125	2.50	8.00 to 15.00	2500 "	Carriages if notified.
" " "	"	Prospect Cottage	Mrs. E. Black	¼	25	2.00	8.00 to 12.00	2500 "	" "

Post Office.	Railway Station.	Hotel or Boarding House.	Name of Proprietor.	Miles from Station.	Capacity.	Price per Day.	Price per Week.	Altitude above Sea.	How Reached from Railway Station.
Gouldsboro, Wayne Co., Pa	Gouldsboro	Simons House...	W. L. Haven.....	—	25	1.50	7.00	1970 ft.	Opposite D. L. & W. Station.
Sherburne, Chen'go Co., N.Y.	Sherburne	Hotel Daniels....	Ferguson & Nash	—	75	2.00	7.00 to 10.00	1040 "	Near station.
" " "	"	Spring House....	C. H. Reynolds..	1	50	2.00	8.00 to 12.00	1040 "	Free carriage if notified.
Cortland, Cortland Co., N.Y.	Cortland	Messenger House	O. L. Ingraham .	¼	60	2.00 to 2.50	10.50	—	Bus and electric cars.
Richfield Springs, Otsego Co., N. Y.	Richfield Springs	Spring House....	T. R. Proctor ..	⅛	300	4.00	according to room, etc.	1750 "	Hotel stages meet all trains.
" " "	" "	Kendalwood......	G. W. Tunnicliff.	¼	200	3.00	16.00 to 21.00	" "	Free bus to all trains. Illustrated book on application.
" " "	" "	Cary Cottage.....	Edward Cary....	¼	200	2.00	10.00 to 15.00	" "	Bus to all trains.
" " "	" "	The National....	S. P. Barker......	¼	200	2.00	7.00 to 14.00	" "	" "
" " "	" "	Fuller House.....	N. D. Jewell.....	¼	100	3.00	15.00 to 16.00	" "	" "
" " "	" "	Tunnicliff Co'ges	C. E. Tunnicliff & Mrs. J. F. Getman	¼	100	3.00	12.00 to 20.00	" "	" "
" " "	" "	Schuyler	Fred Feldman...	—	200	2.00	10.00 to 15.00	" "	Opposite D. L. & W. Depot.
" " "	" "	Greeman's Ap'ts	Henry Greenman	⅛	25	—	—	" "	Two doors from Spring House. All large airy rooms, with bath, electric light, etc. Send for diagram.
" " "	" "	Gladstone......	J. A. Storer......	⅛	100	—	—	" "	Apartments en suite, with bath. To rent furnished.
" " "	" "	Palmer Cottage..	Vilroy Palmer...	⅛	—	—	—	" "	Rates on application for the season. To rent furnished.
" " "	" "	Cushman Cott'ge	J. B. Cushman...	⅛	—	—	—	" "	" "
" " "	" "	Hotel Earlington	E. M. Earle & Son	⅛	350	4.00	according to room.	" "	Bus to all trains.
" " "	" "	St. James Hotel.	E. M. Earle & Son	⅛	300	3.00	12.00 to 18.00	" "	" "
Utica, N. Y..................	Utica	Baggs Hotel......	Kelly & Johnson.	acr's str'et	150	4.00	according to room, etc.	—	Across the street. Uniformed porter meets all trains.
"	"	St. James	Smith & White..	—	90	2.00 to 2.50	—	—	One block. Porter meets all trains.
Oswego, N. Y................	Oswego..........	Doolittle House..	J. G. Bennett....	⅛	500	3.00	14.00 to 18.00	819 "	Free carriage meets all trains.
" "	"	Ringold House..	Mrs. A. M. Ringold	⅛	50	1.50 to 2.00	5.00 to 10.00	" "	Carriage if notified.
" "	"	Lake Shore Ho'se	C. E. Keyes......	opp.	200	2.00 to 3.00	7.00 to 14.00	" "	
" "	"	Park House......	D. J. Brown......	¼	150	2.00	5.00 to 10.00	" "	Bus meets all trains.
Dansville, Livingston Co., N. Y.	Dansville.........	Sanatorium......	J. Arthur Jackson	¾	300	3.50	17.50 to 49.00	1400 "	" "
Fultonville, N. Y............	Fultonville.......	Cobble Stone Hall	....	—	125	Rea-s'ble.	——	500 "	" "

LIST OF HOTELS AND BOARDING HOUSES
TAKING SUMMER BOARDERS
ON OR NEAR THE LINES OF THE
DELAWARE, LACKAWANNA & WESTERN RAILROAD.
LAKE KEUKA, BATH & HAMMONDSPORT RAILROAD.

Post Office	Railway Station.	Hotel, Boarding House or Farm House.	Name of Proprietor.	Rods from Station.	Capacity	Price Per Day.	Price Per Week.	Altitude Above Sea	Remarks. How Reached from Railway Station.
Hammondsport, Steuben Co., N. Y.	Bath, N. Y.	Fairchild's House	C. H. Whittleton	10	60	$2.00	$8.00 to 12.00	780 ft.	All are contiguous to depots or landings, but carriages are available when required.
" "	"	Steuben House	W. H. & J. P. McCormick	20	50	2.00	6.00 to 10.00	740 "	
" "	"	Grand Central	A. Haffner	20	30	1.50	5.00 to 8.00	780 "	
" "	"	Ruby Cottage	B. Baker	10	30	1.50	5.00 to 8.00	780 "	
Grove Spring, Steuben t o., N. Y.	"	Grove Sp'gs Hotel		16	250	3.00	14.00 to 20.00	780 "	
Catawba, Steuben Co., N. Y.	"	Gibson House	W. H. Taylor	10	100	2.00	8.00 to 12.00	760 "	
Keuka, " "	"	Keuka House	Washborn & Wright	10	50	2.00	8.00 to 12.00	780 "	
Hammondsport, " "	"	Ogoyago House	Farrell & Bailey	12	75	2.00	8.00 to 12.00	780 "	
" "	"	Idlewild Hotel		12	50	2.00	8.00 to 12.00	780 "	
Penn Yan, Yates Co., N. Y.	"	The Ark	F. U. Schwartz	00	50	2.00	8.00 to 12.00	780 "	
Keuka University, "	"	Univ. B'd'g H'se		30	100	2.00	8.00 to 12.00	780 "	

CAYUGA LAKE HOUSE

SHELDRAKE, SENECA CO., NEW YORK.

CHARMING SUMMER RESORT ON CAYUGA LAKE.

Hotel has all modern appointments, including Elevator and Electric Lights.

OPEN JUNE 15th, AND CLOSES ABOUT SEPTEMBER 15th.

TRANSIENT RATES, $2.50 PER DAY AND UPWARDS.

SPECIAL RATES MADE FOR FAMILIES FOR THE SEASON.

FIRST-CLASS LIVERY IN CONNECTION.

HOPS EVERY SATURDAY EVENING.

Billiards.   Bowling.   Lawn Tennis.   Boating.   Fishing

NO MOSQUITOES.   NO DAMPNESS.   NO MALARIA.

For particulars and pamphlet address

DUDLEY S. PHINNY, PROPRIETOR.

CHAUTAUQUA THE SUMMER TOWN ON CHAUTAUQUA LAKE.

THE HOTEL ATHENÆUM.

"*Change of occupation, not idleness, is true recreation.*"

NOT A DULL DAY ALL SUMMER.

Chautauqua is charming in its natural location, artistic in its architecture and landscape gardening, perfect in its water supply and drainage. It offers a delightful, interesting, and stimulating Summer life, with varied forms of physical and mental recreation and entertainment. There is no other town like it in the world. Famous lecturers, readers and musicians, teachers from colleges and universities come yearly to Chautauqua to charm and inspire its citizens. This town, attractive to all people, is especially **an ideal resort for families**.

The **Hotel Athenæum** is an establishment of the first class, equipped and managed in accordance with the best modern methods. The corridors are broad and straight; staircases are widely separated from elevator shaft. Danger from fire is reduced to a minimum.

Since last Summer steam heat has been introduced, the electric light system extended, and important improvements made. Prices: Table board, *without room*, $10.50 per week. Room and board from $14 to $24—according to location. Rooms without board in July from $5 to $21 per week. Rooms can be engaged for September without board. Special rates to families and large parties. Persons, so desiring, can room at hotel and obtain cheaper table board at cottages near by.

For full details, address

W. A. DUNCAN, Secretary, Syracuse, N. Y.

Mountain House — DELAWARE WATER GAP, PA.

TWENTY-FIFTH SEASON

RATES: PER WEEK, $10.00; PER DAY, $2.00

HIGH LOCATION
MOST CONVENIENT TO ALL POINTS OF INTEREST

Mrs. THEO. HAUSER & SON

THE GLENWOOD,
DELAWARE WATER GAP, PA.
ELEVATION, 1,500 FT.   CAPACITY, 200.

High, cool and attractive. Fine Driving, Boating, Bathing and Fishing. Large well shaded lawns, pure spring water, electric bells, hot and cold baths, livery. Cuisine and service first-class. Convenient to all points of interest. Coach meets all trains.

TERMS MODERATE, FOR CIRCULARS ADDRESS   *JOHNSON BROS.*

A. A. DAME, PRESIDENT.   O. T. SUMNER, SECRETARY.

DAME & TOWNSEND CO.,
(SUCCESSORS TO JAMES O. MORSE.)

ESTABLISHED 1849.

Wrought Iron Pipe and Boiler Tubes,

**Manufacturers of all kinds of Brass and Iron Fittings
for Steam, Gas and Water,**

STEAM AND WATER GAUGES, STEAM TRAPS, GATE VALVES,
RADIATORS, RAILWAY, MILL AND ENGINEERS' SUPPLIES

GAS AND STEAM FITTERS' TOOLS, ETC.,

76 JOHN, and 29, 31 & 33 PLATT STREET,

NEW YORK.

Delaware, Lackawanna & Western R. R. Co.

FAMILY TICKET AND COMMUTATION TARIFF.

Commutation tickets will be furnished on application, at the several stations, and at 429 Broadway, New York City.

These tickets are subject to the rules and regulations of the Company, and must only be used by the persons named thereon. If offered by any other person, conductors will take up the ticket and collect fare.

Personal baggage will be checked on these tickets to the extent of 150 pounds.

These tickets will be valid for sixty (60) rides between the stations, and during the month named on face of ticket, and must be shown whenever required by conductors or ferry-masters.

They give the right of passage only on passenger trains that are advertised to stop at the stations named on ticket.

☞ Tickets are not valid for passage unlesss the ticket for preceding month is surrendered to conductor on first trip on which the ticket for the current month is used. School tickets good for 46 rides per month will be issued to scholars only, on presentation of certificate signed by the principal of the school or college which the scholar is attending. Printed form of certificates can be procured at the stations.

Fifty trip tickets, valid for one year from date of sale, for use by purchaser, a member of, a visitor to, or a servant in the family of, the purchaser, are issued at rates given herein. These tickets may be purchased at the stations, or at 429 Broadway, New York City.

BETWEEN NEW YORK AND	\multicolumn{12}{c	}{RATES FOR CONSECUTIVE MONTHS.}	Sum of Monthly Rates.	Yearly Rates.	Rates for 50-Trip Family Tickets.
	1st Month.	2d Month.	3d Month.	4th Month.	5th Month.	6th Month.	7th Month.	8th Month.	9th Month.	10th Month.	11th Month.	12th Month.			
Harrison	$5 50	$5 50	$5 50	$5 00	$5 00	$5 00	$5 00	$4 50	$4 50	$4 00	$3 50	$3 50	$3 50	$55 00	$55 00	$5 00
Newark	5 50	5 50	5 50	5 00	5 00	5 00	5 00	4 50	4 50	4 00	3 50	3 50	3 50	55 00	55 00	5 00
Roseville	5 50	5 50	5 50	5 00	5 00	5 00	5 00	4 50	4 50	4 00	3 50	3 50	3 50	55 00	55 00	5 00
Grove Street	6 50	6 50	6 50	6 00	6 00	6 00	6 00	5 00	5 00	5 00	4 50	4 50	4 50	66 00	61 00	6 25
East Orange	6 50	6 50	6 50	6 00	6 00	6 00	6 00	5 00	5 00	5 00	4 50	4 50	4 50	66 00	61 00	6 50
Brick Church	6 50	6 50	6 50	6 00	6 00	6 00	6 00	5 00	5 00	5 00	4 50	4 50	4 50	66 00	61 00	7 00
Orange	6 50	6 50	6 50	6 00	6 00	6 00	6 00	5 00	5 00	5 00	4 50	4 50	4 50	66 00	61 00	7 50
Highland Avenue	7 00	7 00	7 00	6 50	6 00	6 00	6 00	5 00	5 00	5 00	4 50	4 50	4 50	68 00	63 00	8 75
Mountain	7 50	7 50	7 00	6 50	6 00	6 00	6 00	5 00	5 00	5 00	4 50	4 50	4 50	69 00	64 00	9 50
South Orange	8 00	8 00	7 00	6 50	6 00	6 00	6 00	5 00	5 00	5 00	4 50	4 50	4 50	70 00	65 00	10 00
Maplewood	8 50	8 50	8 00	7 00	6 50	6 00	6 00	5 00	5 00	5 00	4 50	4 50	4 50	73 00	68 00	11 25
Wyoming	9 00	9 00	9 00	7 00	6 50	6 00	6 00	5 00	5 00	5 00	4 50	4 50	4 50	75 00	70 00	12 50
Milburn	9 00	9 00	9 00	7 00	6 50	6 00	6 00	5 00	5 00	5 00	4 50	4 50	4 50	75 00	70 00	12 50
Short Hills	9 50	9 50	9 50	7 50	6 50	6 00	6 00	5 50	5 00	5 00	4 50	4 50	4 50	78 00	73 00	13 75
Huntly	9 50	9 50	9 50	7 50	6 50	6 00	6 00	5 50	5 00	5 00	4 50	4 50	4 50	78 00	73 00	13 75
Summit	9 50	9 50	9 50	7 50	6 50	6 00	6 00	5 50	5 50	5 00	4 50	4 50	4 50	78 00	73 00	13 75
New Providence	10 00	10 00	10 00	8 50	7 50	6 50	6 00	5 50	5 50	5 00	4 50	4 50	4 50	79 00	74 00	15 00
Chatham	10 00	10 00	10 00	8 00	7 00	6 50	6 00	5 50	5 50	5 00	4 50	4 50	4 50	82 00	77 00	16 25
Madison	10 50	10 50	10 50	8 50	7 50	7 00	6 00	5 50	5 50	5 00	4 50	4 50	4 50	85 00	80 00	17 50
Convent	11 00	11 00	11 00	9 00	8 00	7 50	6 50	6 00	5 50	5 00	4 50	4 50	4 50	90 00	85 00	18 75
Morristown	11 00	11 00	11 00	9 00	8 00	7 50	6 50	6 00	5 50	5 50	5 00	4 50	4 50	90 00	85 00	20 00
Mount Tabor	12 00	12 00	11 00	10 00	9 00	7 50	6 50	6 00	5 50	5 50	5 00	5 00	5 00	95 00	90 00	25 00
Denville	12 00	12 00	11 00	10 00	9 00	7 55	6 50	6 00	5 50	5 50	5 00	5 00	5 00	95 00	90 00	26 25
Morris Plains	11 50	11 50	11 50	9 50	8 50	8 00	6 50	6 00	5 50	5 50	5 00	4 50	4 50	93 00	88 00	22 50
Rockaway	13 00	13 00	13 00	9 00	8 50	6 50	6 00	5 50	5 50	5 00	5 00	5 00	5 00	100 00	95 00	26 25
Dover	14 00	14 00	13 50	11 00	10 00	9 50	8 00	7 00	6 50	6 00	5 50	5 00	5 00	110 00	105 00	27 50
Port Oram	15 00	15 00	13 50	11 00	10 00	9 50	8 50	7 00	7 00	6 50	6 00	6 00	6 00	115 00	110 00	28 75
Mount Arlington	16 50	15 50	13 50	11 00	10 00	8 50	7 50	7 00	7 00	6 50	6 00	6 00	6 00	120 00	115 00	31 25
Hopatcong Station	18 00	15 50	13 50	13 00	11 50	11 00	9 50	8 50	8 00	7 50	7 00	7 00	7 00	130 00	125 00	32 50
Stanhope	18 00	15 50	13 50	13 00	11 50	11 00	9 50	8 50	8 00	7 50	7 00	7 00	7 00	130 00	125 00	35 00
Waterloo	19 00	16 50	14 50	13 50	12 00	11 50	10 00	8 50	8 00	7 50	7 00	7 00	7 00	135 00	130 00	37 50
Hackettstown	20 00	17 00	15 00	14 00	12 50	12 00	10 50	9 00	8 50	7 50	7 00	7 00	7 00	140 00	135 00	41 25

NEWARK & BLOOMFIELD BRANCH.

BETWEEN NEW YORK AND	\multicolumn{12}{c}{RATES FOR CONSECUTIVE MONTHS.}	Sum of Monthly Rates.	Yearly Rates.	Rates for 50-Trip Family Tickets.
	1st Month.	2d Month.	3d Month.	4th Month.	5th Month.	6th Month.	7th Month.	8th Month.	9th Month.	10th Month.	11th Month.	12th Month.			
Ampere	$6 00	$6 00	$6 00	$5 50	$5 50	$5 50	$5 00	$5 00	$5 00	$4 50	$4 50	$4 50	$60 00	$55 00	$6 00
Watsessing	6 50	6 50	6 50	6 00	6 00	6 00	5 00	5 00	5 00	4 50	4 50	4 50	66 00	61 00	7 00
Bloomfield	6 50	6 50	6 50	6 00	6 00	6 00	5 00	5 00	5 00	4 50	4 50	4 50	66 00	61 00	7 50
Glen Ridge	6 50	6 50	6 50	6 00	6 00	6 00	5 00	5 00	5 00	4 50	4 50	4 50	66 00	61 00	8 25
Montclair	6 50	6 50	6 50	6 00	6 00	6 00	5 00	5 00	5 00	4 50	4 50	4 50	66 00	61 00	8 75

PASSAIC & DELAWARE BRANCH.

	1st	2d	3d	4th	5th	6th	7th	8th	9th	10th	11th	12th	Sum	Yearly	50-Trip
West Summit	10 00	10 00	9 50	7 50	6 50	6 00	5 50	5 50	5 00	4 50	4 50	4 50	79 00	74 00	16 25
Murray Hill	10 00	10 00	9 50	7 50	6 50	6 00	5 50	5 50	5 00	4 50	4 50	4 50	79 00	74 00	17 50
Berkeley Heights	10 50	10 50	10 00	8 00	7 00	6 50	6 00	6 00	5 50	5 00	5 00	5 00	85 00	80 00	18 75
Gillette	10 50	10 50	10 00	8 00	7 00	6 50	6 00	6 00	5 50	5 00	5 00	5 00	85 00	80 00	21 25
Stirling	11 00	11 00	10 50	8 50	7 50	7 00	6 50	6 50	6 00	5 50	5 00	5 00	90 00	85 00	22 50
Millington	11 50	11 50	11 00	9 00	8 00	7 50	7 00	7 00	6 50	6 00	5 00	5 00	95 00	90 00	23 75
Lyons	11 50	11 50	11 00	9 00	8 00	7 50	7 00	7 00	7 00	6 50	5 50	5 50	97 00	92 00	25 00
Basking Ridge	12 00	12 00	11 00	9 00	8 00	7 50	7 00	7 00	7 00	6 50	5 50	5 50	98 00	93 00	26 25
Bernardsville	12 00	12 00	11 00	9 00	8 00	7 50	7 00	7 00	7 00	6 50	5 50	5 50	98 00	93 00	27 50
Mine Brook	12 50	12 50	11 00	9 00	8 00	7 50	7 00	7 00	7 00	6 50	5 50	5 50	99 00	94 00	30 00
Far Hills	13 00	13 00	11 00	9 00	8 00	7 50	7 00	7 00	7 00	6 50	5 50	5 50	100 00	95 00	31 25
Peapack	14 00	14 00	13 50	11 00	9 50	9 00	7 50	7 00	7 00	6 50	5 50	5 50	110 00	105 00	33 75
Gladstone	14 00	14 00	13 50	11 00	9 50	9 00	7 50	7 00	7 00	6 50	5 50	5 50	110 00	105 00	35 00

BOONTON BRANCH.

	1st	2d	3d	4th	5th	6th	7th	8th	9th	10th	11th	12th	Sum	Yearly	50-Trip
Secaucus	6 00	6 00	5 50	5 00	5 00	5 00	4 50	4 50	4 50	4 00	4 00	4 00	58 00	55 00	3 75
Kingsland	6 00	6 00	5 50	5 00	5 00	5 00	4 50	4 50	4 50	4 00	4 00	4 00	58 00	55 00	6 25
Lyndhurst	6 50	6 50	6 00	5 50	5 50	5 00	5 00	5 00	4 50	4 50	4 50	4 50	64 00	60 00	7 50
Delawanna	6 50	6 50	6 00	6 00	5 50	5 50	5 00	5 00	4 50	4 50	4 50	4 50	65 00	61 00	8 75
Passaic	6 50	6 50	6 50	6 00	6 00	6 00	5 00	5 00	4 50	4 50	4 50	4 50	66 00	61 00	10 00
Clifton	6 50	6 50	6 50	6 00	6 00	5 50	5 50	5 00	5 00	4 50	4 50	4 50	67 00	62 00	11 25
Paterson	7 00	6 50	6 50	6 00	6 00	6 00	5 50	5 50	5 00	5 00	5 00	5 00	69 50	65 00	12 50
West Paterson	7 00	6 50	6 50	6 00	6 00	6 00	5 50	5 50	5 50	5 00	5 00	5 00	69 50	65 00	12 50
Little Falls	7 00	7 00	7 00	6 50	6 50	6 50	5 50	5 50	5 00	5 00	5 00	5 00	72 00	67 00	16 25
Mountain View	7 50	7 50	7 50	7 00	6 50	6 50	6 00	5 50	5 00	5 00	5 00	5 00	76 00	71 00	17 50
Lincoln Park	8 00	8 00	8 00	7 50	6 50	6 50	6 00	5 50	5 00	5 00	5 00	5 00	78 00	73 00	18 75
Whitehall	9 00	9 00	8 00	7 50	6 50	6 50	6 00	6 00	5 50	5 00	5 00	5 00	80 00	75 00	20 00
Montville	10 00	10 00	10 00	8 00	7 00	6 50	6 50	6 00	5 50	5 00	5 00	5 00	85 00	80 00	20 00
Boonton	11 00	11 00	10 50	9 00	8 00	7 00	6 50	6 00	5 50	5 00	5 00	5 00	90 00	85 00	20 00

CHESTER BRANCH.

	1st	2d	3d	4th	5th	6th	7th	8th	9th	10th	11th	12th	Sum	Yearly	50-Trip
Kenvil	15 50	14 50	13 50	12 00	11 00	10 50	9 00	7 50	7 00	6 50	6 00	5 00	118 00	113 00	31 25
Succasunna	16 00	15 00	14 00	12 50	11 00	10 50	9 00	7 50	7 00	6 50	6 00	5 00	120 00	115 00	32 50
Ironia	17 00	16 00	15 00	13 50	11 50	10 50	9 00	7 50	7 00	6 50	6 00	5 50	125 00	120 00	33 75
Chester	19 00	17 00	15 00	14 00	12 50	12 00	10 50	9 00	7 00	7 00	6 00	6 00	135 00	130 00	37 50

SUSSEX R. R.

	1st	2d	3d	4th	5th	6th	7th	8th	9th	10th	11th	12th	Sum	Yearly	50-Trip
Andover	20 00	17 00	15 00	14 00	12 50	12 00	10 50	9 00	8 50	7 50	7 00	7 00	140 00	135 00	43 75
Newton	22 00	18 00	16 00	14 50	13 00	12 00	10 50	9 00	8 50	7 50	7 00	7 00	145 00	140 00	47 59

W. F. HOLWILL,

General Passenger Agent.

OF NEW YORK,

Organized February 3, 1892.

DAYNES & CO., Attorneys for the Underwriters,
27 AND 29 PINE STREET, NEW YORK CITY.

The Century Fire Lloyds composed of one hundred individual Underwriters of high commercial standing and sound rating, write fire insurance at equitable rates upon desirable risks situated in all parts of the United States.

Applications are invited from brokers of good standing upon the usual terms.

27 AND 29 PINE STREET,

NEW YORK CITY.

Policies written on behalf of fifty subscribers up to $5,000 on first-class sprinkled risks, and up to $2,500 on desirable mercantile and manufacturing risks.

MENDELSON & CO., Attorneys and Managers.

KNOWLES STEAM PUMP WORKS,

NEW YORK, BOSTON, MASS.,
93, 95 AND 97 LIBERTY STREET.　　FACTORIES,　　183 AND 185 DEVONSHIRE STREET.
PHILADELPHIA,　　WARREN, MASS.　　CHICAGO, ILL.,
518 ARCH STREET.　　　　　　　　163 SOUTH CANAL STREET.
117 Queen Victoria St., London, E. C., England.

MANUFACTURERS OF ALL KINDS OF

STEAM POWER, ELECTRIC AND COMPRESSED AIR PUMPING MACHINERY

FOR EVERY POSSIBLE DUTY.

Simple High Pressure, Compound Condensing and Electric Mining Pumps for Lifts of 2,000 ft. and under. Also Vertical Steam and Electric Sinking Pumps.

SEND FOR ILLUSTRATED CATALOGUE.

American Railway Supply Co.,

Successors to Hoole Manufacturing Co.,

24 PARK PLACE, ⁌ NEW YORK.

Manufacturers of

BAGGAGE, HOTEL AND TIME CHECKS,

BADGES, MEDALS, UNIFORM CAPS AND BUTTONS.

UNIFORM BUTTONS FOR CORPORATIONS

— A SPECIALTY —

THE RICHELIEU & ONTARIO NAVIGATION CO.
GENERAL OFFICES:
228 ST. PAUL ST., MONTREAL.

ROYAL MAIL LINE.

Between Toronto, Kingston, Montreal and intermediate ports, composed of the following first-class iron steamers: "Spartan", "Corsican", "Passport" and "Algerian".

Leaving Toronto daily (Sundays excepted) at 2 o'clock P. M., calling at Bowmanville, Port Hope, Cobourg, Kingston, Clayton, Alexandria Bay, and other intermediate ports, arriving at Montreal at 6.30 P. M., connecting with the steamers for Quebec and the Saguenay.

All these steamers pass through the enchanting scenery of the Lake of the Thousand Islands and the Exciting Rapids of the St. Lawrence.

THE MONTREAL AND QUEBEC LINE.

Composed of the magnificent large iron steamers "Quebec" and "Montreal".

Will leave Montreal daily (Sundays excepted) at 7 o'clock P. M., calling at intermediate points, and arriving at Quebec at 6.30 the following morning, connecting with the steamers for the Saguenay and the Intercolonial Railway for places in the Maritime Provinces.

THE SAGUENAY LINE.

Composed of the beautiful iron steamer "Carolina", the splendid steel steamer "Canada" and the fine steamer "Saguenay".

Leaving Quebec on the mornings of Tuesday, Wednesday, Friday and Saturday at 7.30.

Tickets and all information may be obtained at the principal railway offices in the United States and Canada.

ALEX. MILLOY, TRAFFIC MANAGER.   C. F. GILDERSLEEVE, GENERAL MANAGER.
MONTREAL. March, 1895.

Built to Satisfy

Our Folding Kodaks are as good as cameras can be made. We don't build them to compete with cheap goods, but for customers who want the best instrument that brains, experience and capital can produce. They embody every practical improvement; and are the best all the way through—best lenses, best shutter, best material, best workmanship—best everything. They are built to satisfy. Our catalogue describes them minutely—postal gets it.

The ? of $

There is no camera "just as good as the Folding Kodak," but there's a next best—the Folding Kodet. Not expensive, but up to date for all that. Simpler in construction than the Kodaks, but splendidly made and finished, and fitted with high grade lenses. Adapted to roll film or glass plates —just the thing for those who want a practical instrument at low price. The 4 x 5 Kodets list from $10.00 to $20.00 and the 5 x 7 from $22.00 to $48.00.

EASTMAN KODAK CO.

23 Styles and Sizes
KODAKS and KODETS
$6.00 to $100.00.
Catalogue Free.

Rochester, N. Y.

1875—1895.
Twenty=first Season.

SPRING HOUSE,
RICHFIELD SPRINGS, - - - - - - - NEW YORK.

THE new Bathing Establishment furnishes all the accepted European methods of treatment (by sulphur water) of Rheumatism, Gout, Catarrh and Skin Diseases.
It contains Sulphur Baths, Turkish and Russian Baths (with sulphur vapor), Douche, Massage, Inhalation and Pulverization rooms, Swimming Bath, Gymnasium, Sun Room, Resting Rooms and other conveniences.
Skilled Masseurs of both sexes.
A full corps of competent attendants.

The SPRING HOUSE (Hotel) and BATH HOUSES open every year from JUNE TO OCTOBER.

Mr. W. G. DOOLITTLE, the Manager, will be at Windsor Hotel, New York, from May 1st to June 15th, to attend to all engagements for rooms.

Illustrated pamphlet on application.

T. R. PROCTOR.

FALL RIVER LINE.

THE Fall River Line long since took place among the foremost transportation systems of the country, and has for many years been recognized as the peer of any of its class by all sorts and conditions of people. The business of this line is continuous throughout the year, all facilities, accommodations, comforts and appliances being equally desirable and perfect in Winter as in Summer. In the course of time these facts have become generally known, until a great majority of the public well understands that at all seasons of the year the Steamboats of this Line are the same great floating hotels, making safe, rapid, sure and satisfactory trips and unfailing connections throughout every period. Its quintette of Steamboats, the

"PRISCILLA," "PURITAN," "PLYMOUTH," "PILGRIM" AND "PROVIDENCE,"

are unequalled in the world elsewhere by similar enterprise; and this vast and restless agency is, indeed, one of the wonders of the century. Music, and all features for the satisfaction or delighting of patrons, are unvarying the whole year round.

FROM NEW YORK.—Steamers leave Pier 28 (old number), North River, foot of Murray Street.
FROM BOSTON.—Trains connecting with Steamers at Fall River (49 miles) leave Park Square Station (N. Y, N. H. & H. R. R.—Old Colony System.)
Tickets by this route are on sale at all of the principal ticket offices in the United States and Canada.

J. R. KENDRICK, PRESIDENT, Boston.   S. A. GARDNER, SUPERINTENDENT, New York.
GEO. L. CONNOR, PASS. TRAF. MGR., New Haven.   O. H. TAYLOR, GEN'L PASS. AGENT, New York.

RICHFIELD SPRINGS
(ON D., L. & W. R. R.)
OTSEGO CO., NEW YORK

AN IDEAL SUMMER RESORT

 On Lake Canadarago, 1,750 feet above the sea level. Famed for its Sulphur Waters, so efficacious in cases of **Rheumatism**, Gout, Neuralgia, Dyspepsia, Malaria, Catarrh, Liver and Kidney troubles, and all Skin affections. The sufferer from **Insomnia** will **sleep** in the bracing life-giving air of Richfield Springs. The Bath House is the most thoroughly equipped in this country . . . .

HOTEL EARLINGTON (OPPOSITE THE BATH HOUSE)

 Will be opened on Saturday, June 29th. The house has been greatly enlarged, refurnished and put in the best of order. Many acres have been added to the already spacious grounds, with trees, shrubbery, etc., making a park equal to the best at any summer resort hotel. New Walks, Tennis and Croquet Grounds have been laid out. Also a Bicycle Track, six laps to the mile, with accommodations for the storage and care of machines. Bicycles to rent, and expert instructors in attendance. The Billiard Rooms and Bowling Alleys are new. The Orchestra will play in the Earlington Park from 10 A. M. to 1 P. M. daily for Tennis and Croquet players, Bicycle riders, and spectators. . . . .

The Earlington Stables are spacious and fitted with every modern convenience and luxury. . . . .

RATES, $21.00 PER WEEK, AND UPWARDS

ST. JAMES HOTEL LOCATED IN THE EARLINGTON PARK

This hotel has just been finished and newly furnished, and fills a long felt want, viz.: a modern hotel complete in all its appointments, at moderate prices. . . . .

OPEN JUNE 15TH TO OCTOBER 15TH

The St. James is steam heated, has electric lights, and bells, Baths and the best sanitary plumbing on every floor, and every convenience to make an ideal Summer and Fall home. . .

RATES, $12.00 PER WEEK, AND UPWARDS

Both of the above hotels will be run by the owners
Messrs. E. M. EARLE & SON
From whom plans and full information
can be obtained

DICKSON MANUFACTURING CO.

BUILDERS OF

STANDARD and NARROW-GAUGE

LOCOMOTIVES

SCRANTON, PA.

JAS. P. DICKSON,	PRESIDENT.
JAMES BLAIR,	VICE-PRESIDENT.
WM. H. PERKINS,	SEC'Y & TREAS.
WM. J. BROWN,	ASST. SEC'Y & TREAS.
SIDNEY BROADBENT, . .	GEN'L SUPERINTENDENT.

ESTABLISHED 1856.

Henry Maurer & Son,

MANUFACTURERS OF

Fire=Proof
Building Materials

OF EVERY DESCRIPTION.

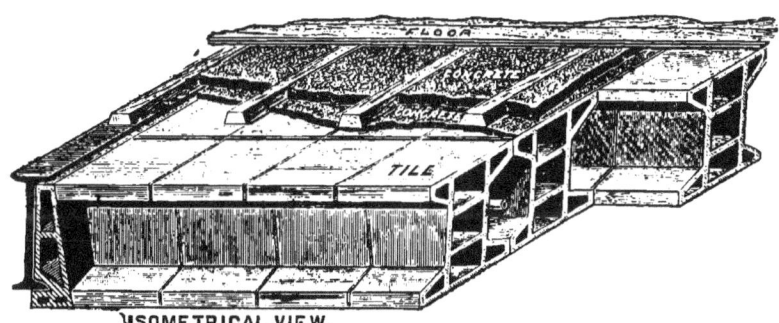

ISOMETRICAL VIEW.
"EXCELSIOR" END CONSTRUCTION FLAT ARCH. [Patented July 21st, 1891.]
25 per cent. lighter and stronger than any other method.

POROUS TERRA COTTA OF ALL SIZES.
FLUE LININGS, FLOOR ARCHES, PARTITIONS,
FURRING, ROOFING, &c.

Fire Brick of all Shapes and Sizes.
CLAY RETORTS FOR GAS WORKS.

OFFICE AND DEPOT:

420 EAST 23D ST., NEW YORK.

WORKS: MAURER, N. J.   P. O. Box No. 1.

(ON CENTRAL R. R. OF N. J.)

The Jackson & Woodin Mfg. Co.,

BERWICK, PA.,

MANUFACTURERS OF

CAR WHEELS FOR FREIGHT OR MINE CARS, ALL SIZES AND WEIGHTS.

FREIGHT CARS

Of all Descriptions and Gauges for Export and Domestic use.

CAST IRON PIPE CAST VERTICALLY FOR GAS OR WATER.

FORGINGS FOR CARS OR SPECIALTIES.

CASTINGS OF EVERY DESCRIPTION.

Branch Castings, Pipe and Bar Iron kept in stock, and all other material furnished promptly at lowest market prices.

WORKMANSHIP AND QUALITY ALWAYS GUARANTEED.

DODGE & BLISS CO.,
WEST END,   JERSEY CITY, N. J.

ON LINE OF D., L. & W. R. R. ALL TRAINS STOP.

Dressed Lumber and Timber
OF ALL KINDS.

Special low prices on car shipment direct from our own Mills at Tonawanda, N. Y., and Norfolk, Virginia.

SPECIALTIES:

ALL KINDS OF HOUSE TRIM, WHITE PINE, NORTH CAROLINA PINE, SPRUCE, HEMLOCK, CYPRESS.

YELLOW PINE, SPRUCE AND HEMLOCK TIMBER AND PINE LATH, ALSO CEDAR, CYPRESS, WHITE PINE SHINGLES.

Manufacturers of Boxes, made up or in Shooks, ready to nail together, in any quantity from 1 to 1,000,000, in any kind of lumber, for all purposes.

SPECIALTY:

PRINTING SPECIAL DESINGS ON ENDS OR SIDES

In one or two colors forming a first-class advertisement.

GOLD CAR HEATING COMPANY,

NEW YORK ADDRESS:
N. E. Cor. Frankfort and Cliff Sts.

CHICAGO OFFICE:
652 The Rookery, E. H. GOLD, Representative.

Upwards of 6,000 Cars and Locomotives equipped with our Systems of Car Heating; also adopted on some of the largest railroads in Europe.

Gold's "Universal" Straightport Coupling,

which couples with Sewall, is the only one extant having an adjustable seat. Supplied with Gold's Automatic Gravity Relief Traps, which are a positive preventive against freezing.

Heft Lubricating Oil Co. - - -

EASTON, PA.

Manufacturers of

- - Lubricating Oils and Greases.

RAILROAD OILS AND GREASES
A Specialty.

ALSO THE NEW PROCESS AXLE GREASE.

RESULTS MAKE REPUTATION

ESTABLISHED 1844

Highest Grade arnishes and Japans

Coach and Car
Piano and Cabinet
House Painters'
and Japanners'

MANUFACTURED BY

MINETT & CO.

60 Pearl Street
NEW YORK

1210 Ridge Ave.
PHILADELPHIA

Works: DELAWANNA, N. J.

✠ GLEN ✣ ISLAND ✠

Steamers leave Pier 18, N. R. (three streets below Barclay Street Terminus of D., L. & W. R. R.), and foot of 32d Street, E. R. For Time Tables see New York Daily Newspapers.

M. C. B. Standard
AUTOMATIC FREIGHT CAR COUPLER.

Locomotive and Car Axles, Coupling Links and Pins.

NEW YORK OFFICE, 66 BROADWAY.
CHICAGO OFFICE, 941 ROOKERY.
ST. LOUIS OFFICE, 219 COMMERCIAL B'LDING.

GOULD COUPLER CO.

Works { BUFFALO, N. Y.
{ DEPEW, N. Y.

M. C. B. Passenger Coupler Used in place of Miller Hook WITHOUT Change in Platform.

Gould Continuous
PLATFORM AND BUFFER.
GOULD VESTIBULE.

RUBBER GOODS

AIR BRAKE HOSE	BELTING
CAR HEATING HOSE	SHEET PACKING
SIGNAL HOSE	PISTON PACKING
STEAM HOSE	GASKETS
TENDER HOSE	VALVES
TANK HOSE	MATS and STEP TREADS
GARDEN HOSE	SPECIAL MOULD GOODS
TUBING	BICYCLE TIRES

NEW YORK BELTING & PACKING CO. LTD

PIONEERS AND LEADERS   **12 PARK ROW**

Goods are Best ; Prices are Right   NEW YORK

Stroud's Self=Basting Roasting Pan.
FIRST PRIZE AT COLUMBIAN WORLD'S FAIR.

Is in Use and has been Endorsed by Thousands.

DOES AWAY WITH HAND BASTING.

Requires no attention ; has no cover ; the Cook can see the meat if so inclined.

EVERY PAN GUARANTEED.

	10 X 14	10 X 15	11 X 17
Prices in Steel, ea.	.65	.85	$1.00
White Enameled Steel, ea.......	1.75	2.00	2.25

Stroud's Oyster and Clam Steamer has met with great popular favor.

We have numerous testimonials see one from Hotel Brunswick.

June 22d, 1894.

JAMES STROUD, 1263 Broadway, N. Y,
  DEAR SIR :—I have used your Oyster and Clam Steamer in the hotel, and am pleased to say that it gives entire satisfaction. It preserves the juice of Oysters and Clams intact and pure ; insures quick service and is an ornament to the table.
  I can also speak in terms of praise of your Self-Basting Pan for roasting meat, and would strongly recommend it to every housekeeper.

Very truly yours,
FRANCIS KINZLER,
Of Hotel Brunswick Co.

Also endorsed by the Waldorf Hotel, Imperial, etc.

PRICES OF CLAM STEAMERS :
Small................$3.50 each.   Large...............$4.50 each.

Manning, Maxwell & Moore
RAILWAY AND MACHINISTS' TOOLS
AND SUPPLIES
WE CARRY IN STOCK

The largest and most complete assortment of Tools and supplies of every description in the United States for

RAILWAY SHOPS, MACHINE SHOPS, FACTORIES, BOILER ROOMS, BOILER MAKERS, ENGINE BUILDERS, AND ALL PLACES WHERE MACHINERY AND POWER IS USED

GENERAL SALES AGENTS FOR

THE POND MACHINE TOOL CO.
Metal Working Machine Tools
THE PEDRICK & AYER CO.
Special Tools for Railway and Machine Shops
THE SHAW ELECTRIC CRANE CO.
Shaw Three Motor Electric Traveling Cranes

Nos. 111 and 113 LIBERTY ST., NEW YORK

NO. 424 TELEPHONE BUILDING
PITTSBURGH, PA.

NO. 60 S. CANAL STREET
CHICAGO, ILL.

J. ROGERS MAXWELL, Pres.
ALFONSO DE NAVARRO, 2d Vice-Pres.

JOSE F. DE NAVARRO, Vice-Pres.
HOWARD W. MAXWELL, **Treas.**

HENRY GRAVES, JR., Sec'y.

ATLAS PORTLAND CEMENT

WARRANTED EQUAL TO ANY AND SUPERIOR TO MOST OF THE FOREIGN BRANDS.

OFFICIAL TESTS, Nos. 3567 and 3568, made by the **Department of Docks,** New York, March 31, 1894, being part of contract No. 464 for 8,000 barrels.

Tensile Strength, 7 days, neat cement..........................622 lbs.
"   "   7 days, 2 parts sand to 1 of cement..........332 lbs.
Pats steamed and boiled..Satisfactory.

All our product is of the first quality, and is the only American Portland Cement that meets the requirements of the U. S. Government and the New York Department of Docks. We make no second grade or so-called improved cement.

ATLAS CEMENT COMPANY,

143 LIBERTY STREET,   NEW YORK CITY.

This New House
··· For Sale ···
AT MONTCLAIR, N. J.
Containing 11 Rooms and Bath.

Hardwood trim, including floors. Open fire-places in almost every room handsomely mantled and tiled. Artistic arrangement evident in the whole design. Lot, 100 x 210. House, 48 x 31. Situated on high ground in the most attractive and aristocratic section of the town.

For terms and particulars address owner,

96 LLEWELLYN ROAD,
COR. MELROSE AVENUE,
MONTCLAIR, N. J.

*S*cience rules the

K-E-A-T-I-N-G

World's Lightest Frame By Science's Aid.
World's Lightest Bicycle By Science's Aid.

S-t-r-a-i-n o-f p-e-d-a-l-i--n-g i-s **w-i-t-h** t-h-e g-r-a-i-n o-f t-h-e s-t-e-e-l i-n-s-t-e-a-d o-f a-c-r-o-s-s t-h-e g-r-a-i-n a-s i-n a s-t-r-a-i-g-h-t-f-r-a-m-e-d b-i-c-y-c-l-e

Do You Race?
The KEATING Jumps at the Finish.

FREE CATALOGUE.

Keating Wheel Company,
HOLYOKE, MASS.

BRADLEY & SMITH,
MANUFACTURERS OF BRUSHES
—FOR—

Railroads, Painters and Families,

ALSO FOR EXPORT TRADE.

251 PEARL STREET, NEW YORK.

THE BURNET CO.,
77 MAIDEN LANE, NEW YORK,

RAILWAY, STEAMSHIP, MILL AND MINE SUPPLIES.

———— SPECIALTIES ————

Steam, Oil and Air Brake Hose, R. R. Forges, Anvils,
Rubber Belting, Locomotive Jacks, Vises,
Leather Belting, Lub. Oils and Gases,
Wood Split-Pulleys, Tube Expanders, Drills,
Iron Pulleys, Files, Globe Packing,
Shovels, Chains, Salamander Fire
Wheel Barrows, Proof Composition,
Alba Packing, P. P. P. Packing.

We Solicit Specifications for Supplies, on which we will affix our Lowest Price.
On Application will Send our Catalogue.

KNIVES, FORKS, SPOONS, SALTS. TEA WARE, FERN DISHES, CHAFING DISHES, Etc.

HOTEL WARE A SPECIALTY.
BEST GOODS AND LOWEST PRICES IN AMERICA.

SILVER METAL MFG. CO.   FACTORY, OSWEGO, N. Y.

N. Y. CITY OFFICE, No. 607 CABLE BUILDING.

EDWARD CLIFF, President and Manager.   JNO. C. N. GUIBERT, Secretary and Treasurer.

VOSE & CLIFF MANUFACTURING CO.,
Room 108, No. 39 Cortlandt Street, New York,

MANUFACTURERS OF

KING'S FLEXIBLE SIDE BEARING

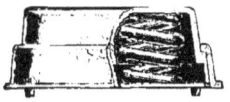

This device secures reduced wear of wheel flanges; greater durability for trucks; longer life for cars; economy in freight service.

Adopted as standard by Boston & Albany; Delaware, Lackawanna & Western; New York Central & H. R.;

Pat. Nov. 8, '81; Mar. 6, '83.   N. Y., Susquehanna & Western, and other railroads; Delaware & Hudson Canal Co.; Burton Stock Car Co., and Eastman Stock Cars.

Sample and Trial Set Furnished if Desired.

LAPPIN BRAKE SHOES.
CAST IN ONE PIECE
WITH ALTERNATE SPACES OF CHILLED AND SOFT IRON.

They Preserve the Tires and Outwear all other Shoes.

Sample Sets of Flanged or Plain Shoes for Locomotives or Cars furnished for test free of charge.

THE LAPPIN BRAKE SHOE CO.,
39 & 41 Cortland St.,   =   =   =   NEW YORK.
Works: BLOOMFIELD, ESSEX CO., N. J.

CAMPBELL & THAYER,
89 Maiden Lane,   NEW YORK,

Manufacturers of

··LINSEED OIL··

Raw, Refined and Boiled, in Casks and Barrels

—— ALSO ——

LINSEED CAKE.

EAGLE BRAND THE BEST
NO TAR   # ROOFING   **NO TAR**

It is superior to any other Roofing for House, Factory or outbuildings; it costs half the price of shingles, tin or iron; it is easily applied by anyone. Send for estimate and state size of roof. Write at once.

RUBBER PAINT!

The best known Paint in the world for tin, iron or shingle roofs, fences, barns and outbuildings; it costs only 60 cents per gallon in barrel lots, or $4.50 for a 5-gallon tub. Color, dark red. Will last for years; it is guaranteed not to peel, crack, scale nor wash off, and it is fire-proof against sparks.

Excelsior Paint & Roofing Co.,   155 Duane St., New York.

FOUNDED 1837.
THEO. W. MORRIS & CO.
GLASS

WINDOW GLASS, POLISHED AND CRYSTAL PLATE, FRENCH AND GERMAN MIRROR PLATES, ROUGH AND RIBBED GLASS, CATHEDRAL, ONDOYANT, FLORENTINE, OPALESCENT, ORNAMENTAL CUT AND COLORED GLASS.

WIRE GLASS.

474, 476 and 478 GREENWICH STREET, NEW YORK.

ESTABLISHED 1857.

ROMER & CO.,
Patent Jail Locks, Night Latches
and Railroad Padlocks
FOR DOMESTIC AND EXPORT TRADE.

NOS. 275, 277 AND 279 PASSAIC STREET,
Between D., L. & W. and Erie R. R. Depots,
NEWARK, N. J., U. S. A.

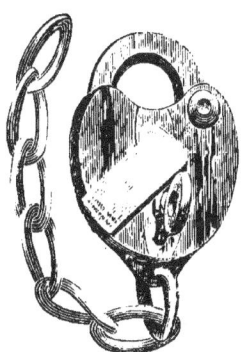

PENNSYLVANIA BOLT & NUT CO

MANUFACTURERS OF

REFINED BAR IRON

MACHINE BOLTS		HOT PRESSED AND
TRACK BOLTS	BOILER AND BRIDGE RIVETS	COLD PUNCHED
BOLT ENDS	CAR FORGINGS AND ARCH-BARS	SQUARE AND HEXAGON
LAG SCREWS	STRUCTURAL AND ELECTRICAL FORGINGS	NUTS
GIMLET POINTED	TURNBUCKLES	CHAMFERED AND
COACH SCREWS		TRIMMED NUTS
		WASHERS

LEBANON, PENNA.

BATH OFFICE.

MILLER'S
TURKISH, ELECTRIC,
AND ROMAN BATHS.

41 W. 26th St., New York City.

HOT-AIR, ELECTRO-THERMAL,
GALVANISM, MASSAGE.

Best Ventilated, Best Conducted and
Most Carefully Administered
Baths in the Country.

QUIET, CLEANLINESS,
CULTURE, REFINEMENT.

HOURS:
Gentlemen—Week-days, 6 to 8 A. M.
2 to 11 P. M.; Sundays,
6 A. M. to 6 P. M.
Ladies—Every week-day,
9 A. M. to 2 P. M.

Massage treatment given at residence.

Rooms with or without meals can
be had in connection with the Baths.

C. H. HAYNES, Proprietor.

RIVER FARM HOUSE, ✢ E. T. CROASDALE, PROPRIETOR.

DELAWARE WATER GAP, PA.

Pleasantly Situated. One mile from the Depot and each of the two principal Hotels. Rooms large and pleasant. Good Horses and Carriages, with careful drivers, furnished at moderate prices. . . . . .

BOARD : $10 per Week or $2 per Day, according to room occupied, etc. Children from $5 to $10 per Week.

Open from May to November.

For Particulars, address,

E. T. CROASDALE.

CLAIRMONT & CO.,
Opticians,

129 East 23d Street,
BET. LEXINGTON & 4TH AVES.,
ADJOINING CHURCH.

535 Fifth Avenue,
BET. 44TH & 45TH STS.,
NEW YORK.

Louis F. Mazzetti,
CATERER AND CONFECTIONER

MAIN STORE,

867 SIXTH AVENUE,

S. W. Cor. 49th St., NEW YORK.

TELEPHONE CALL, "402 38TH ST."

BRANCHES :

300 COLUMBUS AVENUE, N. W. Corner 74th Street.
Telephone Call, "132 Columbus."

1064 MADISON AVENUE, Between 80th & 81st Streets.
Telephone Call, "348 79th Street."

44 W. 125TH STREET, Bet. 5th & Lenox Aves.
Telephone Call, "152 Harlem."

The New Manhattan Mohair Skirt Binding.

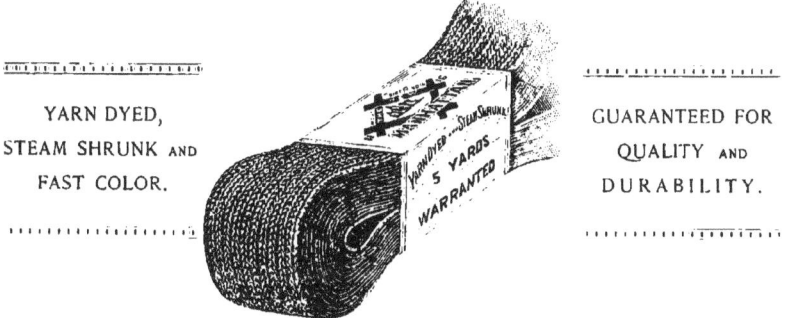

YARN DYED,
STEAM SHRUNK AND
FAST COLOR.

GUARANTEED FOR
QUALITY AND
DURABILITY.

If you cannot obtain this Braid from your dealer, send us 20 cents for a five yard piece of any color.

Manufactured by
15 & 17 MERCER ST.
NEW YORK.

Please mention this book.

FERDERICO LESPONA, Proprietor.   ESTABLISHED 1879.

BODEGA ESPAÑOLA

IMPORTED
WINES, LIQUORS, OILS, OLIVES, CAPERS, CIGARS,
AND OTHER SPANISH, FRENCH, ITALIAN
AND DOMESTIC DELICACIES.

WE SEND BY EXPRESS VIANDS FROM CUBA ONLY TO THE UNITED STATES
GUAVA JELLY MANGO, MAMEY, GUNABANAS, JICACOS, Etc.

TRY OUR BACALAO.

97 MAIDEN LANE,   **NEW YORK.**

BOSTON & LOCKPORT BLOCK CO.

162 COMMERCIAL STREET,
BOSTON, MASS.

33 SOUTH STREET,
NEW YORK.

MANUFACTURERS OF
IRON, STEEL, AND WOOD TACKLE BLOCK,
WAREHOUSE AND RAILROAD TRUCKS.

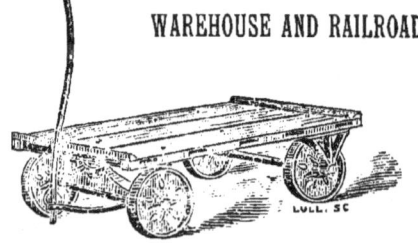

W. F. HOLWILL, President.   L. B. FOLEY, Secretary.   J. B. SAVINE, Attorney.

New York State Mortgage, : : :
: : : Bank and Savings Association
181 BROADWAY, N. Y. (ROOM 45).

SHARES, $200

OWN YOUR HOME
AND
STOP PAYING RENT.

This Association will loan you the money to buy or build a home, or pay off a mortgage, and allow you to repay the loan in monthly instalments, just as you now pay rent. To those who do not wish to acquire homes, the shares of the Association are an exceptionally good investment; they provide a place to 'deposit money once a month, with interest from date of deposit, or to withdraw deposits at any time. Bonds and Mortgage of this Association continue during the period covered by the existence of the series of shares borrowed on, or the option is given to pay all or any part of the mortgage at any time. There is no danger of loans being called in every two or three years.

Shares, One Dollar per month.   Shares can be subscribed for at any time.

MILLER'S HOTEL,

37, 39 AND 41 WEST 26TH STREET,
NEW YORK CITY,

Between Fifth and Sixth Avenues, near Broadway and Madison Square Park.

A CLEAN, QUIET, COMFORTABLE HOTEL-HOME.

In the centre of Retail Trade, the Shopping District, the Principal Theatres, Amusement Halls, Art Galleries, Hotels and Churches.

Within three minutes' walk of Broadway, Fifth Avenue, Sixth Avenue and Twenty-third Street, with their lines of Stages, Cable Cars, Horse Cars and the Elevated Road leading to all parts of the City.

◂―AMERICAN PLAN.―▸
PERMANENT AND TRANSIENT GUESTS.

Rates, $2.50 Per Day.   A few Large Rooms, $3 to $5.

Special Rates for Excursion Parties, and for families, transiently or by the year.

SEND FOR CIRCULAR AND COPY OF HOTEL MESSENGER.

Turkish, Electric and Roman Baths connected with the Hotel.

CHARLES H. HAYNES, Proprietor.

Westcott Express Company

✻
✻
✻
WILL CALL FOR AND CHECK BAGGAGE DIRECT FROM HOTELS, RESIDENCES OR BUSINESS HOUSES IN NEW YORK, BROOKLYN OR JERSEY CITY TO DESTINATION.

Special arrangements made for the transportation of household packages, family marketing, wash hampers, etc., during the Summer Season.

CABS AND COACHES FURNISHED
AT REASONABLE RATES.

Messengers of the Westcott Express Co. are on all incoming trains over the D., L. & W. R. R. to arrange for the prompt transfer of passengers and baggage to any part of NEW YORK, BROOKLYN, JERSEY CITY OR HOBOKEN.

EXECUTIVE OFFICE, 14 PARK PLACE, NEW YORK.
TELEPHONE, 1296 CORTLANDT.

• • BRANCHES • •

111 4th Ave.	Foot West 42d St., W. S. R. R.	338 Fulton St., Brooklyn.
942 Broadway.	" Franklin St., "	19 Bergen St., "
314 Canal St.	" Barclay St., D., L. & W. R. R.	726 Fulton St., "
Grand Central Depot.	" Christopher St., " "	20 and 22 Dean St., "
235 Columbus Av., cor. 71st St.	53 West 125th St., Harlem	106 Broadway, Williamsburg.

STORAGE furnished on application at any of the above offices.

www.ingramcontent.com/pod-product-compliance
Lightning Source LLC
Chambersburg PA
CBHW020844160426
43192CB00007B/783